Read Write In...

Literacy and Language
Handbook

4

Janey Pursglove and **Charlotte Raby**

Series developed by **Ruth Miskin**

OXFORD
UNIVERSITY PRESS

OXFORD
UNIVERSITY PRESS

Great Clarendon Street, Oxford, OX2 6DP,
United Kingdom

Oxford University Press is a department of the University of Oxford.
It furthers the University's objective of excellence in research, scholarship, and education
by publishing worldwide. Oxford is a registered trade mark
of Oxford University Press in the UK and in certain other countries

First Edition published in 2013

British Library Cataloguing in Publication Data
Data available

ISBN: 978-0-19-833081-3

7 9 10 8 6

Paper used in the production of this book is a natural, recyclable product
made from wood grown in sustainable forests. The manufacturing process
conforms to the environmental regulations of the country of origin.

Printed in Great Britain by Ashford Colour Press

Acknowledgements

Cover: Chuck Groenink

Illustrations by: Leo Broadley; Anthony Browne; Ross Collins; Lee Cosgrove;
Clare Ellsom; Lizzy Finlay; Chuck Groenink; Lemniscates; Garry Parsons; Korky Paul;
Andrés Martínez Ricci; Ariel Sela; David Semple; Jeanne Willis

Design by Q2A

INSPIRATIONAL SUPPORT FOR TEACHERS
For free professional development
videos from leading experts, plus other
resources and free eBooks, please go to
www.oxfordprimary.co.uk

HELPING YOU ENGAGE PARENTS
We have researched the most common concerns
and worries parents have about their children's
literacy and provide answers and support in
www.oxfordowl.co.uk

This site contains advice on how to share
a book, how to pronounce pure sounds,
how to encourage boys' reading, and much
more. We hope you will find the site
useful and recommend it to your parents.

Contents

Introduction

What is Literacy and Language?

Literacy and Language is a complete literacy programme for children in Years 2–6 (Primary 3–7). It is designed to stimulate and challenge children's thinking and create enthusiastic, lifelong readers and writers.

It provides explicit guidance for developing children's reading comprehension and writing composition with support for teaching grammar, vocabulary development, critical thinking and spoken language. It gives you all the support you need to teach outstanding, consistent literacy lessons every day, and to deliver the new National Curriculum confidently.

The core purpose of the programme is to ensure that children, as the National Curriculum aims state:

> read easily, fluently and with good understanding

> develop the habit of reading widely and often for both pleasure and information

> acquire a wide vocabulary

> use grammar correctly

> appreciate our rich and varied literary heritage

> write clearly, accurately and coherently, adapting their language and style in and for a range of contexts, purposes and audiences

> use discussion in order to learn; they should be able to elaborate and explain clearly their understanding and ideas

> are competent in the arts of speaking and listening, making formal presentations, demonstrating to others and participating in debate

Literacy and Language resources for each year:

an **Anthology** of complete stories, plays, poems and non-fiction texts	a **Pupils' Book** containing writing, grammar, comprehension and vocabulary activities related to the Anthology texts	a **Homework Book** providing further practice and consolidation of grammar points and writing tasks	**Software** with a wide variety of teacher-led activities and teacher support, for use on an interactive whiteboard	a **Handbook** giving clear day-by-day lesson plans for each Unit

Resources

Anthology

Literacy and Language is based on Anthologies of carefully chosen complete stories, plays, poems and non-fiction texts by leading children's authors including Michael Morpurgo, Jeremy Strong, Roger McGough, Geraldine McCaughrean, Jamila Gavin, Ted Hughes and Kaye Umansky.

The range of stories, plays, poems and non-fiction texts in *Literacy and Language* provide an opportunity for children to study texts which are absorbing, challenging and deep enough to dive into, while being accessible to all children.

The children's increasing familiarity with a wide range of stories, plays, poems and non-fiction texts will generate a desire for more reading for pleasure. Wider reading lists are provided for every Unit.

> All the texts in the Anthology are complete and are just the right length for children to read during the lesson and to develop reading stamina.

> All the fiction and non-fiction texts include rarer vocabulary, which the children explore through Word power activities prior to reading the text.

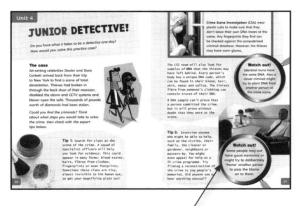

> Each non-fiction text is a model of a particular form with a clear purpose, aimed at a specific audience. The high-interest, often humorous non-fiction texts provide further stimulus for reading widely and often.

Pupils' Book

Lively activities in the Pupils' Book develop children's writing, grammar, comprehension and vocabulary skills. The activities are linked to the Anthology texts and help children consolidate and apply what they are learning.

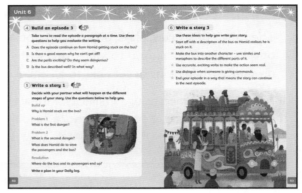

> **Grammar** is taught in context and through writing to make it meaningful for children.

> Each Unit has **activities on 'Power words'** – ambitious words to enhance children's spoken vocabulary and ultimately their vocabulary for writing.

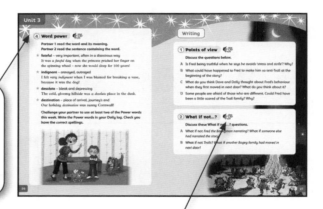

> **Partner work** is embedded in the programme – many of the activities are rooted in discussion, which helps to develop children's spoken English.

Homework Book

The Homework Book contains weekly activities which allow children to practise and embed the grammar, writing and other language and literacy skills they have learnt in the lessons.

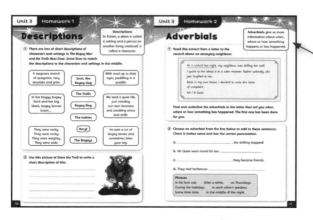

> The activities are accessible and engaging, with age-appropriate glossaries and information boxes to ensure children can work independently at home.

Software

The Software is integral to the programme and is used for whole class teaching.
It contains a range of resources to support your teaching.

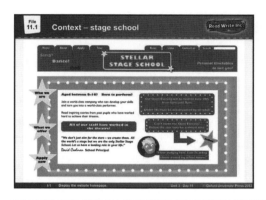

There are fully illustrated texts, including stories, plays, poems and non-fiction texts from the Anthology, to display and explore as a class.

Audio and video clips are used to introduce drama activities or stimulate discussion.

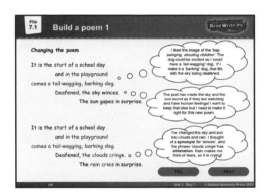

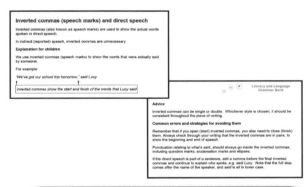

There are **modelled writing scripts** for the teacher to show how a text is built up, including how to 'Think out loud' to show children how to develop ideas.

A **Grammar Bank** gives teachers clear explanations about every aspect of grammar in the new National Curriculum and practice tests for children (see p.9).

Files include:

- video, audio performances of the poems and plays, radio interviews, music and images
- drag and drop language activities
- writing plans which can be printed out for class use
- 'Think out loud' teacher scripts for modelled writing
- 'Power words' for classroom display
- ready-prepared 'Write a story' texts for modelled writing
- editable timetables.

The Software booklet provides more detailed information about the features of the Software.

All this support makes it possible for you to teach an outstanding literacy lesson every day.

Teaching Handbook

Teachers are given comprehensive, structured support from the detailed day-by-day lesson plans in the Teaching Handbook and timetables.

Overview timetables are provided in the Teaching Handbook and as editable files on the Software.

An overview of each Unit includes assessment criteria for reading and writing.

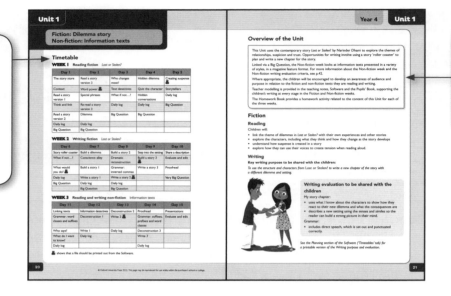

Lesson plans give detailed guidance for each activity.

Activities are clearly matched to the new National Curriculum.

Children write every day, building up ideas, planning, developing longer pieces of writing, then evaluating, editing and proofreading their work.

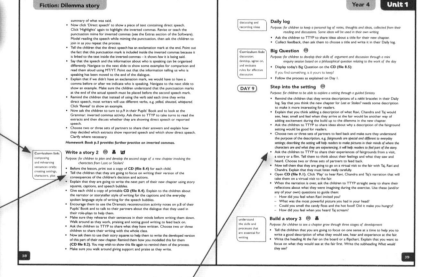

Partner work ensures that every child is speaking every day, enriching their spoken English.

What will children be taught?

Comprehension skills

At the heart of *Literacy and Language* is the enjoyment of and engagement with a variety of texts. Children are encouraged to take their own meaning from each text, becoming independent and critical thinkers. Comprehension activities are designed to help children to infer, summarise, question, clarify, predict and argue a point of view. The children also make connections between texts and their own experiences. The programme approach integrates reading, writing, thinking, and spoken language in all activities, to ensure the daily development of children's comprehension and wider literacy skills.

Grammar

Children are taught the importance of using grammar correctly, so they can communicate clearly and convey their meaning effectively. Comprehensive guidance is provided for teachers, supported by engaging Software, Pupils' Book and Homework Book activities.

Children meet examples of the grammar point they will study in the context of the story, playscript, poem or non-fiction text in the Anthology. The teacher then explains the grammar concept to the children, often using the Software and an activity in the Pupils' Book. Children are also taught the grammatical terms. When the teacher models the writing process the grammar concept is included so that children can see how to use it in their writing. When children do their main writing task they are reminded to include the grammar point as it is listed in the evaluation criteria. Children consolidate their knowledge of the grammar concept through activities in the Homework Book.

Grammar Bank

A Grammar Bank on the Software provides teachers with explanations about every aspect of grammar in the new National Curriculum. It contains a detailed, cross-referenced glossary of grammar terminology with clear examples and 'test yourself' exercises for teachers, with answers included. There are also grammar tests for children that provide practice in the type of questions they will meet in the English Grammar, Punctuation and Spelling Test.

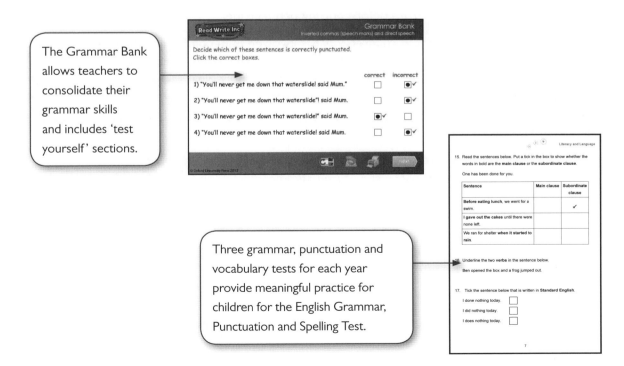

The Grammar Bank allows teachers to consolidate their grammar skills and includes 'test yourself' sections.

Three grammar, punctuation and vocabulary tests for each year provide meaningful practice for children for the English Grammar, Punctuation and Spelling Test.

Writing

Daily writing is at the heart of *Literacy and Language*. Alongside the main, extended writing activities, opportunities are taken every day to create shorter pieces of writing. This allows children to focus on very specific skills, build up their confidence and stamina for writing, and develop their understanding of audience and purpose.

As the new National Curriculum recommends, children are shown the process of writing. Using the resources for modelled writing and 'Thinking out loud', you can show what is involved in being a writer: making choices, alterations and additions while monitoring for sense and meaning. This de-mystifies the writing process for children while demonstrating the 'magic' of creating different effects with language. Writing in action shows children the power of language.

What they read, talk about and see through teacher modelling encourages children to experiment with language to express their thoughts and ideas accurately and independently. Most importantly, daily writing opportunities help children to develop a belief in themselves as writers.

Vocabulary development

The greater the children's vocabulary and the complexity of the language they hear and read, the richer their writing will be. The stories, plays, poems and non-fiction texts in the programme all include ambitious vocabulary. Before children read the texts, they are taught the meanings of more challenging words – both in the context of the story and in real life situations. The teacher and children use the vocabulary throughout the lesson, but also through the week, until the words become familiar. These new words and phrases are displayed and collected from one week to the next, keeping the favourite and most useful words displayed throughout the programme.

Spoken language

The new National Curriculum places huge emphasis upon spoken language. It states, 'The quality of and variety of language that pupils hear and speak are vital for developing their vocabulary, grammar and their understanding for reading and writing.'

Teaching children to articulate their thoughts and ideas out loud and to communicate what they know and understand is critical to the success of *Literacy and Language*. Children are taught to orally rehearse what they will write before putting pen to paper.

Teachers 'Think out loud' to show children what is involved in becoming an effective reader and writer. You can show children how you clarify and modify your understanding of what you read – how you infer and predict; build pictures in your mind; identify what's important; summarise key points; and importantly, persevere when things get tricky. In the same way, children are expected to 'Think out loud' with a partner to check their own understanding so their thinking is made clear to themselves as well as to you.

Literacy and Language uses carefully constructed partner work to make this possible. *Read Write Inc.* partner work is pacey, structured and meaningful – it keeps the children engaged throughout the lesson. Children answer every question with a partner, comment on each other's ideas, clarify each other's thinking, and build upon each other's thoughts and ideas. The teacher listens in carefully, selects children to give feedback and then selects others to build upon what they say. The teacher asks questions to take their thinking further and clears up any misconceptions.

Spelling

Read Write Inc. Spelling covers the National Curriculum spelling requirements and can be used alongside *Literacy and Language*.

How does the programme work?

Literacy and Language comprises six Units of work per year group. The Units are designed to be used over three weeks, but can also be used more flexibly, e.g. over a longer period if necessary as there is ample material and stimulus in the programme to extend tasks.

Whilst all literacy skills are developed throughout the programme, each week has a *particular* focus:

- Week 1 Reading fiction
- Week 2 Writing fiction
- Week 3 Reading and writing non-fiction

Children write every day in their Daily log (notebook) so that writing becomes a habit. They record their thoughts, ideas, and reactions to the text, often as mind maps and story maps – some of which they will draw on for extended writing activities in Weeks 2 and 3.

Grammar activities are woven into the programme on the Software and in the Pupils' Book. In addition, the Homework Book provides an opportunity for children to consolidate and practise their grammar, writing and other literacy skills at home.

Thinking and discussion skills are practised through a daily 'Big Question' which is a philosophical question that children debate so that their spoken language is developed every day.

Week 1: Reading fiction

The story store
The main story (or poem or playscript) the children study in each Unit is introduced via a brief discussion of other texts containing similar themes, some of which will be familiar to most children. Summaries of these texts are provided in the Story store on the Software. This activity helps children to make connections between texts and their own experiences.

Read a story versions 1, 2 and 3
Literacy and Language uses a three layers of text approach to teaching reading and writing. Children are introduced to the text via Story version 1, 2 and 3.

Story version 1 introduces the children to the characters, setting, and plot through about ten sentences – the 'bare bones' of the story. This allows all children to access the basic story straight away. The ending is never revealed at this stage to ensure the children are motivated to want to read the full story.

Story version 2 is a little longer than Story version 1. It gives the children more information about the characters, setting and plot. This shows children how language can be used to change or develop readers' understanding of texts.

Reading Story version 1 and Story version 2 first means that when the full story is revealed in Story version 3, which is in the Anthology, the children can focus all their attention on the subtleties, nuances and their own interpretations of the text. The staged and guided access into the story means that children who need more support are undaunted by a challenging text and can immerse themselves in the world of the story as successfully as the children who need least support.

Week 2: Writing fiction

Build a story 1, 2 and 3
Having explored a text through three layers of meaning, from its simplest level to its most complex, children then see a new text being composed through the planning, oral rehearsing,

drafting and editing stages. The teacher shows how a story is 'built up' via three layers of development (Build a story 1, 2 and 3). Using the pre-prepared resources, you are fully supported in the role of a writer as you model the composition of a text. This modelled writing deepens children's understanding of the writing process and enables them to compose confidently themselves.

Write a story 1, 2 and 3
With your support, the children then mirror the process you have modelled, drafting and revising so that they write ambitiously and accurately as they compose their own extended piece of writing.

The Software provides two versions of a story being written – Write a story 1 and Write a story 2. Through drama activities, teacher modelling and partner work, children build on these story frameworks, adding their own ideas, developing sentences and using them as models for planning their own plots, structures and characters. These prepare children to write the full story – Write a story 3.

Week 3: Reading and writing non-fiction
The fiction and non-fiction texts in each Unit are linked via one of the 'Big Questions' that children debated in the Fiction weeks. Children explore examples of the non-fiction text type, focusing on audience, purpose, form and style through Deconstruction 1, 2 and 3 activities which are designed to reveal the conventions of specific text types. Then they use what they have learnt to plan and draft their own pieces of writing, with an audience in mind, through Write a… 1 and 2 (discussion text/explanation text/instruction text, etc. depending on the text type). A final piece is then written (Write a… 3) presented and evaluated through self and peer assessment.

Core activities
The core activities encourage children to engage fully with the text as they explore character, motivation, settings and themes.

Word power
Powerful, evocative vocabulary is explained and explored before children encounter it in the story, play, poem or non-fiction text. Teachers and children are also encouraged to use the 'Power words' outside the context of the story to ensure they become part of the children's own vocabulary store.

Think and link
Used at different points in the programme, this ensures that children question what they are reading and connect it to their wider reading, own experiences and current understanding of the world.

What if not…?
An opportunity for children to speculate on how a story would change if the writer altered any one aspect of character, plot or setting, developing their awareness of how one is affected by the other, e.g. in *Beauty and the Beast*, we ask 'What if not *a handsome prince?* What if the Beast had turned into *a frog* when Beauty kissed him?'

Build a sentence
Build a sentence is used to build a vivid, engaging description. The starting point is often a single word or a short phrase which is chosen because it is particularly powerful or unusual. The activity is used, with My turn/Your turn, to build up a sentence from a simple fragment to an ambitious, complex sentence that provides children with a model of good writing in microcosm. Teachers model making choices out loud, making changes and improvements, and repeating their sentence to themselves to ensure they can remember it. Sentences can be built up out loud, or written down.

Jump in

The purpose of Jump in is to help children remember vocabulary and phrases from the story. Jump in is used in *Literacy and Language* on subsequent readings of the fiction texts, to help children remember and assimilate the 'Power words' and 'Special phrases'. Once they get to know the story, ask them to join in the reading of the words in bold. Exaggerate particular words and phrases and use actions and facial expressions to help.

Daily logs

Children write in a Daily log (notebook) to:

- record responses to what they have read, thought and talked about
- experiment with vocabulary and text structures
- make notes, mind and story maps, diagrams and plans
- collect and paste related artefacts – tickets, photos, leaflets and drawings from home.

Big Question

A 'Big Question' is asked at the end of Days 1–8 and discussion should take about 10 minutes. These questions explore an idea linked to an aspect of the text covered that day, e.g. after reading a story about two Victorian children living on the streets, the children debate: Does hunger mean the same thing to everyone? The aim of the Big Question is to develop spoken language and argument skills. Children learn to justify ideas with reasons, negotiate, evaluate and build on the ideas of others, select the appropriate register for effective communication, as well as think in a deeper way about the more abstract issues that come from the text. Children are encouraged to express their opinions and enjoy a context in which there may be no right or wrong answers, just their own carefully considered opinions.

On Day 10 children vote on which Big Question to revisit and explore more fully as a 'Very Big Question' (see p.41). This provides an opportunity for children to develop or revise their opinions. See the Very Big Question organisation below on p.17.

On Day 11 the non-fiction text is introduced through a brief re-examination of one of the Big Questions already discussed in the fiction weeks, helping children to make links between their own ideas and contextualising the new non-fiction text. For example, in Unit 4 children first study a playscript about a court case, and one of the Big Questions is: How do we know when we have justice? This is briefly revisited on Day 11 when introducing a non-fiction text about detectives looking for evidence to try and solve a crime.

Picture Books in Year 2

The same concepts and structures are used in *Literacy and Language* across Years 2–6. In Year 2, however, the Story store is enhanced by the use of high quality picture books as an introduction to the themes to be explored in the Anthology story, play or poem.

Authors and illustrators include Tony Ross, Anthony Browne, Jeanne Willis and Korky Paul.

Differentiation – guided assistance

It has been assumed that children in the *Literacy and Language* groups will all be fluent readers but not necessarily working at the same comprehension level. Differentiation is achieved by the amount of support pupils need in order to learn something new. The guidance in *Literacy and Language* ensures that children who need least support receive the necessary challenge and that others receive the necessary assistance to understand the texts they read and to write confidently.

The range of teaching and learning strategies embedded within the *Literacy and Language* resources allow you to ensure that all children develop their ability to understand the texts they read, use the spoken word confidently and become accomplished writers.

Teachers support and challenge the children by:

- developing comprehension using the three layers of text approach for reading, allowing access to engaging and challenging texts for all children
- modelling your thought processes in planning for writing and editing using 'Think out loud' and the three layers of text approach for writing
- preparing children for writing using oral rehearsal
- providing differentiated writing frames where necessary
- asking and encouraging children to ask questions, with an emphasis on allowing thinking and talking time
- using partner and small group work developed to a high level to provide peer support and challenge
- encouraging use of the Daily logs to enrich and extend children's thinking, providing a 'safe' place for recording thoughts and ideas and to experiment with short pieces of writing
- using Challenge activities in Years 5 and 6 for class extension work.

Assessment and marking

Assessment is integral to the whole *Literacy and Language* programme. Partner discussion helps teachers assess what and how children are learning throughout the lesson.

The specific focus for both reading and writing is set out at the beginning of each Unit, along with the key purpose and evaluation criteria for children's main writing composition. Each set of partners is provided with a copy of the writing Evaluation criteria (see the Planning section of the Software, and navigate to the 'Timetables' tab for these) at the start of the writing process and this is used as a guide for editing and evaluating their own and their partner's work. The criteria are included in the Pupils' Book for selected Units, and as PowerPoints on the Software, to show that they are integral to the writing process. They also form the basis for the teacher's marking. Teachers are encouraged to mark the children's work thoroughly and give advice on their next steps based upon the Evaluation criteria.

Commenting on Daily logs

Teachers explain that the Daily log is an important part of being a writer – it is to a writer what a sketch book is to an artist. The children know that the logs will not be 'marked' in the same way as their exercise books. Teachers read the children's notes and ideas and respond with thoughtful notes and suggestions. These should be written in pencil, not pen; it will be like a dialogue on paper. Children should be aware that their privacy will be respected and that ideas from their Daily log will not be shared with others without their permission. Although the Daily log is for notes and ideas, it should be stressed that this book is special – it is not a rough book or jotter. Children can leave the front page empty so that, at the end of the year, they can make a contents page for the year's work.

How do you get started?

Book training

Ruth Miskin Training provides a one- or two-day in-school training course or a one-day central training course. A knowledgeable and experienced trainer ensures you can teach the new National Curriculum confidently, using *Literacy and Language*. Please note: *Literacy and Language* should be taught by qualified teachers.

Appoint the *Literacy and Language* leader. Choose a confident and organised teacher to meet the other teachers every week for 20 minutes to discuss one particular aspect of *Literacy and Language*, demonstrate lessons to teachers, observe other teachers, evaluate children's progress and teachers' marking.

Training can be booked at: www.ruthmiskintraining.com

How does the programme fit with Read Write Inc. Phonics?

As soon as children have completed *Read Write Inc. Phonics*, or are reading at NC Level 2a, they are ready to start *Literacy and Language*. Children who finish *Read Write Inc. Phonics* during Year 2 join a Year 2 *Literacy and Language* class. Children who finish in Year 3 join a Year 3 *Literacy and Language* class, and so on. We develop the same teaching strategies and principles used in *Read Write Inc. Phonics*:

Full participation: this is fundamental to *Literacy and Language*. Teachers use 'Think out loud' to show the children how to analyse, plan and organise their ideas. 'My turn/Your turn' is also used to practise key activities and, crucially, partner work ensures that all children participate in the whole lesson.

Positive teaching: children learn at a much faster pace in an assertive and positive climate. They talk more readily in an atmosphere free from anger and tension. Praise for effective partner work is crucial.

Pace: each Unit has been planned to take three weeks. However, teachers might choose to add in extra time for some activities. You may also want to plan time for children to present and publish some of their final compositions.

Purpose: every part of the lesson has a very clear purpose. Please read the explanation behind the core activities on p.12. It is important to make the purpose of each activity transparent and easy to understand using child-friendly language.

Passion: this is a very supportive and detailed programme, which is why it works so well. However, it is the energy, enthusiasm and passion that teachers put into the lessons that bring the teaching and learning to life. Passionate teaching has impact.

Setting up Literacy and Language in your classroom

Timetable 70 minutes for *Literacy and Language* lessons. We also recommend that schools plan for an additional 20 minutes for Storytime every day. Suggested stories and poems to read to children are listed on www.ruthmiskintraining.com. In the Overview chart on pp.18–19, there are also suggestions for stories and books for wider reading which will link to the themes and genres explored in the Units.

Management signals

Use these signals to ensure teaching is effective and consistent throughout the school.

The 'stop' signal: when all children are engaged in partner work, you need to be able to get their attention quickly and easily without raising your voice. Hold your hand in the air and do not talk whilst it is raised. When children see the signal they should finish what they are saying and raise one hand in response. Do not start talking until everyone has returned the signal and you have lowered your hand.

'My turn/Your turn' signal (MT/YT): there are times when you will need children to copy what you do. *My turn:* touch your chest with your palm when it's your turn. *Your turn:* open your palm to children when it's their turn.

The 'Turn to your partner' signal (TTYP): before you ask a question, tap two fingers together to warn children they will need to turn to their partners to answer. Explain that the 'hands up' system for answering questions will not be used. Ask children to put one hand on their head if they need clarification or have a question to ask.

The 'Perfect partner position': partners should sit side-by-side and shoulder-to-shoulder. (If they face each other the noise level increases.) Number the partners 1 and 2. Children keep the same number for the duration of the whole Unit. See the Planning section of the Software and navigate to the 'Extras' tab for further guidance on choosing partners, and activities to ensure partners work effectively together.

Planning and preparation

All the planning is ready for you to use. However, a thorough understanding of the programme's multi-layered and integrated approach to teaching fiction, non-fiction and grammar is vital. The more prepared you are, the more successful your children will be.

First, gain a thorough overview of the whole Unit. Read the story and non-fiction texts in the Anthology, followed by the teachers' notes in the Handbook, and the activities in the Pupils' Book and Software. You will see how the individual layers unfold; how the reading activities feed into the writing and how the 'Big Questions' weave together the fiction and non-fiction texts. Each activity builds upon the next.

Study the timetable at the beginning of each Unit – it provides an overview of the activities for each day and shows when you need to print out any files from the Software such as evaluation sheets, modelled writing prompts, words for display, etc.

Prepare for your lessons using the teaching notes for the Unit. You could also use and adapt the flexible planning sheets on the Software.

Organising discussion

Setting ground rules for discussion
The ground rules for discussion should inform the whole school policy on teaching and learning so they become fundamental to every lesson in every curriculum area. Children should be taught, explicitly, the rules for working in a group or with a partner and take part in regular

evaluations of what makes for effective discussion – see the Planning section of the Software, and navigate to the 'Extras' tab for the Effective discussion poster. Although the rules are similar for all ages, children's responses increase in complexity and sophistication year-by-year.

Display the Effective discussion poster in a prominent position. Praise the children for specific behaviour when partners co-operate successfully.

Short answers
Explain to the children that you will sometimes require a one- or two-word answer to questions – use a finger and thumb to show 'small'. This action tells partners to turn back to you quickly once they have said their answer to their partner.

One, two, three: if there is only one answer to the question, say '*One, two, three*,' and ask children to call out the answer together.

Popcorn: if there are lots of different one-word answers use Popcorn – children call out their answers in the pauses between other answers.

Wave: sweep your arm across the room in a wave. Children call out their answer as your arm sweeps over them.

Longer answers to explain why
Ask a question, then ask partners to TTYP (Turn to your partner). Listen in to different partnerships each time, sometimes building on their ideas. Do not get too involved with one partnership as it is important to observe how well all sets of partners work together – particularly in the early days. Do not give children too long to answer or let the discussion tail off. Importantly, make sure children carry on talking until you raise your hand to stop. It is very disruptive to discussion when children raise their hands/show thumbs or use any other signal to show that they have an answer ready. Select partnerships with helpful contributions to feed back to the group or do this on their behalf.

In-depth answers to consider different viewpoints, challenge claims politely, negotiate an agreement
As above but go backwards and forwards, asking other partnerships to build on the contributions of others.

Very Big Question organisation

For the extended 'Very Big Question' discussion, make sure the children are seated so that they can all see each other. Set aside 20–30 minutes to allow a full discussion. Act as the facilitator and avoid taking over or dominating the discussion. Ensure that all children are allowed to express their points of view and make every attempt to elicit responses from other children to what has been said rather than simply accepting a series of opinions with no real acknowledgement of others' ideas and opinions.

You can vary the way you organise the children, e.g. have a whole group discussion; smaller groups or pairs who discuss and then come together as one large group. Avoid 'jigsawing' as you want the children to develop their ability to sustain and deepen discussions beyond their first responses.

The Big Questions and the Very Big Questions are not just about developing language and social skills. They are vital opportunities for children to explore ways of thinking about and perceiving the world, themselves and others and of universal themes and ideas stimulated by their reading.

Overview chart

Unit	Unit 1	Unit 2	Unit 3	
Main grammar focus for the Unit	Inverted commas	Paragraphs	Adverbials including fronted adverbials	
Fiction text/s	*Lost or Stolen?* by Narinder Dhami (A dilemma story)	'The Balloons' by Oscar Wilde 'My Sari' by Debjani Chatterjee 'At the End of a School Day' by Wes Magee (Poetry)	*The Bogey Men and the Trolls Next Door* by Kaye Umansky (A story in narrative verse)	
Fiction focus	This Unit explores the themes of relationships, suspicion and trust. Children use a story 'roller coaster' to plan and write a new chapter for *Lost or Stolen?* by Narinder Dhami.	This Unit explores three poems with the theme of moments to remember: everyday moments shaped into poems. The emphasis is on enjoying the poets' use of language to create images and emotions. Children are encouraged to experiment with language and form to create their own poem in free verse.	In this Unit children read a story told in rhyming narrative verse. They use drama and discussion to look at some of the serious issues behind the humour in the story. Strands of the story are then picked out to form the basis of the children's own writing.	
Suggestions for wider reading	*Cinderella: A Fairy Tale* – Charles Perrault and Loek Koopmans *Cendrillon: A Caribbean Cinderella* – Robert D. San Souci and Brian Pinkney *The Egyptian Cinderella* – Shirley Climo and Ruth Heller *Snow White in New York* – Fiona French *Snow White* – Josephine Poole and Angela Barrett	*Heard it in the Playground* – Allan Ahlberg *The Puffin Book of Utterly Brilliant Poetry* – Brian Patten (Editor) *Don't Tell the Teacher* – Gervase Phinn *I Like This Poem* – Kaye Webb (Editor) *Boy: Tales of Childhood* – Roald Dahl *Matilda* – Roald Dahl *The Worst Witch Collection* – Jill Murphy	*Trolls Go Home (Troll Trouble)* – Alan MacDonald *The Secret Book of Trolls* – Danny Willis *Troll Wood* – Kathryn Cave and Paul Hess *Jabberwocky and other poems* – Tig Thomas *Night of the Gargoyles* – Eve Bunting and David Wiesner *Science Verse* – Jon Scieszka and Lane Smith	
Non-fiction text/s	'Gadget Magic' 'The Greatest Gadget of Them All?' (Information texts)	'Your Alien Experiences' 'The Daily Blab' (Journalistic recounts)	'The Stellar Stage School' 'How the Voice Works' (Explanation texts)	
Non-fiction focus	Children look at information texts presented in a variety of styles, in a magazine feature format. They create and present their own information texts. Then they plan a presentation to pitch a new gadget to potential investors.	Children explore recounts and journalistic texts. They learn about the main features of recounts through reading and analysing some journalistic reports. They then write their own newspaper report.	Children explore the language and organisational features of explanation texts through examples of visual, verbal and written explanations. They create their own explanations in a variety of forms, culminating in the delivery of an explanatory lesson on how to get the 'pop star look'.	

	Unit 4	Unit 5	Unit 6
	Plurals, possession and apostrophes	Standard English	Nouns and pronouns
	The Fly and the Fool by Lou Kuenzler (A playscript)	*Runaways!* by Jim Eldridge (A story with a historical setting)	*Sugarcane Juice* by Pratima Mitchell (A story from another culture)
	In this Unit the children explore a playscript set in Vietnam. They look at the differences between how the characters see themselves and how others see them. The children then write an ending for a new playscript based on the traditional tale of Rumpelstiltskin.	This Unit focuses on a story set in Victorian times. Children explore the setting and use it to immerse themselves in the story. The setting and period then provide inspiration for their own writing.	This Unit explores a story from another culture, set in Pakistan. Children look closely at the vivid descriptions and action so that they can borrow language, ideas and structure such as dialogue to use in their own writing. They then write an additional episode of the story using the ideas and techniques that they have explored.
	Children of the Dragon: Selected Tales from Vietnam – Sherry Garland and Trina Schart Hyman *Stories from Around the World* – Heather Amery and Linda Edwards *Illustrated Stories from Grimm* – Ruth Brocklehurst, Gill Doherty and Raffaella Ligi *Brothers Grimm Folk Tales* – The Brothers Grimm, Michael Foreman and Brian Alderson	*Hetty Feather* – Jacqueline Wilson and Nick Sharratt *Smith* – Leon Garfield *Street Child* – Berlie Doherty *Cecily's Portrait* – Adèle Geras *Lizzie's Wish* – Adèle Geras	*Haroun and the Sea of Stories* – Salman Rushdie *Stories from India* – Anna Milbourne and Linda Edwards *The Wheel of Surya* – Jamila Gavin *Seasons of Splendour: Tales, Myths and Legends of India* – Madhur Jaffrey and Michael Foreman *Rickshaw Girl* – Mitali Perkins and Jamie Hogan
	'Junior Detective!' (Evaluating evidence)	'London Herald' (Newspapers)	'VIPER! – Critic's Review' 'VIPER! – A Film Trailer' (Persuasive writing)
	Children read an explanation about how the police use different sorts of evidence to prove who has committed a crime. Next they look at several pieces of evidence and evaluate them, choosing two to present to a 'court'.	Children broaden their knowledge of Victorian times by exploring journalistic texts that are typical of the period. They will learn about the features of newspaper articles and entries. Then they write their own entry for a class newspaper set during the Victorian era.	Children develop their understanding of persuasive techniques used in advertising so that they can create their own marketing campaign with a clear message. They analyse a film trailer and a poster and design their own versions for a new film.

Fiction: Dilemma story
Non-fiction: Information texts

Timetable

WEEK 1   Reading fiction   *Lost or Stolen?*

Day 1	Day 2	Day 3	Day 4	Day 5
The story store	Read a story version 3	Who changes most?	Hidden dilemma	Creating suspense 🖨
Context	Word power 🖨	Text detectives	Quiz the character	Storytellers
Read a story version 1	Special phrases	What if not...?	Hidden conversations	Daily log
Think and link	Re-read a story version 3	Daily log	Daily log	Big Question
Read a story version 2	Dilemma	Big Question	Big Question	
Daily log	Daily log			
Big Question	Big Question			

WEEK 2   Writing fiction   *Lost or Stolen?*

Day 6	Day 7	Day 8	Day 9	Day 10
Story roller coaster	Build a dilemma	Build a story 2	Step into the setting	Share a description
What if not...?	Conscience alley	Dramatic reconstruction	Build a story 3 🖨	Evaluate and edit
What would you do? 🖨	Build a story 1	Grammar: inverted commas	Write a story 3	Proofread
Daily log	Write a story 1	Write a story 2 🖨		Very Big Question
Big Question	Daily log	Daily log		
	Big Question	Big Question		

WEEK 3   Reading and writing non-fiction   Information texts

Day 11	Day 12	Day 13	Day 14	Day 15
Linking texts	Information detectives	Deconstruction 2	Proofread	Presentations
Grammar: word classes and suffixes	Deconstruction 1	Write 2 🖨	Grammar: suffixes, prefixes and word classes	Evaluate and edit
Who says?	Write 1	Daily log	Deconstruction 3	
What do I want to know?	Daily log		Write 3	
Daily log			Daily log	

🖨: shows that a file should be printed out from the Software.

© Oxford University Press 2013. This page may be reproduced for use solely within the purchaser's school or college.

Overview of the Unit

This Unit uses the contemporary story *Lost or Stolen?* by Narinder Dhami to explore the themes of relationships, suspicion and trust. Opportunities for writing involve using a story 'roller coaster' to plan and write a new chapter for the story.

Linked via a Big Question, the Non-fiction week looks at information texts presented in a variety of styles, in a magazine feature format. For more information about the Non-fiction week and the Non-fiction writing evaluation criteria, see p.42.

Where appropriate, the children will be encouraged to develop an awareness of audience and purpose in relation to the fiction and non-fiction texts they are reading and writing.

Teacher modelling is provided in the teaching notes, Software and the Pupils' Book, supporting the children's writing at every stage in the Fiction and Non-fiction weeks.

The Homework Book provides a homework activity related to the content of this Unit for each of the three weeks.

Fiction

Reading

Children will:

- link the theme of dilemmas in *Lost or Stolen?* with their own experiences and other stories
- explore the characters, including what they think and how they change as the story develops
- understand how suspense is created in a story
- explore how they can use their voices to create tension when reading aloud.

Writing

Key writing purpose to be shared with the children:

To use the structure and characters from Lost or Stolen? *to write a new chapter of the story with a different dilemma and setting.*

Writing evaluation to be shared with the children

My story chapter:

- uses what I know about the characters to show how they react to their new dilemma and what the consequences are
- describes a new setting using the senses and similes so the reader can build a strong picture in their mind.

Grammar:

- includes direct speech, which is set out and punctuated correctly.

See the Planning section of the Software ('Timetables' tab) for a printable version of the Writing purpose and evaluation.

Fiction: Dilemma story
Lost or Stolen? by Narinder Dhami

[handwritten:] Resources for display; bracelets, wool, Indian sweets

Resources

🔲 **PB** Pupils' Book, pp.4–13
🔲 **A** Anthology, pp.4–17
🔲 **CD** CD on Interactive whiteboard, Unit 1
🔲 **GB** Grammar Bank on CD
🔲 **HB** Homework Book, pp.4–6

READING FICTION

DAY 1

Curriculum link:
listening to and discussing a wide range of fiction; identifying themes

The story store 🔘CD

Purpose: for children to encounter themes to be explored in the main Anthology text

- Tell the children that every day we face choices and make decisions that affect other people. Explain that in some situations the choices and decisions are simple and some are much more difficult.

- Say that a difficult or tricky problem is called a dilemma. Write the word *dilemma* on the board or a flipchart. Say the first sentence below, and then use MT/YT (My turn/Your turn) to say the phrase '*What a dilemma!*': '*Should Sam tell the teacher who was cheating in the test? What a dilemma!*' (MT/YT)

- Repeat with the next two sentences:
  '*Should Charlie swap the birthday present from his gran for that computer game he really wants? What a dilemma!*' (MT/YT)
  '*Should Emma admit that it was her who broke mum's favourite vase? What a dilemma!*' (MT/YT)

- Remind the children that many stories have a character that faces a dilemma and has difficult choices to make. Display **CD (file 1.1)** to show the first of two summaries from traditional stories. Use MT/YT to read the summary.

- Ask the children to TTYP (Turn to your partner) to say which story they think this is from and then to Popcorn (see Introduction p.17) their answers. Clarify that it is from the story of *Snow White*.

- Click 'Dilemma' to show the dilemma the character faced. Use MT/YT to read it aloud.

- Click 'Next' and read out and explore the second story summary (from the fairy tale *Cinderella*). Click 'Dilemma' to show the dilemma Cinderella faced. Use MT/YT to read it aloud.

- TOL (Think out loud) about a dilemma you have had to face (don't make it too dramatic) and then ask the children to TTYP to share a dilemma they have faced.

Context 🔘CD

[handwritten:] ✻ Write here definition of dilemma

Purpose: for children to become familiar with specific cultural facts and vocabulary needed to understand the story

- Tell the children that they are going to be hearing and reading a special new story in which one of the characters faces a dilemma. Explain that there are some facts and information that some children might not know, about a festival called Raksha Bandhan. Say that this festival is important in our new story.

- Display **CD (file 1.2)** to show the first image and information about Raksha Bandhan. Talk it through, making sure that the children understand the basic meaning of the festival.

- Navigate through the slides to show more images and information, including the tradition and symbolism of *rakhis*. Talk through each slide but don't reveal the link between these and the full story of *Lost or Stolen?* at this point.

<table>
<tr><td>

Curriculum link:
predicting

</td></tr>
</table>

Read a story version 1

Before the lesson, you may wish to watch the video demonstrating Read a story version 1 (with a Year 5 story). This can be found in the Extras section of the Software.

Purpose: for children to become familiar with Story 1; the bare bones of Lost or Stolen?

- Tell the children that they are now going to hear the bare bones of the new story and we are going to call it Story version 1.
- Read the bare bones of the story aloud to the children. Don't reveal any surprises or the ending of the story.
  Story version 1
  1. A girl and her brother have a cousin who visits every day.
  2. They don't like their cousin.
  3. Something goes missing.
  4. Someone faces a dilemma.
  5. It is the festival of Raksha Bandhan.
  6. Something is given to someone.
  7. Something is found.
- Use MT/YT to re-read each point. Exaggerate intonation and emphasis for effect. This will help the children to 'hold' the basic story in their minds. Show your interest in and excitement about the new story.
- Tell the children that even though this is just the bare bones of the story, the words were already creating pictures in your mind of the characters and the action. Explain that you are going to re-read the story and you would like them to close their eyes and make pictures in their own minds as you read.
- Now ask them to TTYP to share one or two images they conjured from the words. Choose two or three sets of partners to share their thoughts with the whole group.

drawing and justifying inferences

Think and link

Purpose: for children to make links and connections between other stories they know, their own experiences and the new story

- Now display **CD (file 1.3)** to show Story version 1 to the children.
- TOL about a time when you noticed something had gone missing and you didn't know whether it had been lost or stolen, e.g. your keys. Talk about the feelings you had and if you ever found the missing item.
- Now ask the children to TTYP to share their own experiences of something going missing. Choose two or three sets of partners to feed back and encourage them to make connections between their own experiences, your experience and any of the stories they have discussed.
- Ask them to record their own experience using two or three sentences in their Daily log.

predicting; identifying how language, structure and presentation contribute to meaning

Read a story version 2

Purpose: for children to see how Story version 2 'grows' the new story, by providing additional information; for children to become more familiar with the story before they hear it for the first time

- Say that it is time to find out a bit more about the new story. Explain that the story has been developed and then read it aloud with varied intonation and appropriate emphasis.
  Story version 2
  1. A girl called Chandra and her brother Ravi have a cousin who visits every day in the summer holidays.
  2. They don't like their cousin, Taj, because he is always boasting about his expensive possessions. He seems to have everything he wants.

3. It is the day before the festival of Raksha Bandhan, celebrating brothers and sisters. Chandra and Ravi are cross that Taj will be joining them for the festival.
4. Someone's prize possession goes missing. Has it been lost or stolen? Who could have stolen it? Someone thinks they have all the answers but they face a dilemma.
5. It is the day of the festival of Raksha Bandhan and the item is still missing.
6. Chandra gives something very special to someone.
7. Chandra, Ravi and Taj each find something valuable.

- Ask the children to TTYP to share how the pictures in their minds changed as they heard the story with the extra information.
- Now ask them to TTYP to share one or two images again. Take feedback and TOL about how incredible it is that words can make and change pictures in our minds.
- Now click 'Next' to display this version on **CD (file 1.3).** Click 'Highlights' to reveal the extra information to show how the story has been developed.
- Close the CD file and ask the children to TTYP to take turns telling the story to each other. Explain that Partner 1 will begin, and when you say '*Stop and swap*', Partner 2 will take over. Keep repeating the *stop and swap* process until they have finished telling the story so far.
- Explain that when they hear the full story by author Narinder Dhami, they will find out even more about Chandra, Ravi and Taj and the difficult dilemma.

Daily log

Curriculum link: discussing and recording ideas; predicting

Purpose: for children to keep a personal log of notes, thoughts and ideas, collected from their reading and discussions. Some ideas will be used in their own writing

- Ask the children to TTYP to remind each other what the word *dilemma* means.
- Collect answers from one or two sets of partners and use their responses to build a clear definition. Write it on the board or a flipchart. Use MT/YT to say the definition.
- Hide your definition and tell them to write their own definition in their Daily log.
- Now ask the children to TTYP to share ideas about what the dilemma in the new story might turn out to be.
- Ask them to record their own ideas in their log. Choose a few sets of partners to share and explain the reasons behind their ideas.

Big Question (CD)

discussion; develop, agree on, and evaluate rules for effective discussion

Purpose: for children to develop their skills of argument and discussion through a mini enquiry session based on a philosophical question relating to the work of the day

- Display today's Big Question on the **CD (file 1.4)**:

  Can a friend be like a brother or sister?

- Ask the children to TTYP to talk about this question. Collect feedback and write some responses on the board.
- Click 'Prompts' to show some statements that may help to encourage discussion.

DAY 2

Read a story version 3 🄰 (teacher only) 🄿🄱

checking that the text makes sense, asking questions, drawing inferences

Purpose: for children to hear and enjoy the full version of the story for the first time

- Tell the children that they are now going to hear the whole story for the very first time. TOL about which parts you are looking forward to hearing about.
- Ask the children to TTYP to share what they are looking forward to in the story.
- Now read the full story from the Anthology pp.4–13 aloud to the children, with great enjoyment, enthusiasm and appropriate intonation.
- At the end of the story, ask the children to look at the Read a story version 3 activity on p.4 in their Pupils' Book. Guide them as they TTYP to discuss the questions and feed back to the class.

Curriculum link: discussing words and phrases that capture the reader's interest and imagination

Word power

Purpose: for children to increase their knowledge of and application of rarer vocabulary and synonyms

> *incessantly   exasperated   trepidation   despondent*

- Before the lesson, print out the Power words and their synonyms from printable **CD (file 2.1)** and display them on your Story wall.
- Tell the children that there were some words in the story they heard yesterday that the author chose because they are powerful.
- Display **CD (file 2.2)** to show the Power words. Use MT/YT to say the first word. Click 'Synonyms' to show the synonyms for the word and a sample sentence.
- Ask the children to repeat the sentence using MT/YT, giving dramatic emphasis and actions as you say it. Repeat the process for the rest of the words.
- Let the children hear you use the words in your teaching and conversation throughout the day in an exaggerated or ironic fashion e.g. *'I arrived at school today with great* trepidation.' *or 'I seem to have talked* incessantly *this morning, children!'*
- Encourage them to use the words with friends and family so that they become embedded in the children's own spoken (and eventually, written) vocabulary.
- Remind them that these powerful words are on the Story wall for this Unit and are there for everyone to use. Praise them if they use one of the words.

discussing words and phrases that capture the reader's interest and imagination

Special phrases ⓒⒹ

Purpose: for children to become familiar with Special phrases particular to the story and consolidate their understanding of imagery

> *...the sun shone as brightly as the gold* rakhi *Chandra tied on Ravi's wrist.*
>
> *...they shared delicious Indian jellied sweets that glistened like rubies, emeralds and amethysts.*

- Remind the children that an image is a picture. Say that an artist creates images with paint but a writer creates images with words.
- Tell the children that you are going to show them some Special phrases from the story. Explain that these are special because they are phrases that help to form clear images in our minds.
- Explain that each of these Special phrases uses a simile to create a powerful image. Ask them to TTYP to remind each other what a simile is. Collect answers and examples and clarify if necessary.
- Now display **CD (file 2.3)** to show the first Special phrase. Use MT/YT to read the phrase aloud. TOL about why you think the writer chose this simile.
- Click 'Reveal' to show the second Special phrase and repeat MT/YT to read the phrase, then TOL about the writer's choice.
- Now ask the children to TTYP to choose their favourite Special phrase. Make sure they can explain to their partner what they like about it and why the *image* and *simile* help the reader. Choose some partners to feed back.
- Tell the children that you want them to create some Special phrases. Say that you have chosen parts of the story that they could turn into powerful images by using similes.
- Click 'Reveal' again to show a part of the story. Ask the children to TTYP to share ideas for a simile to create a powerful image of Ravi snapping at Taj, e.g. *...Ravi snapped like a hungry crocodile.*

- Choose two or three sets of partners to feed back and type some examples in the editable box on screen. Ask the children to TTYP to say which one they think is the most effective and why. Collect feedback.
- Click 'Next' to look at another line from the story: 'Taj looked despondent when he turned up.' Ask the children to recall the meaning of the word *despondent* and to Popcorn their answers.
- Remind them that some similes will have *as* _____ *as* ____ instead of *like a* ____. Click 'Reveal' on **CD (file 2.3)** to show the altered version that will allow for a simile.
- Ask the children to TTYP to share ideas for a simile to create a powerful image of how despondent Taj looked, e.g. *Taj looked as despondent as a cat that got caught in the rain when he turned up.*
- Choose two or three sets of partners to feed back and type some examples in the editable boxes on screen. Ask the children to TTYP to say which one they think is the most effective and why. Collect feedback.
- Blank the screen and write these sentences on the board or a flipchart.

  Ravi snapped like a _____·_____

  Taj looked as despondent as a _____

- Now ask them to complete the sentences using similes to write their own Special phrases in their Daily log.

Curriculum link:
showing
understanding
through
intonation, tone
and volume

Re-read a story version 3

Purpose: for children to gain a deeper understanding of the story and to see the text for the first time

- Ask the children to turn to pp.4–11 in their Anthologies and to read the story aloud with their partners. They should read alternate pages each, and ensure they use expression and intonation to convey meaning and impact to their partner. Explain that you will be listening in and looking out for particularly good reading.
- For some groups, you may wish to read aloud to the children first as they follow the text in their own copy so that they can Jump in (see Introduction p.13.) to say the Power words and Special phrases.

Dilemma

Purpose: for children to develop their ability to identify a dilemma in a story

Plenary:
Challenge –
design a K2Y
Version 4
(2 min whiteboard
challenge)

- Remind the children that before they heard the full story, they recorded their ideas about what the main dilemma might turn out to be.
- Now ask them to TTYP to decide:
  - Who faced the main dilemma in the story?
  - What dilemma did they face?
- Write the two questions as headings on the board or a flipchart and then choose two or three sets of partners to share their ideas. Write their answers under the headings, teasing out reasons for their answers and using your own TOLs to explore other possibilities as they arise.
- Now ask them to TTYP to discuss how the dilemma was resolved. Take feedback and clarify if necessary.

Daily log

Purpose: for children to keep a personal log of notes, thoughts and ideas, collected from their reading and discussions. Some ideas will be used in their own writing

record ideas;
composing
and rehearsing
sentences orally

- Ask the children to write down the answers in their own words to the questions:
  - Who faced the main dilemma in the story?
  - What dilemma did they face?
  - How was the dilemma resolved?
- Remind them to rehearse their sentences in their minds until their ideas are fully formed, before writing them down in their Daily log.

Curriculum link:
discussion;
develop, agree on,
and evaluate
rules for effective
discussion

Big Question

Purpose: for children to develop their skills of argument and discussion through a mini enquiry session based on a philosophical question relating to the work of the day

- Display today's Big Question on the **CD (file 2.4)**:

  Are gadgets always good to have?*

- Follow the process as explained on Day 1.

  This Big Question will be revisited on Day 11 – the first day of the Non-fiction week.

DAY 3

Who changes most?

Purpose: for children to explore and develop their own point of view about the development of characters in the story

- Tell the children that the words and actions of characters can show us how they change and develop throughout a story.
- Display **CD (file 3.1)** to show one section from *Lost or Stolen?* Ask them to read it aloud chorally with appropriate intonation and expression to convey meaning.
- Click 'TOL' to show a think bubble and use it and/or your own ideas to say how you would describe Chandra's character based on this part of the story only.
- Now ask the children to TTYP to say how they would describe Taj based on this part of the story only. Take feedback and make sure the children can support their ideas and then repeat the process for Ravi.
- Explain that characters' behaviour can change as the story changes and develops. Now ask them to look at the Who changes most? activity on p.4 of their Pupils' Book.
- Tell them to TTYP to read another section of the story and the statements shown and then discuss which character they think has changed the most. Make sure they understand that there isn't a right answer, you are just looking for their own ideas and opinions.
- Take feedback, making sure the children give reasons for their choices.
- Ask them to write a couple of sentences in their Daily log saying who changes the most during the story and why.

Text detectives

Purpose: for children to develop an awareness of subtext

- Tell the children that the words on a page tell us some of the story but that writers give us lots of extra clues about what characters might be thinking, what makes them behave in certain ways and how other people's actions might be influencing or affecting them.
- Explain that this is like hidden or secret writing, and readers can be like detectives, finding the hidden or secret information that helps us to understand the characters and the story even better.
- Display **CD (file 3.2)** to show an 'iceberg' text/secret text diagram. Use the think bubbles to talk through and explain the diagram.
- Move to the next slide to display text from the story *Lost or Stolen?* Read it out using MT/YT. TOL to explain the diagram.
- On the next slide, click 'Secret text'. Use MT/YT to read the subtext and ask the children to TTYP to say whether they agree and why. Take feedback.

Cut r paste
activity
onto picture
ice-berg?

Fiction: Dilemma story

- Ask the children to TTYP and to look at the Text detectives activity on p.5 of their Pupils' Book. Tell them to complete the activity, matching the writing from *Lost or Stolen?* with the 'secret writing'.

Curriculum link:
drawing inferences; participate in discussion about books

What if not...?

Purpose: for children to consider how the characters' actions affect the plot

- Ask the children to look at the What if not...? activity on p.6 of their Pupils' Book. Model how you TOL about the first What if not...? question: What if not *Ravi's dad who borrowed the games console? What if Taj had borrowed it without asking permission?*

  Ravi and Chandra might still have realised it was missing, but if Taj put the console back after borrowing it then Ravi and Chandra would never know where it had disappeared to. If they suspected Taj they would never quite trust him but would not want to ask him about it. On the other hand, if they caught Taj putting the console back after secretly borrowing it, they would know that he had taken it but couldn't say he had stolen it as he had returned it! I think Ravi and Chandra would be really angry though.

- Explain that this is a discursive response, i.e. you are thinking about the issue from lots of different angles.
- Now ask the children to TTYP to discuss the other What if not...? questions. Collect feedback and encourage others to build upon and develop ideas.
- Encourage the children to use discursive language, e.g. *On the other hand..., It could be..., Maybe...*, to help them to order and articulate their answers.
- Ask them to think of their own What if not...? question with a partner. Choose one pair to feed back, and discuss their question as a class.

discussing their understanding and explaining the meaning of words; write for a range of purposes

Daily log 🔘

Purpose: for children to keep a personal log of notes, thoughts and ideas, collected from their reading and discussions. Some ideas will be used in their own writing

- Remind the children that Chandra gave Ravi and Taj a *rakhi* each. Ask the children to TTYP to explain what a *rakhi* is and why it is given to boys. Choose two sets of partners to share their explanations and clarify where necessary.
- Now ask them to write an explanation of what a *rakhi* is, who it is given to and why, in their Daily log.
- Display **CD (file 3.3)** to show examples of different *rakhis*. Tell the children to choose the *rakhi* they would like to give or receive. Ask them to write a brief description of it in their Daily log.

discussion; develop, agree on, and evaluate rules for effective discussion

Big Question 🔘

Purpose: for children to develop their skills of argument and discussion through a mini enquiry session based on a philosophical question relating to the work of the day

- Display today's Big Question on the **CD (file 3.4)**:

  Is it better to give someone a present or do something for them?

- Follow the process as explained on Day 1.

Hidden dilemma

Purpose: for children to develop their ability to think outside the story to enrich their reading experience

- Remind the children that they were able to identify the main dilemma in the story *Lost or Stolen?*

- Explain that there are two characters that we know about but never hear from or 'meet' in the story. Ask the children to TTYP to identify who the characters are. Now ask them to Popcorn their answer (*Taj's mum and dad*).
- Tell the children to take turns to re-read the story with their partner, one section at a time. Then ask them to TTYP to discuss what information they know about Taj's parents from the story. Take feedback and clarify if necessary.
- Explain that based on what you know from the story, you think Taj's parents have a dilemma of their own. Ask the children to TTYP to say what they think their dilemma is, e.g. *they work very long hours, have lots of money to spend on Taj but no time to spend with him.*
- Collect feedback and generate discussion about whether Taj's parents have to work such long hours or whether they could choose to spend more time with him. Make sure they understand that there isn't a right answer, you are just looking for their own opinions.
- Take a quick vote on who thinks Taj's parents are just doing their best for him and who thinks they should spend less money and more time with him.

Quiz the character ⓒᴰ

Purpose: for children to use hotseating to explore a character's motivations, feelings and actions

- Tell the children that you would like to explore how Taj might feel about his life. Say that you have some questions to use to hotseat Taj.
- Display **CD (file 4.1)** to show the first question. Use MT/YT to read the question and then ask the children to TTYP to share ideas about how Taj might respond.
- Choose two sets of partners to feed back. Click 'Questions' to show the next question. Use MT/YT to say the question and repeat the TTYP and feedback process.
- Keep clicking 'Questions' to reveal two further questions and repeat the whole process.
- Ask the children to TTYP to share ideas about any other questions they would like to ask Taj. Collect feedback. You may wish to record a few of their questions on the board or a flipchart.
- Now tell the children that they are going to take turns being Taj in the hotseat.
- Navigate to the next slide and click on 'Hotseat 1' to show the first two questions again. Explain that Partner 1s will take on the role of Taj in the hotseat and Partner 2s will ask the questions. Model how you would respond to a question.
- Say they may add one more question of their own to ask Taj if they wish.
- Walk around noting empathetic and thoughtful responses from Partner 1s to use as the basis for your feedback to the children.
- Stop the hotseating. Click 'Hotseat 1' to hide the first two questions and click 'Hotseat 2' to show the final two questions again. Explain that Partner 2s will now take on the role of Taj in the hotseat and Partner 1s will ask the questions, then repeat the process above.
- Give feedback to the children based on your observations.

Hidden conversations ⓒᴰ

Purpose: for children to develop the ability to empathise with different kinds of characters

- Tell the children that you have been wondering what kind of conversations Taj's parents might have together and with Taj.
- Display **CD (file 4.2)** to show a scenario. Read it aloud and then click 'Dialogue' to show dialogue. Tell Partner 1s to read Taj's dad's dialogue aloud and Partner 2s to read Taj's mum's dialogue aloud.

- Explain that this is just one possible conversation they could have. Navigate to the next slide and click 'Dialogue' to show different dialogue. Repeat the process of partners reading it aloud.
- Now tell the children to look at the Hidden conversations activity on p.6 of their Pupils' Book. Talk through the prompts to help them to create notes for a short role-play of the conversation between Taj and one of his parents.
- Explain that they can use their notes as a script or just re-read them and then improvise.
- Allow time for partners to plan and practise their role-plays. You may wish each set of partners to perform to the whole group or you could create small groups from three or four sets of partners to perform in turn for each other.
- Walk around listening and noting interesting dialogue and perspectives on the situation and good partner work to use as the basis for your feedback to the children.

<table>
<tr><td>

Curriculum link:
recording ideas;
write for a range
of purposes; read
aloud their own
writing to the
whole class

</td><td>

Daily log

Purpose: for children to keep a personal log of notes, thoughts and ideas, collected from their reading and discussions. Some ideas will be used in their own writing

- Display **CD (file 4.3)** to show two examples of blurbs for *Lost or Stolen?* and read them aloud chorally with the children.
- Tell them that you want them to TTYP to decide which blurb is the most successful and which is the least successful and to explain why. Make sure they understand that there isn't a right answer, you are just looking for their own ideas and opinions.
- Collect responses and encourage them to give reasons for their choices.
- Now tell the children that you want them to write a blurb of their own. Leave the examples on the screen and tell the children they can borrow any words or phrases to help them. Explain that they can choose whether to work alone or with their partner.
- Ask the children to Popcorn any of the Power words or synonyms they heard in the story. Write them on the board or a flipchart and ask them to try to include one in their blurb.
- Choose two or three sets of partners to read out their blurbs to the whole class.
- Over the next couple of days, choose and photocopy a few examples to display on the Story wall for this Unit.

</td></tr>
<tr><td>

discussion;
develop, agree on,
and evaluate
rules for effective
discussion

</td><td>

Big Question

Purpose: for children to develop their skills of argument and discussion through a mini enquiry session based on a philosophical question relating to the work of the day

- Display today's Big Question on the **CD (file 4.4)**:

  What is more important, time or money?

- Follow the process as explained on Day 1.

</td></tr>
</table>

DAY 5

Creating suspense

Dictionaries will be required in this part of the lesson.

Purpose: for children to increase their knowledge of specific vocabulary relating to suspense in stories

- Tell the children that stories with dilemmas in them need to create *suspense*. Display **CD (file 5.1)** to show the word *suspense* and its definition. Read it aloud to the children.
- Click 'Reveal' to show four ways a writer can create suspense.
- Give each set of partners an *Oxford Junior Dictionary* or equivalent. Remind them that because this is a special dictionary written for children, some words are not

listed. Tell them that there are over 10,000 entries in their dictionary. Explain that in the full, adult *Oxford English Dictionary*, there are over 650,000 words.

- Write the title *Suspense in Dilemma Stories* on the board or a flipchart. Remind them how to look up words in a dictionary, using the word *suspense* as an example. Read out the dictionary definition and write it on the board or flipchart.
- Now click 'Reveal' again to show the words *curious*, *confusing*, *choices*, and *surprise*.
- Ask the children to TTYP to look the words up in their dictionary and to write the definitions in their Daily log in their own words. Tell them that if a word is not in their dictionary they will need to TTYP to work it out from the context. Model this by giving an example of the word in a sentence, and guide children towards the correct meaning.
- Choose a different set of partners to share each definition they have recorded with the class.
- Print **CD (file 5.2)** to display on your Story wall for this Unit. The printable file includes different forms of the words and some extra, related words.

Curriculum link:
reading for a range
of purposes

Storytellers

Purpose: for children to practise using their voice to convey suspense and tension and to develop their skills as effective storytellers

- Tell the children that writers can also choose particular words, decide whether to use short or long sentences and use different kinds of punctuation to create suspense.
- Say that as readers, we can use all the things the writer has given to us to create suspense by using our special Storyteller voice. Remind the children that their voice is very special because it can be used like a tool or instrument to create atmosphere and feelings.
- Ask the children to TTYP to think of different ways they could use their voice when telling a story. Collect feedback and write their answers on the board or a flipchart, e.g. *varying volume, speed, pitch, pausing*.
- Explain that they are going to hear an extract from *Lost or Stolen?* being read aloud by an excellent storyteller. Open **CD (file 5.3)** and click 'Play' to hear the extract.
- Ask the children to TTYP to share their thoughts about how the storyteller used their voice to create tension and suspense.
- Say that a good storyteller can take the reader on a roller coaster ride of emotions, speeding up, slowing down, taking us to the very top of the roller coaster and stopping for a second or two before we whizz back down again!
- Ask the children to listen as you play the extract again, and tell them to imagine the roller coaster ride.
- Now ask the children to practise their own Storyteller voices. Tell the children to find the section in their Anthology that starts with line 7 on p.12 – 'Chandra knew that Ravi was still bursting to ask Taj about the console' and ends with '"Sorry…" Dad confessed a little sheepishly' on lines 8–9 on p.13. Partner 1 should read the text in their best Storyteller voice, then Partner 2 can give feedback. Then the partners should swap roles.

discussing and
recording ideas

Daily log

Purpose: for children to keep a personal log of notes, thoughts and ideas, collected from their reading and discussions. Some ideas will be used in their own writing

- Tell the children that suspense can be experienced in many different circumstances in our daily lives. Explain that they are often quite small incidents or moments, not just unusual, dramatic ones.

- Write this stem sentence on the board or a flipchart: *There was a moment of suspense when...*

  > Say it aloud to the children, pausing at the end before adding a simple, everyday example of when you felt suspense (orally – don't write the example down), e.g. '*...I saw a cat about to pounce on a tiny bird! Would the bird fly away in time?*' Repeat with another example, e.g. '*...I was a child at school, and I was told to go to the headteacher's office. Was I getting a reward or a telling off?*'

- Ask the children to TTYP to discuss times when they have felt suspense, e.g. wanting to find out how a story will end, wanting to know if the school netball team won their area match, as they are unwrapping a gift. Choose two or three examples to share, making sure that they use the stem to help them to answer in a full sentence.

- Now tell them to write at least one example in their Daily log. Explain that they can use the same stem sentence or make up their own to create full sentences.

<table>
<tr><td>

Curriculum link:

discussion;
develop, agree
on, and evaluate
rules for effective
discussion

</td></tr>
</table>

Big Question (CD)

Purpose: for children to develop their skills of argument and discussion through a mini enquiry session based on a philosophical question relating to the work of the day

- Display today's Big Question on the **CD (file 5.4)**:

  If you want to learn, do you have to be curious?

- Follow the process as explained on Day 1.

WRITING FICTION

 DAY 6

Story roller coaster (CD)

Purpose: for children to develop their awareness of the development and structure of stories

- Remind the children that when we read a story, it can be a bit like being taken on a roller coaster ride by the writer. We begin the story not knowing what twists and turns the plot will take.

- Explain that like a roller coaster, the story might begin quite slowly and build up and up to an exciting moment or a dilemma like the top of the ride. The story ends when things are sorted out and all is calm again like the end of the ride.

- Tell the children that we can use an image of a roller coaster to see how a writer takes his or her reader through different stages of a story.

- Display **CD (file 6.1)** to show the story roller coaster. Click 'TOL' to show the think bubble. Use this to TOL about the Beginning of a story.

- On the next slide, click 'TOL' and use the think bubble to talk about the Build up in a story.

- Navigate through the slides and repeat the process on each slide until you have completed the story roller coaster ride.

- Now tell the children that the story *Lost or Stolen?* follows this structure. On the final slide, show the structure of *Lost or Stolen?* on the roller coaster and use MT/YT to read the first summary aloud.

- Ask the children to TTYP to summarise what the Build up to the dilemma is in *Lost or Stolen?* e.g. Ravi's new games console goes missing. He thinks Taj has taken it. Collect answers, clarify and paraphrase before typing a summary into the editable text box. You will need to click 'Reveal' to show further text and editable boxes.

- Repeat the process for the Dilemma, e.g. should Ravi confront Taj or not?
- Use MT/YT to read the Decision and action and Consequences summaries aloud.
- Now ask the children to TTYP to summarise what the Ending is in *Lost or Stolen?* e.g. *Ravi and Chandra's father confesses that he borrowed the games console and forgot to put it back. Relief that they didn't accuse Taj. All go off to the fair.* Collect answers, clarify and paraphrase before typing a summary into the editable text box.

> **Curriculum link:** drawing inferences; participate in discussion about books

What if not...?

Purpose: for children to understand how stories can be extended

- Display **CD (file 6.2)** to show a picture of a simple roller coaster that mirrors the story structure of *Lost or Stolen?* Say that this would give you a short, exciting ride with one *peak* before the end.
- Click 'Next' to show a bigger, more complex roller coaster. Explain that this one extends the ride and doubles the excitement by providing two peaks before the end.
- Tell them we could consider the question What if not *a short story? What if it was just a chapter in a much longer story (a novel) involving the same characters?*
- Explain that when stories have chapters, the writer often creates a beginning linked to the end of the first chapter and then builds up to another dilemma and resolution and ending.
- Tell the children that it would mean that the longer story would have more than one peak or dilemma, taking the reader on a longer story roller coaster.
- Click 'Next' to show the more complex story roller coaster diagram on the final slide.
- Ask the children to TTYP to say which kind of stories they prefer – short stories like *Lost or Stolen?* or much longer ones with chapters. Choose two or three to feed back and encourage them to explain the reasons for their answers.

What would you do?

Purpose: for children to explore their own responses to hypothetical dilemmas

- Before the lesson, print out and cut up enough copies of **CD (file 6.3)** for each set of partners.
- Tell the children that just like Ravi, we all face dilemmas in life, some that are small and quickly resolved and others that are more complicated to sort out.
- Ask them to look at the What would you do? activity on p.7 of their Pupils' Book.
- Explain that they should take a character each and read through the speech bubbles with their partner. When they have finished reading, ask them to TTYP to talk about which action *they* would take in that situation.
- Choose two sets of partners to share their answers.
- Explain that they are now going to play the game What would you do?
- Give each pair a shuffled set of dilemma cards from **CD (file 6.3)**.
- Tell them to pick a card, discuss the dilemma and what they would do and then shuffle the cards before picking another one. Walk around as they play the game, noting different choices and points of view to follow up on in your feedback.
- Choose different sets of partners to share one dilemma they discussed and say what decisions they made about what they would do in that situation and why.
- Try to use words such as *choices, decisions,* and *consequences* to structure the feedback session.

Curriculum link:
write for a range
of purposes

Daily log

*Purpose: for children to keep a personal log of notes, thoughts and ideas, collected from their
reading and discussions. Some ideas will be used in their own writing*

- Ask the children to TTYP to discuss why a story can be like a roller coaster.
  Collect feedback and paraphrase their ideas.
- Now ask them to write two or three sentences in their Daily log explaining in
  their own words why a story is a like a roller coaster. You may wish to ask the
  children to complete a quick sketch or diagram to show their understanding.

discussion;
develop, agree on,
and evaluate
rules for effective
discussion

Big Question 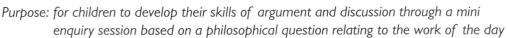

*Purpose: for children to develop their skills of argument and discussion through a mini
enquiry session based on a philosophical question relating to the work of the day*

- Display today's Big Question on **CD (file 6.4)**:

  How do we know right from wrong?

- Follow the process as explained on Day 1.

Build a dilemma 

Purpose: for children to see how a new storyline could be developed for existing characters

- Explain that you really liked the characters Ravi, Chandra and Taj and would like to
  extend the story *Lost or Stolen?* by adding a new chapter. You are in the role of the
  writer from now on.
- Say that one of the characters will face a different kind of dilemma and you have
  chosen one of the dilemmas from the What would you do? game.
- Display **CD (file 7.1)** to show the dilemma. Read it aloud to the children.
- Say that you used the story roller coaster to make a plan to help you to build the
  new dilemma into a new chapter involving Ravi, Chandra and Taj.
- Click 'Next' to show the incomplete story roller coaster for the new chapter. Use
  MT/YT to read the notes for the *Beginning, Build up* and *Dilemma*.
- Explain that these notes helped you to write a draft of the new chapter up to this
  point. Go to the next slide to show the draft and read it aloud to the children.

Conscience alley

Purpose: for children to develop their ability to empathise with a character's situation

- Tell the children that Chandra's decision of whether to support Ravi or Taj adds
  suspense to the dilemma and will have a dramatic effect on the rest of the chapter.
- Ask the children to TTYP to share what they know about Chandra's character
  from the story *Lost or Stolen?*
- Take feedback and write their answers on the board or a flipchart, e.g. *calm, kind,
  gets fed up with Taj's boasting, cheerful, sensible, sense of humour.*
- Now ask them to TTYP to share ideas about who she is likely to support and why.
- Write the word *conscience* on the board. Explain that our *conscience* is like a voice
  in our minds telling us what is right and what is wrong. Ask the children to decide
  who *they* think Chandra should agree with – Ravi or Taj – and why. Ask them not
  to reveal their decisions.
- Organise the children so that they form two lines, facing each other. Say that this
  is an alley called Conscience alley.
- Choose one child to be Chandra. Tell the children that Chandra is going to walk
  slowly down the alley and they are going to give their advice as she passes them.
- At the end of the activity, ask 'Chandra' to reveal what her decision would be and why.

Curriculum link:
plan writing by
discussing writing
that is similar

Build a story 1

Purpose: for children to see a new chapter grow through three stages of development

- Tell the children that you are now going to focus on the next part of the new chapter. Display **CD (file 7.2)** to show the story roller coaster from the point when the dilemma occurs.
- Use this to remind the children that a *decision* leads to an *action*, pointing to the relevant parts of the roller coaster and linking the decision to the thoughts and ideas they have already had about Chandra's choices.
- Navigate to the next slide to show the decision Chandra must make and remind the children that it adds suspense because the reader doesn't know what she will do.
- Tell the children that you are going to show them the bare bones of the next part of the chapter. Click 'Decision' to reveal Chandra's decision and then click 'Next' to navigate to the statement and question. Use MT/YT to read each sentence.
- Say that the question helped you to develop this part of the new chapter. Now click 'TOL' to show the think bubble. Use this to answer the question.
- Explain that this helped you to write a draft of this part of the new chapter, about the *decision*. Click 'Next' to show the draft and then ask the children to read it out chorally.
- Click 'TOL' and explain that you are drafting your new chapter in the past tense, so it matches the original story. Remind the children that the decision leads to an *action*. Click 'Action' to begin the same process and work through the remaining slides to develop this part of the new chapter.

composing
and rehearsing
sentences orally;
creating settings,
characters, plot

Write a story 1

Purpose: for children to plan and develop the first stage of a new chapter involving the characters from Lost or Stolen?

- Display **CD (file 7.3)**. Remind the children that Chandra could have made a different *decision*, leading to a different *action*. Click 'Decision' to reveal Chandra's alternative decision.
- Click 'Next' to show the statement and questions. Use MT/YT to read each sentence.
- Tell the children that the questions will help them to develop this part of their new chapter. Ask them to TTYP to discuss possible answers to the questions.
- Draw one or more large think bubbles on the board or a flipchart. Choose two or three sets of partners to feed back. Write some of their suggestions inside the think bubbles.
- Now ask them to write their own ideas in in their Daily log and to draw a think bubble shape around them.
- Tell the children that they should now use these notes to help them to write a draft, as you modelled for them in Build a story 1, to develop their new chapter.
- You may wish to give your own brief demonstration, using your notes on the board or flipchart to begin to write a draft to get them started. Remind them to rehearse their sentences in their minds before they write them down.
- Next, explain that they are now going to focus on the *action* part of the new chapter. Click 'Action', then move to the next slide and use MT/YT to read the statement and questions.
- Tell the children that they are going use the questions again to help them to develop this part of their new chapter and repeat the process above.

- Ask the children to TTYP to read out their drafts to each other and check they make sense. Ask them to make corrections if necessary.
- Choose two or three sets of partners to read parts of their drafts out to the class. Now tell the children to TTYP to share what they liked about the extracts.

Curriculum link: participate in discussion; record ideas

Daily log

Purpose: for children to keep a personal log of notes, thoughts and ideas, collected from their reading and discussions. Some ideas will be used in their own writing

- Remind the children of the Conscience alley activity they took part in earlier.
- Ask them to TTYP to share whether they would have supported Ravi or Taj if they were in Chandra's situation and why.
- Now tell them to write a sentence or two to record what their decision would have been, and why, in their Daily log.

discussion; develop, agree on, and evaluate rules for effective discussion

Big Question (CD)

Purpose: for children to develop their skills of argument and discussion through a mini enquiry session based on a philosophical question relating to the work of the day

- Display today's Big Question on the **CD (file 7.4)**:

  Is it right to give advice to someone?

- Follow the process as explained on Day 1.

(DAY 8)

Build a story 2 (CD)

Purpose: for children to see a chapter grow through three stages of development

plan writing by discussing writing that is similar; recording ideas

- You may need to allow time for the children to complete their Write a story 1 task in the first part of this lesson.
- Tell the children that you now want to focus on the consequences of Chandra's decision and the actions the children took to resolve their dilemma.
- Display **CD (file 8.1)** to show the new chapter so far over two slides. Remind them that this is *your* version and theirs will be different.
- Click 'Next' to move to the third slide to show the story roller coaster diagram. Ask the children to TTYP to say what they think the consequences might be for Chandra, Ravi and Taj when they arrive home on time but unhappy. Collect feedback.
- Say that you had an idea about the consequences. Click 'Next' to show the scenario on the story roller coaster. Tell the children that you are going to show them how you developed the idea to continue your new chapter.
- Remind them that in Week 1 they thought about conversations that characters could have had without the reader knowing. Say that you had an idea about a surprise for the children that could have been organised by Ravi and Chandra's parents while they were at the fair alone.
- Ask the children to TTYP to share ideas about what the surprise might be. Choose two or three sets of partners to feed back.
- Display **CD (file 8.2)** to show the new chapter, when the children arrive home on time but are gloomy and unhappy, until their parents reveal the surprise.
- Explain that you have used the captions and speech bubbles as the 'bare bones' of the final part of your new chapter to help you to write the full version with dialogue. Go through each of the bare bones slides.
- Next, navigate to the slides that show the full text. Read it aloud to the children with appropriate intonation and expression to convey meaning.
- Say that you used lots of the words from the bare bones version to help you. Click 'Highlights' to show the words you used.

- Remind the children that the text on the speech bubbles became dialogue and you had to add the appropriate punctuation, pronouns, nouns and verbs when you had removed the speech bubbles.
- Click 'Dialogue' to show these changes and talk them through with the children.

Dramatic reconstruction PB

Purpose: for children to become familiar with a scenario to be used as the basis for their writing

- Ask the children to look in their Daily log at their Write a story 1 draft. Remind them that this was where they wrote about Chandra's decision to support Ravi and use the tickets for extra rides at the fair.
- Tell them that you now want them to focus on the consequences of Chandra's alternative decision and the actions the children took to resolve their dilemma.
- Say that you have been thinking about how the children and their parents would behave when the children finally arrived home late. Ask the children to TTYP to share ideas about what the different characters might be feeling, e.g. *furious, worried, betrayed, scared, anxious, disappointed, guilty, upset, defiant*

  and saying, e.g.

  'Where on earth have you been?' 'We trusted you!' 'We are really sorry.' 'How can we ever trust you again?' 'We didn't mean to be so late!' 'You have ruined our special day.' 'It was Ravi's idea!' 'We had a surprise for you and now it is ruined!' 'We thought you wouldn't mind if we were a bit late.'

- Collect the children's words and phrases and write these on the board or a flipchart. Use MT/YT to say some of the phrases with appropriate intonation and body language.
- Now create groups of four by joining sets of partners together. Explain that they are going to create a short (no more than 3 minutes) improvised role-play of the *consequences* of their actions – what happens when they get home late?
- Ask them to look at the Dramatic reconstruction activity on p.8 of their Pupils' Book and talk through the scene and instructions. Give the children time to allocate roles, discuss ideas, and practise their role-plays.
- Ask the groups to perform their role-plays simultaneously. Walk around listening and noting effective dialogue and empathetic responses to feed back on. You may wish to photograph the role-plays for display.

Grammar: inverted commas CD PB HB

Purpose: for children to revise and develop their ability to punctuate direct speech accurately and to understand the difference between direct speech and reported speech

- Remind the children that if someone is speaking we call it *direct speech* because the person (or character in a story) is speaking directly to someone else.
- Explain that if someone is explaining what someone else has said, we call it *reported speech* because someone is reporting what another person (or character in a story) has said.
- Tell the children that it is quite easy to recognise the difference in spoken word form but it is only clear in written form if we follow the punctuation rules.
- Say that you have a piece of writing to show them that is based on the same situation they used as the basis for their role-plays. Display **CD (file 8.3)** to show the text containing reported speech.
- Read the text aloud and explain that there are no inverted commas (speech marks) because what was said is being reported by someone else. Click 'Highlights' to show what is being reported. Explain that when we report what someone else has said, we usually change the wording slightly or just give a rough summary of what was said.

- Now click 'Direct speech' to show a piece of text containing direct speech. Click 'Highlights' again to highlight the inverted commas. Revise or teach the punctuation mime for inverted commas (see the Extras section of the Software). Model reading the speech while miming the punctuation, then ask the children to join in as you repeat the process.
- Tell the children that the direct speech has an exclamation mark at the end. Point out the fact that this punctuation mark is included inside the inverted commas because it is linked to the text inside the inverted commas – it shows *how* it is being said.
- Say that the speech and the information about who is speaking can be organised differently. Navigate to the next slide to show some examples for comparison and read them aloud using MT/YT. Point out that the information telling us who is speaking has been moved to the end of the dialogue.
- Explain that if we didn't have an exclamation mark, we would have to have a comma before or after we indicate who is speaking. Navigate to the next slide to show an example. Make sure the children understand that the punctuation marks at the end of the actual speech must be placed before the second speech mark.
- Remind the children that instead of using the verb *said* each time they write direct speech, most writers will use different verbs, e.g. *yelled*, *shouted*, *whispered*. Click 'Reveal' to show an example.
- Now ask the children to turn to p.9 in their Pupils' Book and to look at the Grammar: inverted commas activity. Ask them to TTYP to take turns to read the extracts and then discuss whether they are showing direct speech or reported speech.
- Choose two or three sets of partners to share their answers and explain how they decided which extracts show reported speech and which show direct speech. Clarify where necessary.

Homework Book p.5 provides further practice on inverted commas.

Write a story 2

<table>
<tr><td>

Curriculum link:
composing
and rehearsing
sentences orally;
creating settings,
characters, plot

</td></tr>
</table>

Purpose: for children to plan and develop the second stage of a new chapter involving the characters from Lost or Stolen?

- Before the lesson, print out a copy of **CD (file 8.4)** for each child.
- Tell the children that they are going to focus on writing their version of the consequences of the children's decision and actions.
- Explain that they are going to write the next part of their new chapter using story squares, captions, and speech bubbles.
- Give each child a copy of printable **CD (file 8.4)**. Explain to the children about the narrator or storyteller style of writing for the captions and the everyday spoken language style of writing for the speech bubbles.
- Encourage them to use the Dramatic reconstruction activity notes on p.8 of their Pupils' Book and to talk to their partners about the dialogue that they used in their role-plays to help them.
- Make sure they rehearse their sentences in their minds before writing them down. Walk around as they work, praising and noting good writing to feed back on.
- Ask the children to TTYP to share what they have written. Choose two or three children to share their writing with the whole class.
- Now ask them to use their story squares to help them to write the developed version of this part of their new chapter. Remind them how you modelled this for them **(CD file 8.2)**. You may wish to show this file again to remind them of the process.
- Make sure you walk around giving support and praise as they write.

Daily log

*Purpose: for children to keep a personal log of notes, thoughts and ideas, collected from their
reading and discussions. Some ideas will be used in their own writing*

- Ask the children to TTYP to share ideas about a title for their new chapter.
- Collect feedback, then ask them to choose a title and write it in their Daily log.

discussion;
develop, agree on,
and evaluate
rules for effective
discussion

Big Question

*Purpose: for children to develop their skills of argument and discussion through a mini
enquiry session based on a philosophical question relating to the work of the day*

- Display today's Big Question on the **CD (file 8.5)**:

  If you find something, is it yours to keep?

- Follow the process as explained on Day 1.

DAY 9

Step into the setting

Purpose: for children to be able to explore a setting through a guided fantasy

- Remind the children that they wrote descriptions of a *rakhi* bracelet in their Daily
  log. Say that you think the new chapter for *Lost or Stolen?* needs some description
  to make it more interesting for readers.
- Explain that you think adding a description of what Ravi, Chandra and Taj would
  see, hear, smell and feel when they arrive at the fair would be another way of
  adding excitement during the build up to the dilemma in the new chapter.
- Ask the children to TTYP to share ideas about why a description of the fairground
  setting would be good for readers.
- Choose two or three sets of partners to feed back and make sure they understand
  the purpose of the description, e.g. *fairgrounds are special and different to everyday
  settings; describing the setting will help readers to make pictures in their minds of where the
  characters are and what they are experiencing, it will help readers to feel part of the story.*
- Ask the children to TTYP to share their experiences of fairgrounds from a visit,
  a story or a film. Tell them to think about their feelings and what they saw and
  heard. Choose two or three sets of partners to feed back.
- Now tell them that they are going to go on a virtual visit to the fair with Taj, Ravi and
  Chandra. Explain that they must listen really carefully.
- Open **CD (file 9.1)**. Click 'Play' to hear Ravi, Chandra and Taj's narration that will
  take them on a virtual visit to the fair.
- When the narration is over, ask the children to TTYP straight away to share their
  reflections about what they were imagining during the exercise. Use these (and/or
  any of your own) questions to guide them:
  - How did you feel when Ravi invited you?
  - What was the most powerful picture you had in your head?
  - Could you smell the candy floss and the hot food? Did it make you hungry?
  - How did you feel when you heard Taj scream?

understand
the skills and
processes that
are essential for
writing

Build a story 3

Purpose: for children to see a chapter grow through three stages of development

- Tell the children that you are going to focus on one sense at a time to help you to
  write a good description of what they would see, hear and experience at the fair.
- Write the heading *At the Fair* on the board or a flipchart. Explain that you want to
  focus on what they would see at the fair first. Write the subheading *What would
  they see?*

- Tell the children that you want them to help you to write your description and you have some images to show them. Display **CD (file 9.2)** and move through the slideshow of fairgrounds.
- Ask them to TTYP to share words and phrases to describe what they have seen and also from images they had in their minds during the virtual visit. Collect words and phrases and write them underneath the heading *What would they see?*
- TOL (see example on printable **CD (file 9.3)**) as you model orally rehearsing sentences based on any of the words or phrases you have collected from the children. Add some of your own if necessary.
- Use MT/YT to say each version of the sentences before writing them under the subheading, drawing the children in through TTYP to discuss any changes that would improve the writing, e.g. punctuation, synonyms, adverbs, or openings.
- Ask the children to TTYP to create an oral draft sentence of their own based on what they would see at the fair. Collect examples from a few sets of partners and use MT/YT to allow all the children to say them aloud.
- Explain that you now want them to decide on their opening draft sentence and say it in their minds before writing it down. Tell them that they will get the chance to make changes and improve it later.
- Tell the children that they are going to extend and develop their description using other senses, memory and imagination to help them.

Curriculum link:

creating settings, characters, plot; monitor whether their writing makes sense

Write a story 3

Purpose: for children to plan and develop the third stage of a new chapter involving the characters from Lost or Stolen?

- Tell the children that they are now going to continue to write their own fairground description and you want them to focus on what they would hear at the fair. Write the subheading *What would they hear?*
- Open **CD (file 9.4)** and play the fairground sounds.
- Now ask them to TTYP to share words and phrases to describe what they have heard and also from sounds they imagined during the virtual visit and from their own experiences of fairgrounds.
- Collect words and phrases and write them underneath the heading *What would they hear?*
- Tell the children that our sense of smell is also very powerful in creating feelings and bringing back memories. Explain that they must rely on their own experiences, memories and imagination to describe the smells of the fairground.
- Ask them to TTYP to think of the things that would create smells at the fair, e.g. *food, engine oil, earth*. Collect words and phrases and write them underneath the heading *What would they smell?*
- Repeat the process using TTYP and ask the children to feed back on what they would touch or feel, e.g. *hard plastic seats, cold metal safety bars, wristbands or tickets in their pockets, coconut matting on the helter-skelter, ice cold splashes of water on the log flume, sticky, fluffy candy floss.* Collect words and phrases and write them underneath the heading *What would they touch or feel?*
- Say that they are going to start creating sentences to build their own descriptions of what they would have experienced at the fair with Ravi, Chandra and Taj. Tell the children to look at the Write a story 3 activity on p.9 of the Pupils' Book. Talk through the prompts and remind them that they can borrow any of the words and phrases on the board or flipchart to use in their description.
- Walk around as they work, supporting and noting examples of ambitious vocabulary to refer to when you give feedback.

DAY 10

Share a description

Purpose: for children to read and share their writing

- Ask the children to read through their own description of the fair.
- Now tell them to re-read their description and to underline the parts they are most proud of. Ask them to TTYP to share these with their partner.
- Collect examples of powerful words or phrases they like from their own or each other's writing. Add any exciting vocabulary and Special phrases to the Story wall.

> **Curriculum link:** assessing the effectiveness of their own and others' writing

Evaluate and edit ⓒⒹ

Purpose: for children to evaluate their own and their partner's work against specific criteria and then discuss how they could improve their work

- Display **CD (file 10.1)** and read through the evaluation points using MT/YT.
- As a model, select an example of work where the writing has met the criteria, and share this with the other children, explaining why it works well.
- Tell the children to take turns to read their partner's writing in pairs and discuss together how well each piece of writing has met the criteria.
- Ask children to discuss at least two changes they could make to improve their work.

> proofread for spelling and punctuation errors

Proofread

Purpose: for children to proofread their work and make changes to improve the accuracy of their grammar, punctuation and spelling

- Now ask the children to proofread their work. If you have noticed that several children need to improve on a particular aspect of spelling, grammar or punctuation, use this as a focus for the Proofread activity. Write an example which includes common errors from the children's writing and use this as a model.
- The children should always be checking for standard use of punctuation and correct spelling of common exception words.
- The following points would be particularly relevant for this Unit:
  - checking spelling of ambitious vocabulary choices
  - punctuating direct speech correctly.

> discussion; develop, agree on, and evaluate rules for effective discussion

Very Big Question ⓒⒹ

Purpose: for children to develop their willingness to revise or broaden their opinions and ideas through the exploration of one of the Big Questions in depth

- Explain to the children that they are going to vote to choose one of the Big Questions they have discussed to explore further in this lesson.
- Tell the children the 'rules' for the Very Big Question time:

  Think before you talk. Wait for others to finish before you talk. Good listening.

- Display the Big Question they have voted for on the CD (choose from the Big Questions debated so far in the Unit). Give everyone some time to think about the question. Ask partners to share their thoughts on the question.
- Allow each child to express their opinion. Encourage responses from children to what has been said rather than insisting that each child speaks in turn. Step in to clarify, paraphrase or draw in children who are reluctant to talk.
- As the 'enquiry' develops and changes direction, pause the proceedings occasionally and reframe the question – remember the Big Question is a starting point for genuine enquiry. Repeat thinking time and TTYP to refresh the process and to prevent one or two children dominating.
- Allow time to have a final round where children are asked to think about what has been said and share how their opinion has changed or not as a result of the discussion.

READING AND WRITING NON-FICTION

The Non-fiction week looks at information texts presented in a variety of styles, in a magazine feature format. The content of the magazine is used to stimulate the children to create and present their own information texts. Children then plan a presentation for a new gadget and pitch the idea to a panel. See p.20 for the daily timetable for the Non-fiction week.

Non-fiction

Reading

Children will:

- discover that information texts are written with a specific audience and purpose in mind
- understand how people use different sources of information to help them make decisions and form opinions
- compose research questions and use them to focus on the relevant information
- discover how an article is structured to make it easy for readers to find information, using key features e.g. *headings, subheadings, boxed text.*

Writing

Key writing purpose to be shared with the children:

To write an advice leaflet about keeping your phone safe, and to produce a presentation about a gadget to pitch to a panel.

Writing evaluation to be shared with the children

My leaflet:

- gives clear, useful advice about how to keep your phone safe
- has organisational features, e.g. *headings, bullet points, text boxes.*

Grammar:

- includes imperative verbs e.g. *do, don't.*

My presentation:

- gives useful, interesting information about a gadget based on the notes I made
- is persuasive
- is suitable for the audience (the panel) and purpose (persuading them to invest in the gadget).

Grammar:

- includes correct use of suffixes and prefixes to create nouns and adjectives, if prefixes and suffixes have been used.

See the Planning section of the Software ('Timetables' tab) for a printable version of the Writing purpose and evaluation.

DAY 11

Curriculum link:
reading for a range
of purposes

Linking texts

Purpose: for children's interest in information texts to be stimulated and to provide a link between the fiction and the non-fiction text

- Remind the children that all of our Big Questions helped us to share our opinions about something.
- Display the Big Question from Day 2 on **CD (file 2.4)**:

  Are gadgets always good to have?

- Check that all the children can recall the meaning of the word *gadget* and then ask them to TTYP to recall some of the opinions they shared and take feedback.
- Remind them that in the story, Taj always *had* the latest gadget and Ravi always *wanted* the latest gadget.
- Explain to the children that we use information to help us to decide not only whether something would be good for us but whether we want it.
- Say that they are going to be exploring why information is important to us, where information can be found and how it can be presented. Tell the children that they will have a chance to write and present information about an exciting new gadget.

Grammar: word classes and suffixes

Dictionaries will be required in this part of the lesson.

Purpose: for children to become familiar with vocabulary associated with information texts and to increase their knowledge and use of suffixes to create nouns and adjectives

- Tell the children that there are some words that are useful to know when we want to identify and talk about information texts.
- Display **CD (file 11.1)** to show these words: *inform, knowledge, authority, locate, source.*
- Read the words aloud using MT/YT and then click 'Definition' to show each word and its definition. Read the words and definitions aloud using MT/YT.
- Now navigate to the next slide to show the root words and suffixes grid. Use MT/YT to say the first word. Click 'Reveal' to show the word class. Click 'Reveal' to show a suffix and use MT/YT to say the suffix. Click 'Reveal' to show the new word and use MT/YT to say the word. Click 'Reveal' to show the word class.
- Keep clicking 'Reveal' to fill in the subsequent rows in the table. Draw the children's attention to any letters that have disappeared. For *information/informative*, draw attention to the extra letter shown in red.
- Now use MT/YT to say a sentence for each *new* word, e.g.
  'The location *of the treasure wasn't on the map.'*
  'I looked on the Internet for information *about my favourite band.'*
  'This morning's assembly was very informative.'
  'My mate is really knowledgeable *about snakes.'*
  'Leon talks knowledgeably *about skateboarding.'*
- Ask the children to look at p.10 in their Pupils' Book. Explain the activity to them and then ask them to complete it with their partner.
- All of the words and definitions can be printed from **CD (file 11.2)** to display on your Information texts wall.

Who says?

Purpose: for children to recall and consolidate their knowledge of where information can be found and to begin to think about how we evaluate its reliability

- Tell the children that the Internet supplies us with a huge amount of information but there are many other sources of information.

- Ask them to TTYP and then Popcorn their answers to say where else they might find information about:
  - a word
  - a holiday resort
  - directions to a place
  - a famous person from history such as William Shakespeare

  e.g. *dictionary, thesaurus, leaflets, brochures, friends and family, atlas or maps, satnav device, encyclopaedia, museum.*
- Now tell the children to imagine that they have been told they can have a new mobile phone and they want to do some research to help them to decide which one to buy. Tell them to TTYP to discuss the different places they could get information about the latest phones available.
- Collect feedback and write their ideas on the board or a flipchart, adding any that they miss out, e.g. *the Internet, magazine articles, adverts, shops, knowledgeable friends.*
- Explain that it can be difficult to know which sources we can trust to tell us what we really need to know.
- Ask them to TTYP to discuss which would be their top two sources of information for choosing a new mobile phone. Collect feedback and ask for reasons for their answers, e.g. *I trust a friend's opinion more than an advert; a trained shop assistant might know more than a friend.*
- Tell the children to write the heading *Choosing a New Mobile Phone* in their Daily log. Ask them to record their own top two sources for information underneath the heading, including their reasons why.

What do I want to know?

Purpose: for children to be able to compose questions to aid research

- Say that good research usually begins with a set of questions focusing on what information is required. Ask the children to TTYP to think of four questions that would help them to research the most appropriate mobile phone for them to buy.
- Choose two or three sets of partners to share their questions with the class.
- Now model composing one or two of their oral responses into written form, e.g.
  Child: *I'd ask if it's got like, er, games and stuff on it.*
  Teacher: *So your written question could be 'Is it possible to play games on this phone?'*

Daily log

Purpose: for children to keep a personal log of notes, thoughts and ideas, collected from their reading and discussions. Some ideas will be used in their own writing

- Ask the children to work in pairs to decide which four questions they would use to research what mobile phone to buy.
- Remind them of how you composed the question orally in a form that could be written down. Tell them to take turns to compose their own questions orally before writing them down in their Daily log.
- Now ask the children to look again at their top two sources of information they recorded earlier.
- Ask them to TTYP to discuss how well these sources would help them to answer their research questions and whether they would now change their top two sources. Collect feedback, encouraging children to explain their answers.

> **Curriculum link:** using non-fiction, know what information they need to look for and be clear about the task

DAY 12

Information detectives CD

Purpose: for children to develop their ability to identify and record information

- Tell the children that not only are there many different places where information can be found, but there are many ways it can be presented, given or shown.
- Explain that the information that we really need or want can sometimes be surrounded by words and phrases that have a different purpose, e.g. *to add interest to something dull, to persuade us to buy something, to provide extra information that isn't absolutely necessary.*
- Ask the children to look at the first page of 'Gadget Magic' magazine on p.14 of their Anthology. Say that the magazine specialises in providing information about gadgets.
- Explain that the magazine has *teasers* on the first page – say that these are little bits of information about something that is inside the magazine, and they are designed to make you want to read on and find out more information.
- Ask them to look at the first teaser with the heading 'Special Feature' and to follow the text as you read it aloud with appropriate intonation and excitement.
- Use MT/YT with exaggerated intonation to say *'The Greatest Gadget of Them All?'*
- Tell the children to TTYP to try to predict what 'Gadget Magic's' greatest gadget will be and why. You may wish to give them these three to choose from: hand held games console, smart phone, digital camera.
- Collect feedback including reasons for their choices. Ask them to turn to p.16 in their Anthology and take turns to read alternate sections of the article 'The Greatest Gadget of Them All?'
- Say that information about the different features on Ellie's phone is hidden in the article. Tell the children that you want them to TTYP to search 'The Greatest Gadget of Them All?' text to identify as many functions and features on Ellie's phone as possible, e.g. *satnav, music folder, calculator.*
- Explain that they are going to create an information mind map to record the functions and features of Ellie's phone clearly.
- Display **CD (file12.1)** to show the frame of the mind map. Explain the colour coded branch headings and then click 'Reveal' to show an example of how to record information using colour coding, words and symbols or images.
- Ask them to draw their own mind map frame and add the features, functions and symbols to represent them where appropriate. Remind them to TTYP to share information and discuss the most appropriate branches for different functions.

Deconstruction 1 CD

Purpose: for children to develop their ability to think about audience and purpose

- Tell the children that writers and editors also have to think carefully about their readers and the purpose of their writing and publications.
- Display **CD (file 12.2)**. Read the list aloud and ask them to TTYP to say who is the most likely to want to buy or read the 'Gadget Magic' magazine: which gender, what age group?
- Ask them to Popcorn their answers and choose two or three sets of partners to explain the reasons for their choices.
- Now tell the children to share ideas about why 'The Greatest Gadget of Them All?' article was written like a story about Ellie and her family rather than just a list of reasons why a mobile phone is the greatest. Make sure they know that there isn't a right answer, you are just looking for their own ideas and opinions.
- Collect answers and link them to audience and purpose, e.g. *the story makes it more interesting than a list for teenage readers, it is humorous as well as informative.*

Curriculum link: discussing writing similar to that which they are planning to write in order to understand and learn from its structure, grammar and vocabulary

- Click 'Reveal' to show possible options for the purpose of the article. Ask the children to TTYP to discuss what they think the main purpose of the article is from the list.
- Have a quick vote to see what the children perceive as the main purpose of the article. You may wish to ask them to TTYP to put the list in order of most obvious purpose to least obvious purpose. Make sure they understand their personal opinions and reasoning are important here.

Write 1 🅰 🅿🅱 Ⓒⅅ

Purpose: for children to develop their ability to grow an information text from notes

- Ask the children to TTYP to remind each other what a magazine teaser is. Choose a pair to share their definitions.
- Now tell them to look at the teaser on p.15 of their Anthology called 'SPEC-tacular!' and to take turns to read a sentence each. Explain that this gives them a small amount of information about another gadget, the SPEC-tacular glasses.
- Say that the editor of 'Gadget Magic' wants them to write a short article about the glasses for the next issue, written in a similar style to 'The Greatest Gadget of Them All?' article.
- Ask the children to look at the Write 1 activity on p.11 of their Pupils' Book, showing an email from the editor explaining the audience, purpose and length of article she would like.
- Explain that there is also a mind map showing extra information about the SPEC-tacular glasses to use in their article. Display this on **CD (file 12.3)**.
- Ask them to TTYP to read alternate sections of the email. Guide them through the instructions and mind map.
- Tell the children to scan 'The Greatest Gadget of Them All?' article on pp.16–17 of their Anthology to remind themselves of the style of the article. Now tell them to TTYP to discuss how they could begin their 'SPEC-tacular!' article.
- Remind them that they must rehearse their opening sentence in their minds before writing it down.
- Walk around as they work, giving support where necessary. Make sure they know that this is a draft and they can edit their work once they have written their ideas down.

Curriculum link: understand, through being shown these, the skills and processes that are essential for writing for different purposes and audiences

explore, collect and record ideas

Daily log 🅰

Purpose: for children to keep a personal log of notes, thoughts and ideas, collected from their reading and discussions. Some ideas will be used in their own writing

- Tell the children to return to 'The Greatest Gadget of Them All?' article on pp.16–17 of their Anthology. Explain that as well as information about the mobile phone, there is a lot of information about Ellie.
- Ask the children to draw a Role on the wall character shape in their Daily log, large enough to fill most of the page. Model creating one on a large sheet of sugar paper or on a flipchart. See p.89 for a description of Role on the wall.
- Explain that they should TTYP to read through the text again one section at a time in turn. After each section, they must stop and decide what information they have been given or can guess from what is written about Ellie (not the phone).
- Model finding one or two examples, e.g. half-way down p.17 it tells us that she has a cousin called Sophie. Now model writing the information in note form, e.g. *cousin called Sophie*, inside the Role on the wall figure.
- When they have had time to read and record, collect information about Ellie from different sets of partners and add them to your figure. You may wish to display this on your Information texts wall for this Unit.

DAY 13

Curriculum link:
discussing writing
similar to that
which they are
planning to
write; learn the
conventions of
different types of
writing

Deconstruction 2

Purpose: for children to develop their awareness of features of information texts and their purpose. For children to practise scanning texts to identify specific features

Features of information texts

- Remind the children that information texts are usually organised in ways that help to make them easy to read and understand.
- Display **CD (file 13.1)** to show a piece of text. Read it out to the children and explain that it could be organised in a different way to make the information clearer and easier for readers to find.
- Click 'Next' to show the version of the text with headings and subheadings added. Now click 'TOL' and use the think bubble to explain the effect of the change.
- Move through the slides to show more organisational features and think bubbles. Finally, display the whole re-organised text.

Features detectives

- Tell the children that as well as careful reading of a text for particular information, sometimes it is useful to be able to quickly *scan* a text for a general idea of what it is about or what kind of text it is.
- Click on 'Next' to show a definition of the word *scan* from the *Oxford Junior Dictionary*. Use MT/YT to read it aloud.
- Ask the children to open their Anthology at p.14 and to work with their partner to let their eyes scan pp.14–17 to spot examples of the organisational features they have been shown and any others that they can identify.
- Collect examples from two or three sets of partners, clarifying where necessary and checking their understanding of why the features have been used.

identifying ideas
from paragraphs;
write for a range
of real purposes;
using simple
organisational
devices

Write 2

Purpose: for children to develop their ability to identify information and advice; for children to convert continuous prose into an advice and information leaflet

- Tell the children that articles from previous issues of 'Gadget Magic' can be found on the magazine's website and then give each set of partners a copy of printable **CD (file 13.2)**. Don't explain the content or purpose of the article.
- Ask them to TTYP to take turns to read alternate paragraphs. Now ask them to summarise what they think the article is about and its main purpose. Choose two or three sets of partners to feed back. Clarify where necessary.
- Now display **CD (file 13.3)** to show the article on the magazine web-page. Tell them that the local Chief of Police has asked if a journalist from 'Gadget Magic' could write a leaflet giving information about keeping your phone safe.
- Click 'TOL' and use the think bubbles and on-screen prompts over the next slides to model how to begin to separate advice from information, and how to convert the article into a leaflet using organisational features.
- Give each set of partners a selection of coloured pencils. Tell them to TTYP to re-read the printed 'Gadget Magic' article again and to use the instructions to identify the advice, information, headings and slogan using their coloured pencils.
- Now ask the children to look at the Write 2 activity on p.12 of their Pupils' Book. Explain that these are prompts to help them to create a well-organised and useful leaflet for young people.
- Ask them to use their colour-coded article and Pupils' Book notes to plan and create a one or two page leaflet. Remind them to make sure they can say their sentences to their partner before they write them down.

- Walk around as they work giving support, praise and noting things to clarify with the whole class.
- You may need to allocate the first part of Day 14 to allow the children to complete their leaflets.

Daily log

Purpose: for children to keep a personal log of notes, thoughts and ideas, collected from their reading and discussions. Some ideas will be used in their own writing

- Tell the children that technology develops so fast that their parents and grandparents will remember times when gadgets looked very different or didn't exist at all.
- Ask them to look at 'Grandad's Gizmos' on p.14 of their Anthology. Explain the meaning of the word *gizmo*. Allow time for them to TTYP to look at the photograph and read the caption.
- Tell the children that they are going to think of a caption for a different 'Grandad's Gizmo'. Display **CD (file 13.4)** to show a photograph of Dr Martin Cooper holding the first mobile phone in 1973.
- Now ask the children to TTYP to think of a caption to go with the photograph of the first mobile phone.
- Choose two or three sets of partners to share their ideas. Type one of their suggestions into the editable text box.
- Now tell them to draw a quick sketch of the huge mobile phone and write a short piece of information about it, e.g. *First mobile phone, invented by Dr Cooper in 1973.* They can then write a comical caption underneath.

Curriculum link: discussing and recording ideas

DAY 14

proofread for spelling and punctuation errors

Proofread

Purpose: for children to proofread their work and make changes to improve the accuracy of their grammar, punctuation and spelling

- Now ask the children to proofread their work. If you have noticed that several children need to improve on a particular aspect of spelling, grammar or punctuation, use this as a focus for the Proofread activity. Write an example which includes common errors from the children's writing and use this as a model.
- The children should always be checking for standard use of punctuation and correct spelling of common exception words.
- The following points would be particularly relevant for this Unit:
  - making sure that prefixes and suffixes have been added to root words correctly
  - checking spelling of ambitious vocabulary choices
  - checking that capital letters have been used appropriately in headings and subheadings.

Grammar: suffixes, prefixes and word classes

Purpose: for children to develop their knowledge of word classes and how they change when adding suffixes and prefixes

- Ask the children to find the 'I-Spy!' text on p.15 of their Anthology. Explain that this is another teaser for an article. Tell them to TTYP to take turns to read a sentence each of the teaser.
- Ask them to TTYP to describe what a spy does. Collect feedback and clarify if necessary.
- Write the word *spy* on the board or a flipchart. Explain that the word can be a noun or a verb, depending on how it is used, e.g. '*If it is used to describe what someone* is, *it is a* noun. *When it is used to describe what someone is* doing, *it is a* verb.'

- Display **CD (file 14.1)** to show the two entries for the word *spy* in the *Oxford Junior Dictionary*. Read them aloud to the children. Click 'Reveal' and use MT/YT to say the two sentences:
  1. *James Bond is a famous spy.*
  2. *James Bond's gadgets help him to spy on the enemy.*
- Ask the children to TTYP to discuss whether they think the word *spy* is a verb or a noun in each of the sentences. Collect feedback chorally or by choosing sets of partners to share their answers. Ask for explanations for their answers and then clarify if necessary.
- Now tell the children to look again at the 'I-Spy!' text on p.15 of their Anthology and to find the word *unforgettable*. Explain that it is a special word because it is made up of three parts; the root word *forget*, a prefix and a suffix.
- Navigate to the next slide to show the word classes table. Use the column headings to name the parts and click 'Next' twice to show how the word changes from a verb (*forget*) to an adjective (*forgettable*) and again to its opposite adjective (*unforgettable*). Remind them what an adjective is if necessary.
- Read each final word and its definition chorally with the children, putting exaggerated emphasis on the prefix and suffix where appropriate.
- Blank the screen and use MT/YT to say the sentence '*James Bond is a famous spy*'. Ask them to hold the sentence in their minds before writing it down in their Daily log. Tell them to draw an arrow from the word *spy* and to label it as a noun or a verb in this sentence.
- Repeat the same process with the sentence *James Bond's unforgettable gadgets help him to spy on the enemy.*
- Now ask the children to underline the adjective in the first sentence (*famous*) and the second sentence (*unforgettable*).
- Ask them to TTYP to discuss where they could add another adjective in the second sentence. Collect feedback and write some examples on the board or a flipchart, e.g. *James Bond's unforgettable gadgets help him to spy on the* cruel *enemy*.
- Remind them that they could have two adjectives next to each other, e.g. the gadgets could be described as *amazing* as well as *unforgettable* or the enemy could be *wicked* as well as *cruel*.
- Write these sentences on the board or a flipchart and model where commas are needed to separate the adjectives to make the meaning clear, e.g.
  James Bond's amazing, unforgettable gadgets help him to spy on the cruel enemy.
  James Bond's amazing, unforgettable gadgets help him to spy on the cruel, wicked enemy.
- Ask the children to add at least one adjective to their sentence.

Deconstruction 3 🅰 Ⓒ🄳

Purpose: for children to see and analyse formal presentations of information for a specific audience and purpose

- Remind the children that lots of gadgets and inventions we now take for granted were once thought of as ideas that would never work. Ask the children to find the 'Funky Future?' text on p.15 of their Anthology.
- Tell them to TTYP to take turns to read a section each of the text and then choose their favourite future gadget out of the three described. Select a few sets of partners to share their answers and reasons for their choices.
- Explain that inventors need expert advice and money to develop their idea properly and they use information about their idea to persuade people to invest their time and money. Say that this is sometimes called *pitching* an idea.

> **Curriculum link:** retrieve and record information from non-fiction; participate in discussion, listening to what others say

- Tell the children that you are going to show them a clip of a TV programme called *Pitch to the Panel* where inventors have a short amount of time try to persuade a panel of investors to choose their idea to develop.
- Join sets of partners together to form groups of six. Explain that they are going to be in role as the panel (make sure they have their Daily log ready for note-taking). Open **CD (file 14.2)** and click 'Play' to show a presentation about Holo-World.
- Ask them to TTYP to share what they thought of the idea and the presentation.
- Explain that they are going to see the presentation again and then they should jot down any notes about the idea and the way it is presented. Replay the video and allow time for the children to make a few notes.
- Say that they are going to see another pitch. Open **CD (file 14.3)** and play the presentation for the Brain Box. Repeat the process as before.
- When they have made their notes on each presentation, collect feedback from groups. Tease out where the focus was on information about the product and where the focus was on how the information was presented.
- Now ask the children to discuss in their groups which idea or product they would invest in and why and to choose a spokesperson for their group. Conduct a vote and allow each group representative to explain the group's reasons for their choice.

Write 3 PB CD

> **Curriculum link:**
> identifying how language, structure and presentation contribute to meaning; write for a range of real purposes

Purpose: for children to write their own information text to be used as the basis for a presentation for a specific audience and purpose

- Tell the children that they are going to improve the presentation for the Holo-World gadget. Ask them to TTYP to share the notes they have in their Daily log about the first presentation they watched and to discuss how the presentation could be improved.
- Tell them to list three things they think could improve the presentation. Choose two or three sets of partners to share their list, and write their ideas on the board or a flipchart.
- Ask the children to turn to the Write 3 activity on p.13 of their Pupils' Book. Display **CD (file 14.4)** to show the information about Holo-World. Guide them through the notes in the Pupils' Book to explain how they should TTYP to read and use the information about Holo-World and the Top Tips for good presentations.
- Make sure the children understand that they don't have to use all of the information and that they can put it in their own words. It is not a script to learn.
- Remind them that they can also look at their Daily log notes to see what worked well in the presentations they saw, to plan and write a joint presentation with their partner.
- As well as providing sugar paper and felt pens for visual representations, you may wish to arrange for the children to use ICT to make visual aids.
- Explain that they will have the rest of the day's lesson and the first part of their next lesson to complete their informative and persuasive presentations. Tell them that their presentations must be no longer than 3 minutes.
- Walk around as they work, giving support, advice and encouragement where necessary.

Curriculum link: discussing words and phrases that capture the reader's interest and imagination; building a varied and rich vocabulary

Daily log

Purpose: for children to keep a personal log of notes, thoughts and ideas, collected from their reading and discussions. Some ideas will be used in their own writing

- Tell the children that the name of a new gadget or invention is really important and should not only describe what it is but be able to catch people's attention and be memorable.
- Remind them that rhymes, alliteration, puns, word-play and portmanteau words can all help to make a good product name, e.g. the alliteration of Brain Box and the compound word Holo-World from the 'Funky Future?' article in 'Gadget Magic'.
- Ask them to TTYP to think of a new name for Holo-World to use in their presentation. Tell them to write their chosen name in their Daily log and to keep it a secret until presentation day!

DAY 15

read aloud their own writing to a group, using appropriate intonation and controlling the tone and volume so that meaning is clear

Presentations

Purpose: for children to present information for a specific audience and purpose

- Allow time in the first part of the lesson for the children to complete and practise their presentations.
- Remind them of the *Pitch to the Panel* presentations they watched and explain that each set of partners is going to take turns to present or pitch to a panel made up of two other sets of partners.
- Now join three sets of partners together to form groups of six. Start the process of *Pitch to the Panel* by asking one set of partners in each group to begin. The presentations to each panel should take place simultaneously.
- Walk around as the presentations take place, noting good partner work, choice of information and methods of presentation. You may also wish to film or photograph parts of the presentations in progress for display and/or material for discussion and evaluation at the end of the Unit.

assessing the effectiveness of their own and others' writing

Evaluate and edit ⓒⒹ

Purpose: for children to evaluate their work and others' work against specific criteria and then discuss how they could improve the leaflets and presentations

- Display **CD (file 15.1)** and read through the evaluation points on the first slide using MT/YT.
- As a model, select an example of work where the leaflet met the criteria, and share it with the other children, explaining why it worked well.
- Tell the children to look at their leaflets and to discuss with their partner how well they met the criteria.
- Ask children to discuss at least two changes they could make to improve their leaflet.
- Now move to the next slide and repeat the process for the presentations.

Fiction: Poetry
Non-fiction: Journalistic recounts

Timetable

WEEK 1   Reading fiction   Poetry

Day 1	Day 2	Day 3	Day 4	Day 5
The poetry store	Word power 🖶	Multi-syllabic words 🖶	Form 2	Think and link 🖶
Introducing the poem 1	Special phrases	Form 1	What if not...?	Drama
Introducing the poem 2	Read a poem	Haiku	Daily log	Daily log
Introducing the poem 3	Daily log	Daily log	Big Question	Big Question
Daily log	Big Question	Big Question		
Big Question				

WEEK 2   Writing fiction   Poetry

Day 6	Day 7	Day 8	Day 9	Day 10
Zoom in, zoom out	Build a poem 1	What if not...?	Build a poem 3	Form 3
Build an image	Write a poem 1 🖶	Build a poem 2	What do you think?	Evaluate and edit
Daily log	Daily log	Write a poem 2 🖶	Write a poem 3	Proofread
Big Question	Big Question	Daily log	Daily log	Very Big Question
		Big Question		

WEEK 3   Reading and writing non-fiction   Journalistic recounts

Day 11	Day 12	Day 13	Day 14	Day 15
Introduction	Words for recounts 🖶	Grammar: paragraphs	Newspaper vocabulary 🖶	Write 3 🖶
Dramatic reconstruction	Deconstruction 1	Deconstruction 2 🖶	Deconstruction 3	Evaluate and edit
Fact and opinion 🖶	Write 1	Write 2	Role-play	Proofread
Daily log	Daily log	Daily log	Daily log	

🖶: shows that a file should be printed out from the Software.

Overview of the Unit

In this Unit, children explore the poems 'The Balloons' by Oscar Wilde, 'My Sari' by Debjani Chatterjee and 'At the End of a School Day' by Wes Magee. The emphasis is on enjoyment of the poets' use of language to create images and emotions. The texts focus on moments to remember: everyday moments observed, recalled and shaped into poems. Children are encouraged to experiment with language and form to create a poem of their own in free verse.

Linked via a Big Question, the Non-fiction section explores recounts and journalistic texts. For more information about the Non-fiction week and the Non-fiction writing evaluation criteria, see p.72.

Where appropriate, the children will be encouraged to develop an awareness of audience and purpose in relation to the fiction and non-fiction texts they are reading and writing.

Teacher modelling is provided in the teaching notes, Software and the Pupils' Book, supporting the children's writing at every stage in the Fiction and Non-fiction weeks.

The Homework Book provides a homework activity related to the content of this Unit for each of the three weeks.

Fiction

Reading

Children will:

- build strong pictures in their minds, making links between the poems and their own experiences
- explore the effect of poetic techniques, e.g. *repetition*, *alliteration*, and *simile*
- explore the range of forms poetry takes, e.g. *haiku*, *rhyming couplets* and *free verse*
- learn some lines of poetry by heart to recite in a performance.

Writing

Key writing purpose to be shared with the children:

To write a poem in free verse about a small, unexpected event.

Writing evaluation to be shared with the children

My poem:

- describes one particular moment in great detail
- creates strong feelings and makes a vivid picture in the reader's mind
- uses poetic features, e.g. *alliteration*, *simile* and *personification*
- is written in free verse, so I have used line breaks instead of commas to show the reader where to pause when reading aloud.

See the Planning section of the Software ('Timetables' tab) for a printable version of the Writing purpose and evaluation.

Fiction: Poetry

READING FICTION

DAY 1

Curriculum link:
listening to and
discussing a wide
range of poetry,
identifying themes

The poetry store (CD) A

*Purpose: for children to be immersed in
poems that use powerful imagery
to capture everyday moments*

Resources
- **PB** Pupils' Book, pp.14–23
- **A** Anthology, pp.18–25
- **(CD)** CD on interactive whiteboard, Unit 2
- **GB** Grammar Bank on CD
- **HB** Homework Book, pp.7–9

- Tell the children that every day we notice things that are not really important, but we still think and wonder about them – sometimes just for a while, and sometimes for a long time. Give an example of your own, e.g.

  On the way to school today, I passed a black cat. I saw it chasing and then pouncing on a leaf. It reminded me of a black panther stalking and catching its prey.

  There was a tree branch outside my window swaying in the wind, and it looked like a hand waving at me.

- Ask the children to TTYP (Turn to your partner) to share one small thing that they remember about getting ready for school this morning. Take some feedback and ask them to say why they think they remembered that particular moment.
- Explain that poets often make those tiny moments last forever by writing about them. Say that they are going to see two poems that capture a moment that the poets wanted to remember.
- Display **CD (file 1.1)** and tell the children that they are going to hear two short poems (please note: 'The Balloons' is an abridged version). Say that each of the poems focuses on a moment when something ordinary is observed and made special by remembering and exploring it.
- Play the audio of the poems to the children, briefly explaining any tricky words and phrases when each poem has finished (the important thing is to immerse the children in the imagery rather than spend time giving detailed explanations).
- Check they understand that the first poem was inspired by coloured balloons floating in the sky and the second by seeing coloured saris fluttering on a washing line.
- Tell the children to turn to their Anthology pp.18–19 and to TTYP to re-read the poems. Ask them to share with their partner which poem created the clearest images in their minds. Collect feedback and tease out what they think made the images in one poem more powerful than the other.

Similes

- Tell the children that there are lots of similes in the poem 'The Balloons'. Navigate to the next slide to show the poem and click 'Similes' to highlight the relevant parts of the poem. Use MT/YT (My turn/Your turn) to read the similes with the children. Ask the children which simile they think is the best and why.
- Ask them to TTYP to share what a simile is. Collect answers and clarify where necessary, explaining that similes can take two forms using *like* or *as*, e.g. *The cat pounced on the leaf like a panther catching its prey. The cat is as quick as a panther.*
- Say that there is only one simile in 'My Sari'. Ask the children to TTYP to spot the simile in 'My Sari' (p.19 of the Anthology). Take feedback and clarify where necessary. Use MT/YT to read the simile '*It wraps around me like sunshine*'.
- If there is some confusion, explain that the first two lines of the poem say that the saris make the washing line *a rainbow*. Say that this is like a simile but it says *it is* a rainbow, not that it is *like* a rainbow, and so this is called a *metaphor*.

- Tell the children that both poems could also be called *'a moment to remember'* and that this Special phrase is in another poem that they are going to find out about.

Curriculum link: predicting

Introducing the poem 1

Purpose: for children to be introduced to the poem 'At the End of a School Day'

- Tell the children that they are going to hear a new poem that is packed full of wonderful words and phrases that paint pictures in our minds. Say that before they hear the poem, they are going to step into the world of the poem.
- Read the script below, using MT/YT to show some mini-mimes for each section. Immerse the children in the atmosphere and world of the poem without revealing what it is about. Exaggerate intonation, actions, facial expressions etc. to convey the meaning of the poem. It is easier to draw the children into the role-play if you read and act out your script. You may wish to practise the mimes with the children once first.

  It is a warm afternoon in class (mini-mime fanning face and sighing) *and we are tired and restless at the end of a school day. Show me tired! Show me restless!*

  End of lesson! Home time! Shove your homework in your bag (mini-mime stuffing homework into bag).

  Line up, down the corridor, sensibly, slowly (mini-mime marching on the spot).

  Doors open. Burst into the bright sunshine! (mini-mime covering face with hands and revealing, to show bursting through the door into the bright light).

  (Freeze-frame — ask the children to freeze at the point that they burst out of the door.)

- Tell the children to relax the frame and TTYP to say how they feel as they burst through the door. Ask the children to Popcorn (see Introduction p.17) their responses, keeping them in the present tense in role, e.g. *So you feel excited...relieved.*

predicting; identifying how language, structure and presentation contribute to meaning

Introducing the poem 2

Purpose: for children to be introduced to the ideas and images in the poem before they hear the full version

- Ask the children to take up their freeze-frame positions again. Tell them that they are not only about to burst into the sunshine and run out of school, they are also about to burst right into the poem. Continue with the script and mini-mimes below.

  Through the doors and onto the playground (mini-mime running on the spot).

  We are running and shouting (mini-mime shouting whilst running on the spot).

  We skid to a stop! Freeze (freeze-frame skidding to a stop)!

  Why have we stopped?

- Tell the children to relax the frame and TTYP to say why they have stopped. Collect responses, keeping them in the present tense in role, e.g. *Someone's fallen over... You've all seen something strange in the playground... It has started to thunder...*
- Ask the children to take up their last freeze-frame positions again. Continue with the script and mini-mimes below.

  Look down. Stand still. Stare (mini-mime looking down and staring)!

  We kneel down (mini-mime kneeling down).

Very, very carefully, gingerly we pick something up… (mini-mime picking something up from the ground).

We all hold our breath (mini-mime taking a sharp breath in, pausing and slowly breathing out).

A moment to remember… (whisper it together using MT/YT and then TTYP).

Introducing the poem 3 🅰 (teacher only)

Purpose: for children to hear and enjoy the full version of the poem for the first time

- Tell the children that they are now going to hear the whole poem 'At the End of a School Day' for the very first time. TOL (Think out loud) about which parts you can't wait to hear about, e.g. *'I can't wait to hear about what the children have found on the ground in the school playground. I want to know more about the moment that inspired the poet to write the poem.'*
- Turn to pp.20–21 in the Anthology and read the poem aloud to the children with great enjoyment and appropriate intonation. It's important that you just read from your copy and the children don't follow the poem in their copy of the Anthology at this stage. Alternatively there is an audio recording of the poem on **CD (file 1.2)**.
- Ask the children to TTYP to share what pictures the poem created in their minds. Choose two or three sets of partners to share their responses. TOL as you describe the pictures that the poem created in your mind.

Daily log

Purpose: for children to keep a personal log of notes, thoughts and ideas, collected from their reading and discussions. Some ideas will be used in their own writing

- Explain to the children that they are going to collect thoughts and ideas about poems and experiences in their Daily log.
- Ask them to TTYP to share one word, phrase or image they remember from the poem 'At the End of a School Day'. Collect feedback and write their answers on the board or a flipchart, e.g. *the hedgehog looking like an old cricket ball, the bit where the girl picks up the hedgehog.*
- Tell them to write their chosen word, phrase or image in their Daily log.

Big Question 🆎

Purpose: for children to develop their skills of argument and discussion through a mini enquiry session based on a philosophical question relating to the work of the day

- Display today's Big Question on **CD (file 1.3)**:

  When we look at something, do we all see the same thing? *

- Ask the children to TTYP to talk about this question. Collect feedback and write some responses on the board.
- Click 'Prompts' to show some statements that may help to encourage discussion.

  * *This Big Question will be revisited on Day 11 – the first day of the Non-fiction week.*

DAY 2

Word power 🆎

Purpose: for children to increase their knowledge of powerful vocabulary and synonyms

> winces   gapes   frayed   gingerly

- Tell the children that some of the words that the writer used in the poem they heard yesterday are powerful because they aren't used very often.

- Display **CD (file 2.1)** to show a list of the Power words and their definitions/synonyms.
- Look at the words and their definitions with the children and then read the sentences to them. Ask the children to repeat the sentences using MT/YT adding dramatic emphasis and actions as you say them.
- Use the words in your teaching and conversation throughout the day, e.g. *'You were carrying those paintings to the drying rack very gingerly, Tom!'*
- Encourage them to use the words at home with friends and family so that they become embedded in the children's own spoken (and eventually, written) vocabulary.
- Print the words and their definitions/synonyms from **CD (file 2.2)** to display on your Poetry wall for this Unit.

Curriculum link: discussing words and phrases that capture the reader's interest and imagination

Special phrases (CD) (PB)

Purpose: for children to revise some poetic features and become familiar with Special phrases particular to the poem

> *Deafened the sky winces. The sun gapes in surprise.*
> *…runners skid to a stop, stand still and stare*
> *curled up on the tarmac like an old, frayed cricket ball.*
> *tiptoes forward and gingerly, so gingerly*
> *a moment to remember on this warm afternoon in June.*

- Display **CD (file 2.3)** to show some Special phrases from the poem.
- Explain that you have chosen these phrases because they are phrases that we don't use in our everyday talk, so they need explaining, and because they have some important poetic features.
- Use MT/YT to read the first phrase aloud. Click 'TOL' to use the think bubbles and/or your own ideas to draw attention to the poetic features used in some of the phrases, e.g. *imagery, alliteration, simile, repetition, rhythm, rhyme.*
- Navigate through the slides and repeat for each Special phrase.
- Now ask the children to turn to p.14 in their Pupils' Book and look at the Special phrases activity. Explain that you want them to TTYP to read the Special phrases and the effects and to choose their favourite phrase.
- Make sure they can explain to their partner what they like about it. Choose a few sets of partners to feed back.

checking that the text makes sense, asking questions, drawing inferences

Read a poem (A) (PB)

Purpose: for children to gain a deeper understanding of the poem and to see the text for the first time

- Let the children follow their own copy of the poem 'At the End of a School Day' in their Anthology pp.20–21 as you re-read the full version of the poem aloud with great enthusiasm.
- Ask the children to TTYP to read the poem again. Explain that they should read alternate stanzas and read the poem with great expression to convey meaning and impact.
- Now ask the children to turn to p.15 in their Pupils' Book and look at the Read a poem activity. Explain that you want them to TTYP to discuss the questions.
- Collect feedback and build on their responses where possible. Make sure they know that there aren't any right answers – they should give their own ideas and opinions, but must be ready to give reasons for their answers.

Fiction: Poetry

Curriculum link: composing and rehearsing sentences orally; building an increasing range of sentence structures

Daily log

Purpose: for children to keep a personal log of notes, thoughts and ideas, collected from their reading and discussions. Some ideas will be used in their own writing

- Remind the children that there was just one *simile* in 'At the End of a School Day':

  …a small hedgehog
      curled up on the tarmac
          like an old, frayed cricket ball.

- Remind them that there were also similes in the poems 'My Sari': 'It wraps around me like sunshine,'… and 'The Balloons', e.g. 'Dip and drift like satin moons'.
- Now ask them to turn to p.15 in their Pupils' Book and look at the Daily log: similes activity. Explain that you want them to look at the pictures and TTYP to complete the similes. You may wish to model some examples for the children to get them started.
- Choose one or two sets of partners to share their similes. Ask the children to write at least one of the completed similes in their Daily log.

discussion; develop, agree on, and evaluate rules for effective discussion

Big Question

Purpose: for children to develop their skills of argument and discussion through a mini enquiry session based on a philosophical question relating to the work of the day

- Display today's Big Question on **CD (file 2.4)**:

  Are memories important?

- Follow the process as explained on Day 1.

DAY 3

Multi-syllabic words

Purpose: for children to consolidate their understanding of syllables

- Before the lesson, print a copy of the Syllable sums chart for each child or set of partners from **CD (file 3.2)**.
- Tell the children that some of the words in the poems they have read have words with more than one syllable. Remind the children that we call them *multi-syllabic* words.
- Display **CD (file 3.1)** to show some of the multi-syllabic words from the poems. Using MT/YT to say the syllables and then the word.
- Navigate to the next slide and complete the process.
- Navigate to the next slide to display a Syllable sums chart. Use the example to show the children how to count the syllables in the words. Do the next word together and then give each child or set of partners a copy of the chart from **CD (file 3.2)**.
- Explain that you want them to TTYP to complete the rest of the chart in Section A on the sheet. Walk around as they work together, checking their understanding and clarifying where necessary.
- Take feedback. Use your chart on screen to write their answers in the empty cells and consolidate their understanding of syllables.
- Draw their attention to the single-syllable words in Section B on the sheet and ask them to TTYP to try to think of some other single-syllable words. (Section C will be used in a later activity.)

recognising some different forms of poetry; discussing writing similar to that which they are planning to write

Form 1

Purpose: for children to develop their awareness of poetic forms

- Tell the children that just like poets, poems come in all shapes and sizes. Ask: 'Have you ever heard of a haiku *poem?*' Ask them to Popcorn Yes/No responses and then collect feedback from a few children, clarifying the meaning if necessary.

- Remind them that haiku poems have strict rules about how many syllables the poet can use to capture his or her moment to remember.
- Display **CD (file 3.3)** to show the rules for creating a haiku. Explain that if these rules were written as a haiku they would be laid out differently on the page. Navigate to the next slide to show the rules re-arranged into two haikus and use MT/YT to read each line. Click 'Reveal' to show the words split into syllables and use MT/YT to read it again, counting the syllables on your fingers as you read.
- Explain that good haikus are quite hard to write because it is easier to describe an image if we can use any words and phrases that we choose and not have to worry about the number of syllables in them. Say that the limitations of a haiku make you select just the most important words and phrases so they can be very powerful.
- Navigate to the next slide to show the poem 'The Balloons' again. Read the poem aloud to the children and remind them of the meaning of any rarer vocabulary.
- TOL about the pattern of this poem and why it looks different to a haiku, e.g. *'almost every line has seven syllables and each stanza has four lines.'*
- Tell the children you think it would be interesting to take some of the most powerful words and phrases from the poem 'The Balloons' to make a haiku. Ask: *'How many syllables will I need to make a haiku?'* Ask them to Popcorn their answers.
- Click on 'Highlights' to highlight the words that you want to use in your haiku.
- Navigate to the next slide to show the words arranged as a haiku. Click 'Reveal' to show the words split into syllables. Read the haiku aloud using MT/YT, counting the syllables on your fingers as you read it.
- Display **CD (file 3.4)** to show the poem 'My Sari'. Read the poem aloud to the children and remind them of the meaning of any rarer vocabulary.
- TOL about the pattern of this poem and why it looks different to a haiku, e.g. *'every line has eight syllables and the poem is made up of eight lines.'*
- Ask the children to TTYP to choose three words in the poem that they think are the most powerful words. Ask them to Popcorn their chosen words. Take feedback about the reasons behind their choices from a few sets of partners.
- Explain that you could use any of the words in the poem to make the first line of a new haiku poem. TOL as you have a go at creating your own five-syllable line, modelling how you have to keep counting the syllables as you try out different words and phrases.
- Write it on the board and use MT/YT to read the first line of your haiku poem. Now read it chorally, counting the syllables in the line on your fingers as you read.

Curriculum link: learn the conventions of different types of writing

Haiku (CD)

Purpose: for children to develop their ability to experiment with words to create powerful images

- Ask the children to look at Section C on their Syllable sums sheet from **CD (file 3.2)**. Explain that you want them to use the multi-syllabic words and single-syllable words that they looked at in Sections A and B, and other words that they think of, to create their own haikus. Read through the examples given on the sheet using MT/YT. The point of this activity is for children to experiment with using interesting words and structuring them to form a haiku. They don't need to focus on creating a specific image.
- Model how to use some of the words from the sheet and any additional ones to write your own haiku. Show how you edit your work and don't make it look too easy.
- Tell them to experiment in their Daily log, crossing out and trying different words to create an interesting haiku. You may want some partners to write a haiku together.

- Walk around as they work, praising examples of self-editing and experimentation and noting examples to share.
- When they are happy with what they have written in their Daily log, ask them to write their haiku neatly in the space provided on their sheets. Choose as many partners to read out their haikus as time allows.

Daily log (CD)

Curriculum link:
discussing and recording ideas; read aloud their own writing

Purpose: for children to keep a personal log of notes, thoughts and ideas, collected from their reading and discussions. Some ideas will be used in their own writing

- Remind the children that *haiku* is a Japanese word.
- Explain that Japanese writing is made up of symbols. Display **CD (file 3.5)** to show three Japanese symbols.
- Explain that each of the symbols has a meaning. Click 'Reveal' to show the word next to each symbol. Model writing the symbols onto the board or a flipchart.
- Ask the children to choose their favourite symbol and to copy it into their Daily log. They should also write down the meaning of the symbol.

Big Question (CD)

discussion; develop, agree on, and evaluate rules for effective discussion

Purpose: for children to develop their skills of argument and discussion through a mini enquiry session based on a philosophical question relating to the work of the day

- Display today's Big Question on **CD (file 3.6)**:

  Is it better to have rules or to be free to do whatever you like?

- Follow the process as explained on Day 1.

(DAY 4)

Form 2 (CD) A PB

recognising some different forms of poetry; discussing writing similar to that which they are planning to write

Purpose: for children to develop their understanding of rhyming patterns

- Ask the children: *'Do poems have to rhyme?'* and tell them to Popcorn Yes/No responses. Ask one or two children to support their answers, and follow up their responses with a brief class discussion.
- Display **CD (file 4.1)** to show the poem 'The Balloons' again. Ask the children to chant the words in bold.
- Ask the children to TTYP to match up the words which form the end rhymes, e.g. *skies/butterflies, balloons/moons*. Take feedback and clarify where necessary.
- Explain that rhyming patterns can be mapped by using lower case letters to show the pattern. Click 'Rhyme' to show the rhyme scheme of the first stanza and explain the way the notation works.
- Now ask the children to look at the poem 'My Sari' on p.19 of the Anthology. Ask them to TTYP to read the poem, taking it in turns to read two lines each.
- Explain that 'My Sari' has a different rhyming pattern. Tell them that the first three lines would be *a, b, a*. Ask them to TTYP to work out the rest of the rhyme pattern and write it in their Daily log.
- Choose one or two partners to share their answers and/or ask the class to chant the pattern together. Explain that if a poem has two lines together that rhyme (a, a / b, b, etc.) they are called *rhyming couplets*.
- Ask the children to turn to p.16 in their Pupils' Book and look at the Form 2 activity. Explain that they first need to TTYP to think of some words that rhyme with the words in their Pupils' Book and write them in their Daily log.
- Now ask them to use the words that they have written down (and any others they think of) to help them to complete the rhyming couplets. Ask them to write their completed rhyming couplets in their Daily log.

- Give each set of partners a sticky note and ask them to write their best, funniest or favourite rhyming couplet down and stick it on the board or flipchart.
- Choose two or three sets of partners to read out their best, funniest or favourite rhyming couplets.

Curriculum link: drawing inferences; participate in discussion about books

What if not...? (CD)

Purpose: for children to develop their ability to experiment with language and to consider the impact that making changes can have on a text

- Remind the children that not all poems have to rhyme. Display **CD (file 4.2)** to show a What if not...? question: What if not *rhyming*? What if *the poet wanted 'My Sari' to be a non-rhyming poem?*
- Navigate to the next screen to show the poem 'My Sari' again. Use this TOL and/or your own ideas to encourage the children to think about how they could use the poem to create a new *non-rhyming* poem: 'We *could keep the words* line *and* would *because they are hard to change. Then we could use synonyms to change the words that rhyme with them.'*
- Navigate to the next screen to show a selection of synonyms for the rhyming words in the poem. Read each of the words and synonyms using MT/YT.
- Navigate to the next screen to show the first four lines from the poem and a list of the synonyms.
- Use drag and drop to try out different synonyms and draw the children into your own TOL about the effect of the new words, e.g. *'Does the meaning change? Does the emphasis change? How has the rhythm altered?'*
- Navigate to the next screen and repeat the process for the final four lines.
- Navigate to the final screen to show a new non-rhyming poem. This may differ slightly to the version the children created using drag and drop, depending on the choices they made.
- Ask the children to TTYP to discuss whether they prefer the original rhyming poem or the new non-rhyming poem and why. Collect feedback and emphasise that there isn't a right answer – you are just looking for their opinions.

preparing poems to read aloud and to perform

Daily log (A) (CD)

Purpose: for children to keep a personal log of notes, thoughts and ideas, collected from their reading and discussions. Some ideas will be used in their own writing

- Tell the children that you think it's really important to learn some poetry by heart, so they can take it with them anywhere. Say that learning poems by heart can be enjoyable and that when you recite a poem you can put more effort into making it sound interesting and exciting because you don't have to worry about reading the words on the page. Surprise them with any snippets of poetry you can recall yourself and tell them how many years ago you learned them.
- Ask the children to look at the poem 'My Sari' on p.19 of the Anthology. Divide the class into two groups and allocate lines from the poem to each group as follows:

  Group A *Partner 1s: lines 1 and 2, Partner 2s: lines 3 and 4*
  Group B *Partner 1s: lines 5 and 6, Partner 2s: lines 7 and 8*

- Explain that you want them to try to learn their lines by heart for a class performance. You may want to incorporate the performance into next week's work or an assembly.

- Display **CD (file 4.3)** to show some Top Tips for learning poetry by heart. Read each point aloud using MT/YT.
- Tell them to write their allocated lines in their Daily log and draw a few pencil pictures or symbols to help to fix the words in their minds.
- Remind them to try to recite their lines at home each day.

<table>
<tr><td>

Curriculum link:
discussion;
develop, agree on,
and evaluate
rules for effective
discussion

</td></tr>
</table>

Big Question (CD)

Purpose: for children to develop their skills of argument and discussion through a mini enquiry session based on a philosophical question relating to the work of the day

- Display today's Big Question on **CD (file 4.4)**:

  Do our lives have patterns?

- Follow the process as explained on Day 1.

DAY 5

<table>
<tr><td>

identifying how
language, structure
and presentation
contribute to
meaning

</td></tr>
</table>

Think and link (CD)

Purpose: for children to make connections between form and content in poetry

- Display **CD (file 5.1)** to show some poetic terms you have been using. Read the words using MT/YT and then read the lines from the poem 'My Sari' to show examples of them. Click 'TOL' and talk about the poetic features.
- These and other poetic terms can be printed from **CD (file 5.2)** to display on your Poetry wall.
- Remind the children that they have looked at poems that follow rules and have strong rhyming patterns. Tell them that the poem 'At the End of a School Day' is written in the form of *free verse*. Explain that this means it doesn't have a regular rhythm, number of syllables or rhyming pattern.
- Ask the children to look at the poem on pp.20–21 of the Anthology and to TTYP to take turns to read one stanza at a time.
- Ask the children to TTYP and discuss what shows them that this poem has been written in free verse. Take feedback from a few sets of partners and clarify if necessary. Draw the children's attention to the irregular line lengths and irregular number of syllables in each line.
- Ask them to TTYP to think about the shape of the poem. Take feedback and choose a few sets of partners to describe the shape of the poem to the rest of the class. For example, they could talk about how the lines start in different positions.
- Have a class discussion about why you think the poet, Wes Magee, chose this shape for the poem, e.g. *it makes the poem look like the winding path that leads down from the school.*

<table>
<tr><td>

asking questions
to improve their
understanding of
a text; drawing
and justifying
inferences

</td></tr>
</table>

Drama

Purpose: for children to explore deeper meaning in a poem through drama

- Ask the children to look at the poem 'At the End of a School Day' on pp.20–21 of the Anthology. Read the poem aloud to the children, performing it with great dramatic emphasis.
- Remind the children that 'At the End of a School Day' is a narrative poem because it tells a story.
- Explain that we could call the girl who picks up the hedgehog and the children who watch her *characters*. Say that we know what the characters do and how the poem makes us feel because of the way the poet uses words to create moods.
- Tell the children that you wish you could ask the children in the poem, or even the hedgehog, the sky (who *winces*) and the sun (who *gapes in surprise*) lots of questions.

- Ask them to TTYP to think of at least one thing they would like to know about that day or moment to remember. Collect feedback and write some questions on the board or a flipchart.
- Check they can say who or what would be able to tell them the answer and write the name of the character next to the question.
- Repeat the TTYP a couple more times to generate more questions and encourage open as well as closed questions.

Teacher in role

- Explain that you are going to sit in the hotseat and take on the role of some of the characters from the poem.
- Let the children TTYP to choose a character and a question from the ones on the board or flipchart.
- Choose partners to state the character and ask a question. You must answer in role but you can come out of role if necessary to refer to the poem. Make sure you signal that you have come out of role by stepping to the side and explain this to the children. It is important that the children see when you are in role and when you are yourself.

Children in role

- Explain to the children that they are now going to take turns to sit in the hotseat and take on the role of some of the characters from the poem.
- Say that Partner 1s will sit in the hotseat and Partner 2s will ask the questions. Explain that Partner 2s will need to start by choosing a role and a question from the ones on the board or flipchart.
- Give them the opportunity to choose a few characters and questions before using the Stop signal (see Introduction p.16) to halt the hotseating and asking them to swap over.
- Walk around listening in and noting interesting and thoughtful responses.
- Repeat the process as many times as you feel is appropriate with your class. At the end of the activity give feedback and praise based on what you saw and heard.

Daily log 🅰 🆎

> **Curriculum link:**
> discussing and
> recording ideas

Purpose: for children to keep a personal log of notes, thoughts and ideas, collected from their reading and discussions. Some ideas will be used in their own writing

- Ask the children to turn to pp.19–21 in the Anthology and to take turns to read the poems 'My Sari' and 'At the End of a School Day' again with their partners.
- Now display **CD (file 5.3)** and tell the children to TTYP to read the prompts and use them to compare the poems 'My Sari' and 'At the End of a School Day'.
- Ask them to write their responses in their Daily log.
- Choose two or three sets of partners to share their responses with the rest of the class.

Big Question 🆎

> discussion;
> develop, agree on,
> and evaluate
> rules for effective
> discussion

Purpose: for children to develop their skills of argument and discussion through a mini enquiry session based on a philosophical question relating to the work of the day

- Display today's Big Question on the **CD (file 5.4)**:

  Can we ever know what someone else is feeling?

- Follow the process as explained on Day 1.

WRITING FICTION

DAY 6

Zoom in, zoom out

Purpose: for children to develop their ability to use language to describe what they observe

- Display **CD (file 1.3)** to remind the children of the Big Question that they discussed on Day 1: *When we look at something, do we all see the same thing?* Tell them that they are going to see a special image made by a photographer zooming in on and magnifying something.
- Display **CD (file 6.1)** to show the photograph. TOL as you describe what you see (the point is to use description, not to guess what it is). Use your own ideas or click 'TOL' to show a think bubble if you prefer.
- Say that lots of different words appear in your mind as you look at this image. Write two or three words or phrases on the board or a flipchart, e.g. *smooth, cracks, messy, damp*. Ask the children to Popcorn some words of their own for you to write. Encourage them to use different senses, e.g. *cold, hard, quiet*.
- Remind the children that when they read the poems 'The Balloons' and 'My Sari', they turned the words on the page into pictures in their minds. Explain that they are now doing the opposite and turning pictures into words.
- Click 'Zoom out' to show a bit more of the image and ask the children to TTYP to share what they see. Take feedback and add some of their words and phrases to the board or flipchart, e.g. *sharp, jagged, fragile, fluffy*.
- Use every opportunity to develop their confidence and knowledge of language. For example, draw attention to powerful, rarer words that they offer and to antonyms as well as synonyms.
- Move to the next slide to show the whole picture. Ask them to TTYP to say what the whole picture shows.
- Leave up the words you have written on the board or flipchart as you will need them for the next activity.

Curriculum link: composing and rehearsing orally; building a varied and rich vocabulary

Build an image

Purpose: for children to see how similes can be used to build an image

- Ask the children to TTYP to share whether they have ever seen the very special moment when a chick hatches out of an egg. Collect experiences and tell them that this could be described as another moment to remember. Ask them to Popcorn answers to the question: *'Which poem have we looked at that has this Special phrase in it?'*
- Say that you want to try to capture the *moment to remember* shown in the photograph. Explain that you are going to start by creating similes using some of the words. Choose one of the words from those you have written on the board or flipchart, e.g. *fluffy*.
- Now build a simile around it orally. Use the TOL below and/or your own ideas to show your thought process and rejection of more clichéd comparisons.

    Hmm…fluffy. What else is fluffy? A cloud? Cotton wool? A baby's hair?

    I can make a simile, As fluffy as a baby's hair…or fluffy like a baby's hair.

- Write your simile down on the board or flipchart.
- Repeat the process choosing another word or phrase from the ones you wrote on the board or flipchart. This time, ask the children to TTYP to come up with some similes for you to try out orally.

- Take feedback from a few sets of partners and choose two or three similes to write beneath the first one, e.g. *cracks like a wall in an earthquake; as smooth as whipped cream.*
- Ask the children to TTYP to repeat the process with another word, this time without input from you. Collect ideas and similes and write a few on the board or flipchart.

Curriculum link:
discussing and
recording ideas

Daily log

Purpose: for children to keep a personal log of notes, thoughts and ideas, collected from their reading and discussions. Some ideas will be used in their own writing

- Tell the children that they are going to create some more similes using the question: What if not *a chick?*
- Ask them to TTYP to take turns to answer the question: What if not *a chick?* What if *something very surprising or bizarre popped out of the egg?* Give a few examples to get them started, e.g. *a snake, a human, an alien.*
- When you give the Stop signal, ask them to choose one or two of their favourite images and write them down in their Daily log.
- Take feedback and model using some of their ideas to create some similes. Use the following structure but substitute with the children's ideas.

  What if a dragon popped out of the egg, as green as the grass.

  What if a bear popped out of the egg, furry like gran's slippers.

- Now ask the children to TTYP to create some of their own similes using the ideas they recorded in their Daily log, and to write them down. Encourage them to be inventive.

discussion;
develop, agree on,
and evaluate
rules for effective
discussion

Big Question

Purpose: for children to develop their skills of argument and discussion through a mini enquiry session based on a philosophical question relating to the work of the day

- Display today's Big Question on the **CD (file 6.2)**:

  Is it good to surprise people?

- Follow the process as explained on Day 1.

DAY 7

Build a poem 1 (CD)

Purpose: for children to be able to see a poem grow through three stages of development

plan writing by
discussing writing
that is similar

- Tell the children that you have been thinking about moments to remember. Display **CD (file 7.1)** to show pictures of some small but unexpected events in everyday settings.
- Read the caption for each picture and ask the children to TTYP to share similar experiences. Collect lots of responses and use it as an opportunity to generate interest and enthusiasm by encouraging them to embellish their recollections and by sharing your own experiences.
- Tell the children that you decided to write a new poem about one of the events shown in the pictures. From this point on you are in role as the writer.
- Explain that you used some questions to help you to begin writing your new poem. Navigate to the next slide to show a list of questions.
- Ask the children to read the first question aloud chorally. Then click 'Answer' to reveal the answer and read it to them. Repeat this for each of the questions.
- Remind them that you decided to begin by following the pattern of the poem 'At the End of a School Day'. Navigate to the next slide to show the first stanza of the poem. Read it chorally with the children.

- Explain that you are going to show them how you began to build the new poem in different stages. Navigate to the next slide to show the first two versions. Click 'TOL' and use the think bubbles to model the process.
- Navigate to the next slide to show the next two versions. Read them aloud and click 'TOL' to use the think bubbles and your own ideas to show how you developed the poem.
- Navigate to the final slide to show your completed first stanza and read it aloud to the children. Click 'Highlights' to highlight some poetic features and ask the children to TTYP to discuss which poetic features are shown (alliteration and rhyme). Take feedback and clarify if necessary.
- Tell the children that there is a special word that means giving human feelings or characteristics to non-human objects, e.g. *the clouds cringe* and *the rain cries*. Say that this is called *personification*. Write the word on the board or flipchart and ask them to copy it into their Daily log.

<table>
<tr><td>

Curriculum link:
composing
and rehearsing
sentences orally;
creating settings,
characters, plot
</td></tr>
</table>

Write a poem 1

Purpose: for children to develop their confidence and skills in writing poetry

- Before the lesson, print a copy of **CD (file 7.2)** for each child.
- Tell the children that they are going to begin to write their own poem about a dog in their playground.
- Give each child a copy of the writing frames you printed from **CD (file 7.2)** and ask them to TTYP to take turns to read the first stanza in Section A.
- Read the prompts underneath the stanza using MT/YT. Ask the children to TTYP to use the prompts and their own ideas to complete the stanza in Section A. Walk around and listen in, praising good quality discussions and ideas.
- Give them time to complete Section A and then ask them to repeat the process for Section B.
- Collect feedback, expanding on and recording some of their ideas on the board. Remind them that they should try to use some of the poetic techniques they have looked at, such as alliteration and personification.
- Now ask the children to write their first draft of the first stanza of their poem, using their writing frames and the notes on the board or flipchart to help them. They should write this first draft in their Daily log. Remind them that they don't have to stick too closely to the writing frame – they can be as imaginative as they like!
- Remind them that they can look at the original poem any time they want to on pp.20–21 of the Anthology.

<table>
<tr><td>

assessing the
effectiveness of
their own and
others' writing
and suggesting
improvements
</td></tr>
</table>

Daily log

Purpose: for children to keep a personal log of notes, thoughts and ideas, collected from their reading and discussions. Some ideas will be used in their own writing

- Tell the children that it is important to keep reading and working on their poems at this stage. Say that sometimes it helps to discuss your poem with someone else to think about how it could be improved.
- Display **CD (file 7.3)** to show a cartoon of the 'poem doctor' helping a child to improve his poem. Navigate through the slides to look through the cartoon strip and listen to the audio.
- Now ask the children to TTYP to look at their own poem in their Daily log. Tell them to read what they have written so far and to circle or underline one or two sections that they would like some help with.

- Say that Partner 1s will be the poem doctor and Partner 2s will ask for help with their poem. Ask Partner 2s to share what they have written and the sections they are struggling with. Tell them to discuss how to improve their poems with the poem doctor.
- Now ask them to swap roles.
- Make sure they have an opportunity to try out one or two changes in their Daily log.

Curriculum link:
discussion;
develop, agree on, and evaluate rules for effective discussion

Big Question (CD)

Purpose: for children to develop their skills of argument and discussion through a mini enquiry session based on a philosophical question relating to the work of the day

- Display today's Big Question on the **CD (file 7.4)**:

  Is copying always wrong?

- Follow the process as explained on Day 1.

DAY 8

drawing inferences;
participate in discussion about books

What if not…? (CD)

Purpose: for children to develop their ability to experiment with language and to consider the impact of changes made to a text

- Display **CD (file 8.1)** to show the start of your new poem.
- Remind the children that as writers we can change anything we want to experiment with in order to improve on our work. Navigate to the next screen to show the questions: What if not *a dog*? What if *a lion arrived on the playground*?
- Navigate to the next screen to show the parts of the poem that you would want to change if it was a lion instead of a dog that had arrived on the playground.
- Navigate to the final screen to show some alternative words and phrases that you could use to change your poem. Drag and drop the words and phrases into the gaps to experiment with different combinations. Draw the children into your writing by asking them to suggest different combinations and trying out some of their choices. TOL about the effect that the different combinations have on the rest of the poem.

plan writing by discussing writing that is similar;
recording ideas

Build a poem 2 (CD)

Purpose: for children to be able to see a poem grow through three stages of development

- Display **CD (file 8.2)** to show a new version of your poem based on the different combinations that you experimented with in the previous activity.
- Explain that you don't think the last two lines work very well now that you have a lion arriving in the playground instead of a dog. Navigate to the next screen to show the words you would like to change. Ask the children to TTYP to share whether they agree with you and why. Collect feedback and encourage discussion about:
  - the possible response of the clouds and the rain to seeing a lion
  - whether to keep the clouds and the rain or use other parts of the landscape.
- Write their ideas on the board or flipchart and ask them to TTYP and feed back ideas about how the sky/sun/clouds/rain would react to seeing and hearing the lion in the playground.
- Navigate to the final screen to show alternative words for the last two lines of the poem. Drag and drop the words into the gaps to experiment with different combinations. Draw the children into your writing by asking them to suggest different combinations and trying out some of their choices. TOL about the effect that the different combinations have on the rest of the poem. Discuss which combinations create vivid pictures in the reader's mind.

Curriculum link:
composing
and rehearsing
sentences orally;
creating settings,
characters, plot

Write a poem 2

Purpose: for children to develop their ability to experiment with language and make choices for effect

- Before the lesson, print a copy of **CD (file 8.3)** for each child.
- Give each child a copy of the writing frame from **CD (file 8.3)**. Explain to the children that you want them to use the writing frame to begin to create another version of the new poem using the techniques that you have been experimenting with. Say that they can use the words suggested in the boxes or come up with their own ideas.
- Emphasise the need for them to edit and experiment with their lines as much as possible. Remind them that it is fine for them to cross things out and make changes to their work.
- Tell them to rehearse their new lines in their minds before writing them down.
- Walk around supporting, praising and noting good writing, especially the inclusion of poetic techniques.
- To avoid interrupting the children as they are working, write interesting examples on sticky notes as you walk around and stick them up on the board for you to refer to when you give feedback.
- Make sure you give them enough time to complete their stanzas before asking some children to share them with the rest of the class. Give feedback, drawing on some of the interesting examples you stuck on the board whilst they were writing.
- Ask the children to write their completed stanza in their Daily log.

discussing writing
in order to learn
from its structure
and vocabulary

Daily log ▲

Purpose: for children to keep a personal log of notes, thoughts and ideas, collected from their reading and discussions. Some ideas will be used in their own writing

- Ask the children to look at the poem 'At the End of a School Day' on pp.20–21 of the Anthology. Remind the children that the poet Wes Magee chose to set out his poem in a particular way on the page.
- Explain that the poet has chosen where to break the lines and where to start the next line. Ask them to TTYP to share reasons why he may have chosen to do this. Explain that there isn't a right answer to this question, you are just looking for their own ideas and opinions.
- Collect feedback, clarifying and building on their answers.
- Now ask them to look at their own poem in progress in their Daily log. Ask them to experiment with the shape on the page, trying out different patterns and line breaks. Remind them that this is not the final version of their poem yet.
- You may want to model an example on the board or flipchart, e.g.

It is the start of a school day and in the playground
comes
a tail-swishing,
roaring
lion.
Deafened,
the sun hides.
The flowers shrink in shock.

Curriculum link:
discussion;
develop, agree on,
and evaluate
rules for effective
discussion

Big Question

*Purpose: for children to develop their skills of argument and discussion through a mini
enquiry session based on a philosophical question relating to the work of the day*

- Display today's Big Question on **CD (file 8.4)**:

  Is exaggerating the same as lying?

- Follow the process as explained on Day 1.

DAY 9

understand
the skills and
processes that
are essential for
writing

Build a poem 3   (CD)   A

Purpose: for children to see examples of writing that will provide models for their own writing

- Tell the children that you wanted to write another stanza for the poem and to include a simile.
- Say that you looked at 'At the End of a School Day' again and borrowed some of your favourite words and Special phrases to experiment with. Tell them that you now have three versions of a new stanza for your poem.
- Display **CD (file 9.1)** to show your first new stanza (1) and read it aloud using MT/YT.
- Ask the children to look at the poem 'At the End of a School Day' on pp.20–21 of their Anthology and to TTYP to spot the words and phrases you have used. Click 'Highlights' to check that they have noticed all of the words and phrases that you have used from the original poem.
- TOL as you guide them through the process of borrowing words and phrases and using them in a different way to the way the poet used them in the original.
- Navigate to the next slide to show another version of the stanza (2). Read it aloud using MT/YT.
- Ask the children to compare it to your first version (stanza 1) and TTYP to spot the words and phrases you have changed. Draw their attention to antonyms and synonyms that have been used and to the different images created by different words.
- Click 'Highlights' to check that they have noticed all of the words and phrases that you have changed.
- Navigate to the next slide to show a third version of the stanza (3). Read it aloud using MT/YT.
- Tell the children that you want them to think about the image of *fear* being *dumped*. Ask them to think about the pictures the words create in their mind as you read the line *'I dump my fear'* aloud. You may wish to ask the children to close their eyes as you read it.
- Now ask them to TTYP to share what *fear* looked like to them. Take feedback.

What do you think?   PB

*Purpose: for children to develop their ability to evaluate the effectiveness of writers'
techniques and language choice*

- Now ask the children to turn to p.17 in their Pupils' Book and look at the What do you think? activity. Tell them to TTYP to read versions 1, 2 and 3 of your new stanza.
- Explain that you want them to use the questions to help them to evaluate the different versions and choose their favourite words, phrases or lines. Remind them that there are not any right answers to these questions, you are just looking for their own ideas and opinions.
- Collect responses and encourage them to give reasons for their choices.

Curriculum link:
creating settings,
characters, plot;
monitor whether
their writing
makes sense

Write a poem 3 PB

Purpose: for children to develop their ability to write independently

- Tell the children that they are going to write their own version of this new stanza for their own poem.
- Remind them that you used questions to help you to begin your poem (on Day 7). Explain that you are going to show them some discussion questions that will help them to write their new stanza.
- Ask the children to turn to p.18 in their Pupils' Book and to look at the Write a poem 3 activity. Read the first question prompt aloud to the children. Ask them to TTYP to discuss ideas with their partner. Collect responses and write some of them onto the board or a flipchart.
- Repeat for each question prompt.
- Tell them that they are now ready to begin to write their new stanza. Ask them to work in their Daily log and to use stanzas 1, 2 and 3 on p.17 of their Pupils' Book to help them.
- Encourage the children to rehearse their ideas with their partners before they begin to write.
- Walk around as they work, noting any powerful or rarer words or phrases that could be added to your Poetry wall for this Unit.

discussing and
recording ideas

Daily log

Purpose: for children to keep a personal log of notes, thoughts and ideas, collected from their reading and discussions. Some ideas will be used in their own writing

- Ask the children to TTYP to think of at least two possible titles for their poem. Tell them to record their ideas in their Daily log.
- Choose a few sets of partners to share their ideas and add them to your Poetry wall for this Unit.

DAY 10

Form 3 CD

The children will ideally need to have access to IT equipment for this lesson.

Purpose: for children to use IT to develop their awareness of the shape of poems on the page

identifying how
language, structure
and presentation
contribute to
meaning

- Remind the children that they have looked at different forms of poetry and that the poem 'At the End of a School Day' is written in *free verse*.
- Remind them that it isn't just the punctuation that we have to look out for when we read poetry but also the line breaks. Explain that poems form a shape on the page that can affect the way we read the lines. Say that the line breaks are like a form of punctuation.
- Display **CD (file 10.1)** to show the poem 'The Balloons' and click 'Audio' to hear the poem being read. Click 'Shape-shifter' to show the poem again but this time with different line breaks. Click 'Audio' to hear the poem again and ask the children to listen to the effect that the changes in the line breaks has on the way the poem is read. Take feedback and clarify if necessary, drawing attention to the emphasis that is put on the words at the end of each line.
- Navigate to the next slide and repeat the process for the stanza from your new poem.
- Navigate through the remaining slides to show the Top Tips for using IT to experiment with form. Discuss each of the Top Tips and ask the children to think about them in relation to their own poem.
- Now ask the children to type up their new poems.
- When they have typed up their poems, explain that they should use the Top Tips from the presentation to experiment with the shape and layout.

- Remind them to re-read their poem each time they change its shape, until they are happy with the result.
- Now tell them to add one of the titles they recorded in their Daily log on Day 9 to complete their poem.

Evaluate and edit

Purpose: for children to evaluate their own and their partner's work against specific criteria and then discuss how they could improve their work

- Display **CD (file 10.2)** and read through the evaluation points using MT/YT.
- As a model, select an example of work where the writing has met the criteria, and share this with the other children, explaining why it works well.
- Tell the children to take turns to read their partner's writing in pairs and discuss together how well each piece of writing has met the criteria.
- Ask children to discuss at least two changes they could make to improve their work.

Proofread

Purpose: for children to proofread their work and make changes to improve the accuracy of their grammar, punctuation and spelling

- Now ask the children to proofread their work. If you have noticed that several children need to improve on a particular aspect of spelling, grammar or punctuation, use this as a focus for the proofread activity. Write an example which includes common errors from the children's writing and use this as a model.
- The children should always be checking for standard use of punctuation and correct spelling of common exception words.
- The following points would be particularly relevant for this Unit:
  - checking spelling of ambitious vocabulary choices (i.e. those borrowed from the Pupils' Book or Anthology text)
  - reviewing the layout of the poem for impact.

Very Big Question

Purpose: for children to develop their willingness to broaden or revise their opinions through exploring one of the Big Questions in more depth

- See Unit 1 Day 10 for teaching notes on the Very Big Question (p.41).

READING AND WRITING NON-FICTION

The Non-fiction section explores recounts and journalistic texts. The children learn about the main features of recounts through reading and analysing some journalistic reports. They then have the opportunity to write their own report.

See p.52 for the daily timetable for the Non-fiction week.

Non-fiction

Reading

Children will:

- develop their understanding of both personal and newspaper recounts
- understand that recounts are organised in chronological order, in the past tense
- identify the key information in a recount by using the 5Ws – *Who? What? When? Where?* and *Why?*
- learn to identify points of view, facts and opinions in recounts and understand how they change the reliability of the recount.

Writing

Key writing purpose to be shared with the children:

To write an article in the style of a recount, using language and features that are typical of a newspaper.

Writing evaluation to be shared with the children

My article:

- is in chronological order (the order that things happened)
- shares the most important information with the reader by answering the 5Ws
- includes quotations to add detail or give a point of view
- experiments with the language and features of sensationalist newspaper articles, e.g. *revelation, exaggeration, speculation* and *sensation*.

Grammar:

- uses the third person past tense.

See the Planning section of the Software ('Timetables' tab) for a printable version of the Writing purpose and evaluation.

Introduction

Purpose: for children to revise their understanding of simple recounts and develop their awareness of point of view in texts

Curriculum link:
reading for a range of purposes; learn the conventions of different types of writing

- Display **CD (file 1.3)** to show the Big Question from Day 1: *When we look at something, do we all see the same thing?*
- Ask the children to TTYP to recall some of the points they discussed and ideas they explored on Day 1. Collect feedback.
- Remind the children that in the poem 'At the End of a School Day' the narrator is giving us one point of view of an event.
- Explain that because it is a poem, the writer has included poetic techniques such as *simile, alliteration* and *rhyme* and shaped the poem on the page in a particular pattern. Say that the writer has used special words and phrases to make us feel different emotions as we read the poem.
- Tell the children that if the same event had been written as a simple *recount*, it would be very different as it would focus on facts and not on feelings.
- Display **CD (file 11.1)** to show the bare facts of the event in the playground as a recount. Read it chorally with the children.
- Say that this is called a *recount*. It is a clear, factual record of something that has already happened, written for someone who wasn't there.
- Ask the children to TTYP to say whose point of view this recount is written from, e.g. *the girl who picked up the hedgehog, the hedgehog, a teacher, one of the children on the playground.* Tell them to Popcorn their answers and clarify if necessary.
- Click 'Highlights' to reveal the words that help to tell us who wrote the recount.
- Navigate to the next slide to show the same recount rewritten from the point of view of the girl who picked the hedgehog up. Click 'Highlights' to highlight the changes and talk them through with the children.
- Now ask the children to TTYP to share how the account of events would be different if they were recounted by the hedgehog. Collect feedback and build on their answers. Navigate to the next slide to show a third version of events as recounted by the hedgehog.
- Click 'Highlights' to highlight the changes and talk through them with the children. Ask them to TTYP to say why this recount is so different to the first two, e.g. *the perspective of the hedgehog is very different to the children's.*
- Explain that whenever we give an account of something, even if we stick to the facts, we will give a different version to someone else because it will be from our point of view and so we will give special emphasis to different things.

Dramatic reconstruction

building a varied and rich vocabulary

Purpose: for children to experience giving an oral recount in role and to understand that there are differences between oral and written recounts

- Tell the children that they are going to role-play meeting a friend in the park and telling them all about an event. Ask the children to stand up.
- Make sure that the CD file from the previous activity is no longer visible on the screen. Tell Partner 2s that they are the girl in the playground who picked up the hedgehog. Explain that they meet a friend (Partner 1s) in the park the next day and they tell their friend what happened, using their own words. Remind them to use the first person and the past tense and to try to stick to facts. Tell Partner 1s that at this point they should just be listening to the recounts.

- Choose two Partner 2s to share their oral recount with the group. TOL as you tease out a few of the differences between the written and the oral versions, e.g. *use of more emotive language in oral version, less structured, more non-chronological than a written version.*
- Now tell Partner 1s that they are the hedgehog. Say that he meets a fellow hedgehog in the park. Repeat the process.
- When asking children to feed back, this time focus on extra information or personal feelings they may have included that weren't in the written versions, and why that happened.

Fact and opinion

Purpose: for children to be able to identify facts and opinions in texts

- Before the lesson, print a copy of **CD (file 11.3)** for each set of partners.
- Tell the children that recounts are used in everyday life all the time as we tell each other little stories about what has happened to us or what we have witnessed. Remind the children that when they gave their oral recounts about the hedgehog in the playground they had to try to stick to the facts and explain what happened.
- Say that even though we were looking at the events from different points of view, we were not giving opinions or making judgements about what was right or wrong. We just said what happened from our own perspective.
- Tell the children that one place where recounts are given all the time is in a court of law, where the whole focus is on facts and not opinions.
- Display **CD (file 11.2)** to show a Top Tips page from a mock police officers' training manual.
- Explain that this was given to Officer Personal during his training. Read through the Top Tips. Re-read them using MT/YT. Ask the children to TTYP to define *fact* and *opinion*. Choose two sets of partners to share their definitions.
- Tell the children that Officer Personal is now a qualified police officer but still gets in a muddle about fact and opinion. Give each set of partners a copy of **CD (file 11.3)**.
- Explain that this is a transcript of Officer Personal giving evidence in court (explain the word *transcript* if necessary). Say that he can't resist giving his personal opinion instead of sticking to the facts.
- Say that Partner 1s are going to be Officer Personal and Partner 2s are going to be the judge. Explain any unfamiliar vocabulary as necessary, e.g. *cuppa, beat*. Now ask them to TTYP and read their parts.
- Ask the children to TTYP to read through the transcript again and highlight an example of:
  - an opinion
  - information that isn't connected to the event.
- Choose two or three sets of partners to feed back. Clarify if necessary.
- Tell the children that you now want them to underline all of the facts in Officer Personal's speech. Collect feedback and clarify if necessary.
- Explain that you want them to imagine they are giving evidence in court and the judge wants all the facts in the right order so that she/he can build up a picture of exactly what Officer Personal witnessed.
- Ask them to TTYP to discuss the correct chronological order of events, e.g. *10.28am: Officer Personal is sat in the café having a cuppa. 10.30am: The robber pinches the woman's bag. The robber runs off. Next day: Officer Personal sees a man throwing something in the bin outside the café.* This activity is oral but you may wish the children to make notes in their Daily log to help them to order the events.
- Collect examples to share and clarify where necessary.

Curriculum link:
composing
and rehearsing
sentences orally;
recording ideas

Daily log

Purpose: for children to keep a personal log of notes, thoughts and ideas, collected from their reading and discussions. Some ideas will be used in their own writing

- Tell the children two facts and one opinion about the class, e.g. 'this is a large class and it has more boys than girls. It is the best class in the school.'
- Write your statements on the board under the headings *Fact* and *Opinion*.
- Now tell the children to TTYP to share two facts and one opinion about their own family and to write them under the appropriate headings in their Daily log.

DAY 12

Words for recounts

Purpose: for children to become familiar with some words and phrases associated with recounts

- Remind the children that yesterday they heard a lot of words that we use when we talk about recount texts.
- Display **CD (file 12.1)** to show the words and their definitions. Explain that these terms will help us to identify, talk about and write recount texts. Read the words and definitions with the children using MT/YT.
- Print out the words and definitions from the **CD (file 12.2)** and display them on your Journalistic recounts wall for this Unit. Make sure the children hear the words in your teaching and conversation during the day, e.g. *'Can you put these dates in chronological order please? These photos give us a great record of what we did on the trip.'*
- Remember to praise the children when they use the words themselves.

discussing writing
that is similar to
that which they
are planning to
write; checking
that the text
makes sense to
them

Deconstruction 1

Purpose: for children to be able to identify the key features and main points of a more complex recount

- Tell the children that all recounts have the same features but that different recounts can be about very different events. They can be very simple, like the hedgehog in the playground recount, or more complex.
- Ask the children to find the 'Your Alien Experiences' website text on pp.22–23 of the Anthology. Tell them to follow the text as you read it aloud with appropriate intonation and expression to convey meaning.
- Explain that this is a more complex recount but it shares the same features as other recounts. Tell the children that it is useful to think of the 5Ws – *Who? What? When? Where?* and *Why?* to check their understanding of the recount.
- Display **CD (file 12.3)** to show the 5Ws and explanatory think bubbles. Talk through them with the children.
- Now ask the children to TTYP to take turns reading a section each of the Anthology text and summarising it to show their understanding. Walk around as they work, praising and noting clear summarising.
- Point to the first W on screen and ask the children to TTYP to identify it in the Anthology text. Take feedback and then repeat for the next four Ws. When you get to *Why?*, ask the children if the recount explains why it happened.
- Remind the children that there are some key features of recounts. Navigate to the next slide to show a recount features checklist. Talk through the example, showing how a line from the Anthology text is used to illustrate the feature.
- Check the children's understanding of each feature and ask them to TTYP to find an example of each from the text. Use your own Anthology to help you to write or type examples into the empty cells.

Curriculum link:
retrieve and
record information
from non-fiction;
write for a range
of real purposes
and audiences

Write 1 ⓒⒹ

Purpose: for children to develop their ability to write a recount from notes

- Tell the children that a radio show called *Extraordinary Experiences!* interviews people who have had a strange experience. Say that they are going to hear a clip from the show in which a man recounts his extraordinary experience with alien beings.
- Play the audio from **CD (file 12.4)** for the first time.
- Now ask the children to TTYP to summarise what happened to Eddie Brookes. Ask two or three sets of partners to share their summaries.
- Tell the children that Eddie didn't give his recount in strict chronological order. Ask the children to TTYP to speculate why he didn't, e.g. *he was nervous, he was talking from memory, he didn't use notes.* Take feedback and draw out these reasons.
- Tell them that you are going to play the clip again and afterwards you want them to write notes about what happened to Eddie, in chronological order. Remind the children to focus on the most important events of Eddie's experience as they listen to the clip for a second time. Play the clip.
- Ask the children to TTYP to discuss the chronology of events and to write them in note form in their Daily log. Display **CD (file 12.5)** to show an example of brief notes made using bullet points.
- Explain that the owners of the 'Your Alien Experiences' website heard Eddie on the radio and contacted him. They asked Eddie if he would write a short recount of his experiences to go on the website. Tell them that they are going to work in pairs, in role as Eddie Brookes, and they are going to use their own notes to help them to write a recount for the website.
- Click on 'Recount' to show an example of how to turn their notes into a first person recount.
- Remind them to look at their notes, picture themselves as Eddie having this experience, compose their opening sentence and repeat it to their partner before writing it down.
- Walk around supporting and clarifying as they work. When they are happy with their opening sentence ask them to continue to write the rest of the recount.
- When they have finished their writing, join sets of partners together to make groups of four and ask them to share their recounts.

composing
sentences orally;
recording ideas

Daily log 🅰

Purpose: for children to keep a personal log of notes, thoughts and ideas, collected from their reading and discussions. Some ideas will be used in their own writing

- Tell the children that lots of websites have message boards which encourage readers to give their opinion about what they have read on the web pages.
- Ask them to 'post' a message in their Daily log responding to the recount on pp.22–23 of the Anthology.
- Model a couple of opposite responses orally for them, e.g.

Ha! What a lot of rubbish! I think you just had a strange dream. There are no such things as aliens. How can you expect us to believe you?

Very interesting account! I have always believed in aliens and now you have proved they exist!

DAY 13

Curriculum link:
Year 4 Grammar
identifying ideas
drawn from
more than
one paragraph;
organising
paragraphs around
a theme

Grammar: paragraphs

Purpose: for children to revise and consolidate their understanding of the function of paragraphs

- Remind the children that paragraphs can be used to group and organise ideas within texts. Tell them to turn to pp.22–23 of the Anthology and look at the text 'Your Alien Experiences'. Ask them to TTYP to identify how many paragraphs there are in the whole text and to give their answer chorally when prompted.
- Choose two sets of partners to explain how they identified the number of paragraphs. Check their awareness of indentation and how each new paragraph begins on a new line. Clarify if necessary.
- Ask the children to TTYP to share ideas about why or how breaking texts up into paragraphs helps us as readers. Collect feedback and check their understanding of the purpose of paragraphs.
- Now tell the children to turn to p.19 in their Pupils' Book and look at the Grammar: paragraphs activity. Explain that you want them to TTYP to summarise the paragraphs in the 'Your Alien Experiences' text in the Anthology and to organise their notes under the correct subheadings.
- Choose two or three sets of partners to share their summaries for the third paragraph. Check that you and the rest of the class agree. Repeat for the fourth and fifth paragraphs.

Homework Book p.9 provides further practice on paragraphs.

Deconstruction 2 CD

Purpose: for children to be able to identify the features of journalistic recounts

identifying how
language, structure
and presentation
contribute to
meaning; retrieve
and record
information from
non-fiction

- Before the lesson, print a copy of **CD (file 13.3)** for each child.
- Tell the children that because recounts tell us about something that has happened, they can be in different forms. Remind them of the recounts they have looked at already. Display **CD (file 13.1)** to show extracts from the various texts they have already seen. Ask the children to TTYP to try to remember which text each extract is from. Take feedback.
- Explain that all of these recounts were from the point of view of the person involved or witnessing the event and that is why they were written in the first person. Click 'Highlights' to highlight the parts of the texts that show they were written in the first person.
- Remind them that they were also in the past tense because they had already happened. Click 'Highlights' again to highlight the parts of the text that show the event had already happened.
- Tell the children that one of the most common kinds of recounts are newspaper reports and articles.
- Remind them of last week's What if not? question: What if not *a dog*? What if *a lion arrived on the playground*? Say that a dog would not be newsworthy enough to be reported in a newspaper, but a lion would be.
- Display **CD (file 13.2)** to show a news report about a lion appearing in a school playground and read it aloud to the children. Re-read it using MT/YT.
- Use the TOL points below and/or your own ideas to talk through the features which are similar to personal recounts, e.g. past tense, chronological order, the 5Ws; and the features which are different from personal recounts, e.g. third person, quotes from people involved or witnesses.

The opening sentence tells us who *was involved,* what *happened, and* where *and* when *it happened.*

The second paragraph explains how *the lion got into the playground, giving a sense of a chronological order.*

The third paragraph gives us an idea of why the lion appeared and more detail about what happened next, adding to the order of events.

There are two quotes from the witnesses involved.

- Tell the children that this report for *The Sentinel* is appropriate for a serious and formal newspaper that focuses on giving readers the facts and letting them make up their own mind about who might be responsible, what could have happened if the lion hadn't been caught, etc.
- Give each child a copy of **CD (file 13.3)** and ask the children to look at another report from *The Sentinel* in Section A. Ask them to follow the text as you read it aloud with appropriate intonation to convey meaning.
- Now tell them to TTYP to take turns to read one paragraph at a time and summarise what they have read.
- Explain that you want them to TTYP to look at Section B and use it to identify the 5Ws and other features of this journalistic recount. Guide them through the first question and model how to circle, underline or highlight parts of the text to show their ability to locate information.
- Ask them to TTYP to answer the rest of the questions. Give them time to complete this before taking feedback on each question.

Curriculum link:

thinking aloud to explore and collect ideas, drafting and re-reading to check their meaning is clear

Write 2 🄿🄱 🄲🄳

Purpose: for children to use examples of formal newspaper recounts as models for their own writing

- Tell the children that they are journalists and they are going to write a follow up report for *The Sentinel* on the escaped lion story.
- Ask them to turn to pp.20–21 in their Pupils' Book and look at the Write 2 activity. Explain that they have an email from the editor of *The Sentinel* about what she wants them to include in the report, plus some reporter's notes and quotes from the people involved.
- Display **CD (file 13.4)** to show a think bubble with ideas for how you could start the report. Read the think bubble aloud and click 'Write' to model how the notes could be used to create the beginning of a news report. Read the first sentence using MT/YT. Navigate to the next slide and repeat the process.
- Navigate to the third slide and read the prompts aloud to the children. Ask the children to TTYP to discuss what they might include in the next section of the report. Take feedback from a few sets of partners. Navigate through the slides repeating the process for each set of prompts.
- Ask the children to TTYP to read through the activity in their Pupils' Book p.21 and check they understand the task.
- Remind them to rehearse their sentences in their minds before writing them down. Walk around while they write, noting good ideas and imaginative writing.
- Choose two or three children to share what they have written with the group. Pick out good examples of key features to comment on.

learn the conventions of different types of writing, such as the use of presentational devices

Daily log

For this activity you will need a supply of local or national newspapers for children to look at (ensure newspapers are checked for appropriate content first).

Purpose: for children to keep a personal log of notes, thoughts and ideas, collected from their reading and discussions. Some ideas will be used in their own writing

- Join sets of partners together to make groups of four. Give one newspaper and some scissors to each group.

- Explain that newspapers have many different features in them. Write this list on the board or flipchart and ask the children to write it in their Daily log: *headline, photograph, caption, cartoon, sports report.*
- Clarify what each of the features are and show some examples. Allocate a feature to each group and ask them to work together to find two examples of that feature in their newspaper and to cut them out.
- Ask one person from each group to come up to the front and put their examples onto your Journalistic recounts wall for this Unit.
- Tell them to look at a newspaper at home if possible and to bring in any funny or interesting headlines, photographs, captions, cartoons or sports reports to show the group and paste into their Daily log with the correct labels. Children who don't have access to newspapers at home could be allowed to select one or two examples from the Journalistic recounts wall during the next two days.

(DAY 14)

Newspaper vocabulary

Purpose: for children to become familiar with rarer vocabulary

> *revelation   exaggeration   speculation   sensation*

- Tell the children that they are going to be looking at a different style of journalistic recount and they will need to know what some less common words mean when they look at these recounts.
- Display **CD (file 14.1)** to show the words. Read them and their definitions using MT/YT, then read the sentences aloud to the children.
- Remember to try to use the words in your teaching and conversation throughout the day, e.g. *'There has been a lot of* speculation *about which class will win sports day this year.'* Try to make this fun for the children by using the words ironically.
- Praise the children if they use the words.
- Print the words and their definitions from **CD (file 14.2)** to display on your Journalistic recounts wall for this Unit.

Curriculum link:
identifying main ideas drawn from more than one paragraph and summarising these

Deconstruction 3

Purpose: for children to be able to identify features of different types of news reports

- Tell the children that the new owner of the *Gossip Gazette* newspaper, Mr Bigwig, is worried that fewer people are buying his newspaper. Say that he has left an urgent answering machine message for his editor and journalists.
- Tell the children to imagine they are his journalists on the *Gossip Gazette* so they must listen very carefully to his message.
- Play the audio clip from **CD (file 14.3)**.
- Now ask the children to look at the *Daily Blab* report 'School Playground Used for Alien Kickabout!' on pp.24–25 of the Anthology. Explain that this is a recount of the same news story that was in the *The Sentinel* ('Scientists Examine Unusual Rock'), but written in a completely different style.
- Tell them to follow the text as you read it aloud. Now ask them to TTYP to take turns to read alternate sections of the text.
- Display **CD (file 14.1)** again to show Mr Bigwig's words and their definitions. TOL to guide the children to help you to find examples of revelation, exaggeration, speculation and sensation in the *Daily Blab* Anthology text. You may want to write some of their examples from the text on to the board or a flipchart.
- Lead them into thinking and talking about the effect this recount might have on a reader, e.g. *it might make them curious to find out more or even to visit the place where it happened; it could make them feel shocked, excited or even worried and scared.*

Curriculum link:
rehearsing plays
for presentation
and performance
giving
opportunities
to discuss
language, including
vocabulary

Role-play ⓒ 🄿🄱

Purpose: for children to role-play a scenario that they will use as a basis for writing

- Display **CD (file 14.4)** to show the 'Lion in Playground Mystery' report from *The Sentinel*. Remind the children that they have seen this report before (on Day 13).
- Read the report aloud to the children. Check that they understand the formal, serious tone of this report.
- Tell the children that Partner 1s are going to be a reporter for Mr Bigwig's *Gossip Gazette* and Partner 2s are going to be a child who was in the school playground when the lion appeared. Explain that Partner 1s are going to interview Partner 2s.
- Ask them to turn to pp.22–23 in their Pupils' Book and look at the Role-play activity. Tell them to TTYP to read through the first set of prompts on p.22 to help them to plan and practise their role-play.
- Take on the role of the reporter and model how they might begin the interview, e.g. *'So, you were in the playground when the wild beast appeared! What did you think when you first saw the creature?'*
- Give the children enough time to practise their role-plays, then ask them to change roles and repeat the activity. Say that this time Partner 2s should be the reporter and Partners 1s should be a teacher who was in the playground when the lion appeared.
- Ask them to look back at the Role-play activity on p.23 of their Pupils' Book and to read the second set of prompts to help them plan and practise their next role-play.
- When they have practised both role-plays, ask them to decide which one should be used as their performance piece. Divide the class into three groups (of four or five sets of partners). Ask the first group to perform their role-plays while the rest of the class watch. Repeat until all three groups have performed.
- Ask the children to TTYP to share one thing they thought was good about any of the role-plays they saw and why. Collect responses and add your own observations, noting good questions and appropriate use of language in witness recounts.

discussing words
and phrases
that capture the
reader's interest
and imagination

Daily log ⓒ

Purpose: for children to keep a personal log of notes, thoughts and ideas, collected from their reading and discussions. Some ideas will be used in their own writing

- Tell the children that newspaper headlines are designed to make us want to read the whole report or article and so they have to grab our attention.
- Remind them that when they looked at poetry in Weeks 1 and 2 they looked at alliteration and rhyme. Say that because headlines aim to grab our attention, they often use alliteration and catchy rhymes.
- Display **CD (file 14.5)** to show four possible headlines for the story about the lion in the playground written for the *Gossip Gazette*. Use MT/YT to say the headlines in an enthusiastic voice as if you are a newspaper vendor.
- Point out alliteration, rhyme and the use of homophones.
- Now ask them to TTYP to choose their favourite headline. Ask them to write it in their Daily log and then TTYP to make up their own headline.
- Collect ideas and write a few examples on to paper to put on your Journalistic recounts wall for this Unit. Tell them to write their own headlines in their Daily log.

DAY 15

Write 3 ⓒ 🖨

Purpose: for children to develop their ability to select the language and style of a text to suit a particular purpose and audience

opportunities to
write for a range
of real purposes
and audiences

- Before the lesson, print a copy of the writing frames from **CD (file 15.2a)**, **(15.2b)** or **(15.2c)** for each child as appropriate. **CD (file 15.2a)** gives the least support and **CD (file 15.2c)** gives the most support.

- Display **CD (file 15.1)** to show the lion in the playground report again from *The Sentinel*. Remind them that they based their role-plays on this yesterday.
- Say to the children that they are going to help you to re-write the report to make it more suitable for Mr Bigwig's *Gossip Gazette*.
- Read through the report chorally then navigate to the next slide to show an example of a section of the same story written in a different style.
- Ask the children to TTYP to identify how or why it sounds different to the version written for *The Sentinel*. Collect feedback and highlight words and phrases that illustrate their ideas e.g. *narrowly escaped death* and *hungry lion charged*.
- Navigate to the next slides to show the next sections and repeat the process.
- Remind the children of Mr Bigwig's 4 *'tions'*: *revelation, exaggeration, speculation* and *sensation*.
- Navigate to the final slide to show the full report re-written for the *Gossip Gazette*. Read the report aloud to the children.
- Ask the children to TTYP to evaluate the report by identifying which of the 4 *'tions'* have been used and where. Take feedback, asking for clear examples and clarifying where necessary.
- Explain that now it is their turn to write for the *Gossip Gazette*. Remove the re-written report from the screen and give each child a copy of the writing frame from **CD (file 15.2a)**, **(15.2b)** or **(15.2c)** as appropriate. Guide them through the prompts.
- Remind them to rehearse their sentences in their minds before writing them down. Walk around as they work, supporting, clarifying and noting good effort and partner work to mention at the end of the session.

Evaluate and edit

> **Curriculum link:** assessing the effectiveness of their own and others' writing

Purpose: for children to evaluate their own and their partner's work against specific criteria and then discuss how they could improve their work

- Display **CD (file 15.3)** and read through the evaluation points using MT/YT.
- As a model, select an example of work where the writing has met the criteria, and share this with the other children, explaining why it works well.
- Tell the children to take turns to read their partner's writing in pairs and discuss together how well each piece of writing has met the criteria.
- Ask the children to discuss at least two changes they could make to improve their work.

Proofread

> proofread for spelling and punctuation errors

Purpose: for children to proofread their work and make changes to improve the accuracy of their grammar, punctuation and spelling

- Now ask the children to proofread their work. If you have noticed that several children need to improve on a particular aspect of spelling, grammar or punctuation, use this as a focus for the Proofread activity. Write an example which includes common errors from the children's writing and use this as a model.
- The children should always be checking for standard use of punctuation and correct spelling of common exception words.
- The following points would be particularly relevant for this Unit:
  - making sure quotations have been punctuated correctly, using inverted commas
  - checking for correct spelling of more ambitious vocabulary.

Fiction: Narrative verse
Non-fiction: Explanation texts

Timetable

WEEK 1 **Reading fiction** *The Bogey Men and the Trolls Next Door*

Day 1	Day 2	Day 3	Day 4	Day 5
The story store	Synonyms 🖺	Word power 🖺	Re-read a story version 3	Presenting, performing and practising
Read a story version 1	Respond and predict	Special phrases 🖺	Reciting 1	Performance
Think and link	Read a story version 3	Re-read a story version 3	Reciting 2 🖺	Daily log
Read a story version 2	Daily log	Role on the wall 🖺	Daily log	Big Question
Daily log	Big Question	Narrative verse	Big Question	
Big Question		Daily log		
		Big Question		

WEEK 2 **Writing fiction** *The Bogey Men and the Trolls Next Door*

Day 6	Day 7	Day 8	Day 9	Day 10
Points of view	Build a story 1	Build a story 2	Grammar: adverbials	Write a story 3 (continued)
What if not...?	Write a story 1	Write a story 2	Build a story 3 🖺	Share a story
Hear and tell a story 🖺	Daily log	Daily log	Write a story 3	Evaluate and edit
Daily log	Big Question	Big Question		Proofread
Big Question				Very Big Question

WEEK 3 **Reading and writing non-fiction** Explanation texts

Day 11	Day 12	Day 13	Day 14	Day 15
Think and link	Visual explanations	Deconstruction 2	Proofread	Presentation – explanations
Context – stage school	Deconstruction 1	Write 2 🖺	Deconstruction 3	Evaluate and edit
Audience and purpose	Hotseating	Daily log	Write 3	
Daily log	Write 1		Daily log	
	Daily log			

🖺: shows that a file should be printed out from the Software.

Overview of the Unit

In this Unit, children read a story told in rhyming narrative verse. They use drama and discussion to tease out some of the serious issues behind the humour in Kaye Umansky's engaging tale of *The Bogey Men and the Trolls Next Door*. Strands of the story are then picked out to form the basis of the children's own writing.

Linked via a Big Question, the non-fiction section looks at explanation texts. For more information about the Non-fiction week and the Non-fiction writing evaluation criteria, see p.102.

Where appropriate, the children will be encouraged to develop an awareness of audience and purpose in relation to the fiction and non-fiction texts they are reading and writing.

Teacher modelling is provided in the teaching notes, Software and the Pupils' Book, supporting the children's writing at every stage in the Fiction and Non-fiction weeks.

The Homework Book provides a homework activity related to the content of this Unit for each of the three weeks.

Fiction

Reading

Children will:

- make links between the story and their own experiences and prior reading, and between the story and the tradition of oral storytelling and ballads
- explore the language in the story, particularly the use of synonyms
- use evidence from the text to explore the characters
- learn by heart and recite a section of *The Bogey Men and the Trolls Next Door*.

Writing

Key writing purpose to be shared with the children:

To write a new story using some of the characters from The Bogey Men and the Trolls Next Door.

Writing evaluation to be shared with the children

My story:

- is written from the point of view of one of the band members
- gives extra information by including powerful adverbs and adjectives
- uses at least one of the features of Kaye Umansky's style, e.g. *comical images, extra information in brackets, made-up adjectives such as 'trollish'.*

Grammar:

- includes the first person past tense, because I am writing in role as a character.

See the Planning section of the Software ('Timetables' tab) for a printable version of the Writing purpose and evaluation.

Fiction: Narrative verse
The Bogey Men and the Trolls Next Door
by Kaye Umansky

 READING FICTION

Resources

PB Pupils' Book, pp.24–33

A Anthology, pp.26–39

CD CD on Interactive whiteboard, Unit 3

GB Grammar Bank on CD

HB Homework Book, pp.10–12

DAY 1

Curriculum link:
listening to and discussing a wide range of fiction, identifying themes

The story store

Purpose: for children to be introduced to narrative verse form

- Tell the children that many years ago, stories were told orally to groups of people. To help make the stories easier to remember and more entertaining, they were often written in what is called *ballad* or *narrative verse* form.
- Tell them that ballads and stories in narrative verse usually rhyme and have a strong rhythm, rather like songs.
- Explain that the ballads could be about real or imagined events. They could be comic or tragic.
- Display **CD (file 1.1)** to show short extracts from two ballads. Tell the children that one of these is about a real event and the other is about an imagined event.
- Read them aloud to the children and then ask them to TTYP (Turn to your partner) to discuss which ballad they think is about a real event and which one is about an imagined event. Choose two children to feed back and give reasons for their answers.
- Move to the next slide to reveal the news story about the Gresford disaster and read it aloud. Explain to the children that a colliery is a mine where men dig out coal which was used to heat homes before most homes had central heating. Explain that this ballad is based on a true story.
- Move to the next slide to show information about Hilaire Belloc and the ballad of 'George'. Read it aloud to the children.
- You can display the whole of 'George' (and read it aloud if you wish) from **CD (file 1.2)**. Use your own discretion about whether the ballad is appropriate for your class.

predicting

Read a story version 1

Before the lesson, you may wish to watch the video demonstrating Read a story version 1 (with a Year 5 story). This can be found in the Extras section of the software.

Purpose: for children to become familiar with Story version 1, the bare bones of the story

- Tell the children that they are going to be reading another wonderful story written in rhyming verse, but first of all they are going to hear just the bare bones of the story.
- Read Story version 1 aloud all the way through to the children. Do not reveal any surprises or the ending of the final story (Story version 3).

  Story version 1
  1. A family of six and their pet live together and are happy.
  2. They lead a quiet life and avoid trouble.
  3. A new family move in next door. The new neighbours introduce themselves to the family.
  4. Something unexpected happens.
  5. Unkind things are said.
  6. The two families fight with each other. Things go downhill.
  7. A disaster occurs.
  8. Both families panic.
  9. There is no time for fighting. They need to work together – and fast!
  10. Life changes.

- Use MT/YT (My turn/Your turn) and TTYP for each point, breaking down any longer points if necessary. Add in a few mini-mimes and use appropriate intonation to help understanding and for effect. This will help the children to 'hold' the basic story in their minds.

Curriculum link: discussing ideas and predicting

Think and link

Purpose: for children to talk about the pictures, feelings and ideas the words have made in their minds and to make links with their own experiences and other stories they know

- Display **CD (file 1.3)** to show Story Version 1. Talk through each section showing how you link what you know about the story and characters so far with your own experiences and other stories.
- Use TTYP and feedback to allow children to articulate and share ideas and connections, and for you to paraphrase, clarify and extend their thoughts.
- Tell the children that stories are like magic because they create moving pictures in our minds, and feelings and ideas. Explain that everyone's pictures, feelings and ideas are different because the things we have done, seen, watched and read affect how we make sense of the words.
- Say that you had a strong image in your head of what the new neighbours were like – don't share your image though! Ask the children to TTYP to share what pictures, feelings or ideas they had in their minds about the new neighbours.
- Choose two or three children to feed back, encouraging them to think deeply about their own experiences and knowledge of stories.
- Repeat the process with a focus on other aspects of the story so far, e.g. what they imagined the disaster to be, what they think the two families' houses are like, or whether they imagined it as a serious/comical/ghostly story or perhaps a thriller.
- TOL (Think out loud) about your own images, feelings and ideas once the children have shared theirs.

predicting; identifying how language, structure and presentation contribute to meaning

Read a story version 2

Purpose: for children to hear more information about the story and become more familiar with the characters and plot before they hear the full version

- Explain that you now have a bit more information about the new story. Show your enthusiasm about what else they are going to find out from Story version 2. Display **CD (file 1.4)** to show Story Version 2.
- Read it aloud to the children in your Storyteller voice with plenty of dramatic and comic emphasis. Do not reveal any surprises or the ending of the final story.
  Story version 2
  1. Fred and Beryl Bogey, their four children and their pet dog Snot live near the Bogey Bog and are a contented family.
  2. They lead a quiet life, mind their own business and like to avoid any strife.
  3. A new family, the Trolls, move in next door. Dave the Troll introduces his wife Dolly, their children and their cat Tiddles to the Bogey family.
  4. Fred Bogey has heard bad things about Trolls and does not make them welcome at all.
  5. Rudely, Fred says unkind things to Dave and Dolly because he thinks the Trolls will make rotten neighbours.
  6. The two families are at war with each other. Even the children and the pets fight and brawl. Life changes as things go downhill.
  7. Then a catastrophe happens that involves both the Bogeys and the Trolls.
  8. Both families are in a frenzy over the catastrophe.

9. It is a time of crisis. There is no time to fight and brawl. They have to call a truce and work together – fast!

10. Life changes – for better or for worse?

- Immediately after hearing Story version 2, ask the children to TTYP to share how their pictures, feelings and ideas have now changed or developed. Collect feedback and TOL briefly about how your own images have changed.
- Click 'Highlights' to show the additional information about the characters and development of the plot. Click 'TOL' to show think bubbles and use them to share ideas about the effect of the additions and changes.

<table>
<tr><td>Curriculum link:
discussing and
recording ideas</td></tr>
</table>

Daily log

Purpose: for children to keep a personal log of notes, thoughts and ideas, collected from their reading and discussions. Some ideas will be used in their own writing

- Ask the children to look at the Daily log activity on p.24 of their Pupils' Book.
- Tell them to look at the structure of the story mind map and guide them through the instructions. Choose one branch and model on the board or a flipchart how they can record information using words and symbols. Do not model completing the whole mind map.
- Ask them to use your model and the structure in their Pupils' Book to help them to create their own mind map of the story so far across a double page spread in their Daily log. Remind them to leave enough space to be able to add branches and information as they find out more about the story.

<table>
<tr><td>discussion;
develop, agree on,
and evaluate
rules for effective
discussion</td></tr>
</table>

Big Question ⓒⒹ

Purpose: for children to develop their skills of argument and discussion through a mini enquiry session based on a philosophical question relating to the work of the day

- Display today's Big Question on **CD (file 1.5)**:

  If you tell someone a story does it still belong to you?

- Ask the children to TTYP to talk about this question. Collect feedback and write some responses on the board.
- Click 'Prompts' to show some statements that may help to encourage discussion.

Synonyms

Purpose: for children to increase their knowledge of and application of synonyms and to examine how writers use language for effect

- Tell the children that there is a different word in Story version 2 that means the same as *trouble* in Story version 1. Tell them that this *synonym* can be a more powerful way to say the same thing.
- Display Story version 1 and Story version 2 on the **CD (file 2.1)** and click 'Synonyms' to identify the synonym *happy*.
- Click 'Synonyms' again to identify another example of synonymous words and use MT/YT to read them out. Move to the next slide and repeat the process.
- TOL and use TTYP to share examples of how some of these words can change the pictures in our minds as we hear the story by giving us stronger, more precise or more powerful images.
- Print all of these words and their synonyms from the **CD (file 2.2)** and display them on your Story wall.
- Try to use some of these words during the day where appropriate, pointing them out on your Story wall as you say them.

Respond and predict PB

Purpose: for children to use their ideas, experiences and knowledge of other stories to predict how the story will develop and end

- Ask the children to look at the Respond and predict activity on p.25 of their Pupils' Book.
- Tell them to TTYP to read the questions in turn and to discuss their personal responses and ideas about how the story might develop and end.
- Choose two or three sets of partners to share their thoughts and ideas, encouraging them to give reasons for their answers.
- Allow time for the children to record their predictions for the end of the story by adding a *My prediction* branch to the mind map they drew in their Daily log.

Curriculum link: checking that the text makes sense, asking questions, drawing inferences

Read a story version 3 A (teacher only) PB

Purpose: for children to hear and enjoy the full version of the story for the first time

- Tell the children that they are now going to hear the whole story for the very first time. Show your enthusiasm before you start. TOL about which parts you can't wait to hear about.
- Read the full story from the Anthology pp.26–35 to the children with great enjoyment. Use appropriate intonation, facial expressions and body language to add to your storytelling performance.
- At the end of the story, ask the children to TTYP to discuss the Read a story version 3 questions on p.25 of the Pupils' Book. Collect feedback.

discussing their understanding; asking questions to improve their understanding

Daily log

Purpose: for children to keep a personal log of notes, thoughts and ideas, collected from their reading and discussions. Some ideas will be used in their own writing

- Ask the children to look at the mind map they created in their Daily log showing the story so far.
- Tell them that now they have heard the full story, they can add more information to their mind map.
- Explain that they can TTYP to share what they can recall from the story and to help them to decide what to add to their branches and/or what new branches to create, e.g. *ending*.
- Remind them to look at the prediction they wrote in their Daily log about the ending of the story. Tell them to add a sentence or two underneath, briefly explaining the actual ending.

discussion; develop, agree on, and evaluate rules for effective discussion

Big Question CD

Purpose: for children to develop their skills of argument and discussion through a mini enquiry session based on a philosophical question relating to the work of the day

- Display today's Big Question on the **CD (file 2.3):**

  Should we always forgive someone who is unkind to us?

- Follow the process as explained on Day 1.

DAY 3

Curriculum link:
discussing words
and phrases
that capture the
reader's interest
and imagination

Word power

Purpose: for children to develop their knowledge of and application of rarer vocabulary taken from the text

> *fateful   indignant   desolate   destination*

- Tell the children that the writer of *The Bogey Men and the Trolls Next Door* has used a mixture of informal, everyday spoken language and words and phrases that are not commonly used in everyday conversations.
- Display the Power words and their definitions on **CD (file 3.1)**. Look at the words with the children and then read the sentences to them. Ask the children to repeat the sentences using MT/YT, giving dramatic emphasis and actions as you say them.
- Take or create opportunities to use the words during the day, e.g. *'I feel a little indignant that our visitors didn't stay for long after all!' 'It's Monday! It's P.E.! So our destination is…the hall!'*
- Encourage the children to use the words in their everyday conversation so that they become embedded in their spoken (and eventually, written) vocabulary.
- Print these words and their definitions from **CD (file 3.2)** to display on your Story wall.
- Ask the children to look at the Word power activity on p.26 of their Pupils' Book. Tell them to TTYP to complete the activity.

discussing words
and phrases
that capture the
reader's interest
and imagination

Special phrases

Purpose: for children to become familiar with Special phrases particular to the story

> …*Baby Bogey / In his bogey baby buggy.*
> *Fell an atmosphere of chill.*
> *A stagnant stretch of quagmire, / Very desolate and grim.*
> …*a voice like grating gravel*
> *Our dreaded destination – / We were worn out to a frazzle / And quite drenched*
> *with perspiration…*

- Display **CD (file 3.3)** to show the Special phrases from the story. These can be printed off for your Story wall from **CD (file 3.4)**.
- Explain that you have chosen these because they are phrases that we don't use in our everyday talk, because they are from important moments in the story and because they have a special sound or rhythm that is particularly pleasing when we hear or say them.
- Use MT/YT to read the phrases aloud with obvious enjoyment, adding expression, intonation and special emphasis to give further meaning to them.
- Now use the explanations for the choices shown in the table to draw attention to particular features of the phrases or why they are special.
- Ask the children to TTYP to each choose their favourite Special phrase and to explain to their partner what they like about it. Choose some partners to feed back and ask them to read their chosen Special phrase out with expression to show their understanding of its meaning and enjoyment of its sounds and rhythms.

Curriculum link: reading texts that are structured in different ways

Re-read a story version 3

Purpose: for children to gain a deeper und[erstanding]... the text for the first time

- Ask the children to read the story o[n Anthology] pp.26–35 aloud with their partners. They should read alternate [s]ections each and ensure they use expression and intonation to convey [meaning]... that you will be listening in and looki[ng] out for [as a model of] good reading.
- For some groups, you may wish to re[ad]... the text in their own copy so that th[ey]... [can refer to the Pupil Book pump in the Introduction p.131 to try] the Power words and Special phrases.

inferring characters' feelings, thoughts and motives from their actions

Role on the wall

Purpose: for children to develop their ability t... make inferences about characters from what is implied by their words, actions and relationships with other characters

- Before the lesson, print off a blank body outline for each set of partners or each child from **CD (file 3.5)**.
- Explain that as we get to know the story really well, we pick up more and more information and clues about what particular characters are like.
- Display **CD (file 3.6)** to show a body outline. Explain that this represents the character of Dave the Troll.
- TOL as you select appropriate words to describe Dave the Troll from the Characteristics bank and drag the chosen words into the body outline.
- Model using evidence from the story to support your choices, drawing in the children by making occasional choices that they can disagree with and challenge. Don't make it look too easy. Model being uncertain and inferring from what we can read into both the explicit and implicit information.
- Now give the children their own blank body outlines and ask them to TTYP to complete a Role on the wall for Fred the Bogeyman. Explain that they should look at the Characteristics bank and discuss which words are appropriate for Fred. Encourage them to use their own words and phrases as well and to spend time discussing different sides to his character. They can refer to the Anthology for evidence of his character traits.
- Walk around as they work, questioning choices and praising good partner work and thoughtful choices.
- Ask the children to stick their outlines onto the Story wall. Pick out similarities and differences in their choices and between the characters of Fred the Bogeyman and Dave the Troll to stimulate further discussion.

recognise different forms such as narrative poetry

Narrative verse

Purpose: for children to explore how the writer has used a particular form and a variety of language techniques for effect

- Tell the children that as well as creating characters and working out the plot of a story, writers can choose different narrative forms and techniques for all sorts of reasons: to create pace, tone and atmosphere; to make the reader feel emotions; and to encourage the reader to focus on particular words, phrases or details.
- Say that the writer Kaye Umansky chose to write the story of *The Bogey Men and the Trolls Next Door* like a long poem. We can call it a narrative verse – a story told in verse form. Say that it is a bit like the ballads that they looked at in The story store.
- Explain that you are going to choose a few verses to help you to zoom in on the poetic techniques the writer used to create a great story or narrative verse.
- Display two verses from the story on **CD (file 3.7)**. Read the verses chorally.

- Click 'Highlights' and then click 'TOL' to reveal ideas about the poetic techniques and their effects.
- Follow the on-screen prompts to repeat the process for the next two verses, over two slides.
- Display the final two verses and ask the children to TTYP to discuss any features that they think create strong imagery, atmosphere or humour. Make sure the children understand that there isn't a right answer, you are just looking for their own ideas and opinions. Collect feedback and encourage them to support and explain their ideas.

Curriculum link: discussing words and phrases that capture the reader's interest and imagination

Daily log ▲

Purpose: for children to keep a personal log of notes, thoughts and ideas, collected from their reading and discussions. Some ideas will be used in their own writing

- Ask the children to choose their favourite verse from the story. Tell them to TTYP to share their chosen verse and the reasons for their choice.
- Now tell them to copy their favourite verse into their Daily log and to annotate it by underlining and/or circling favourite or powerful words and phrases and examples of rhyme, alliteration, and strong or humorous imagery.
- You may wish to model an example of an annotated verse on the board or a flipchart.

discussion; develop, agree on, and evaluate rules for effective discussion

Big Question ⓒⒹ

Purpose: for children to develop their skills of argument and discussion through a mini enquiry session based on a philosophical question relating to the work of the day

- Display today's Big Question on **CD (file 3.8)**:

  Is it important to be able to get on with everybody?
- Follow the process as explained on Day 1.

(DAY 4)

asking questions to improve their understanding of a text

Re-read a story version 3 ▲

Purpose: for children to deepen their understanding of a story by increasing familiarity with the characters and events

- Ask the children to turn to the story on pp.26–35 of their Anthology and read it silently. Tell them that they can stop to record any thoughts, ideas, questions or favourite words in their Daily log as they read.
- Explain that it is more important for them to think about what they are imagining in their minds and feeling about the characters and events than to finish the whole story this time, as they already know it really well.

Reciting 1 ⓒⒹ

Purpose: for children to explore the tradition of recitation of narrative verse and the reasons for memorising things

- Tell the children that to *recite* something means to say something from memory. Explain that we recite things from memory every day of our lives, without thinking about what we are doing, e.g. when we recite our name, address and telephone number.
- Say that we recite things for many different reasons. Display **CD (file 4.1)** to show one reason and an example. Read it aloud to the children.
- Move to the next slide to show another reason and example. Read it aloud.

- Tell the children that as well as reading poems from a page, they can be good fun to *recite* or perform. Explain that learning a narrative verse or a ballad by heart allows us to make a lot of eye contact with our audience instead of looking down at the page. It also means we can move about freely and not have to keep looking at the words and worrying about losing our place on the page.
- Ask the children to TTYP to share any nursery rhymes, poetry lines or song lyrics that they have memorised and can recite. Choose two or three sets of partners to recite their examples.
- Now ask them to TTYP to say which reason they would give for memorising and learning the verse narrative *The Bogey Men and the Trolls Next Door*. Choose two sets of partners to give their answers, e.g. *for entertainment*. You may wish to reassure them that they will not have to learn the whole story!

Reciting 2

Purpose: for children to practise and develop their memorisation skills

- Before the lesson print one copy of **CD (file 4.2)** for yourself, and a copy of **CD (file 4.4)** for each child.
- Tell the children that it would be really good to be able to recite and perform the narrative verse *The Bogey Men and the Trolls Next Door* but as it is too long for one person to learn, each set of partners will have three verses to learn and recite together for a class performance.
- Now ask them to look at the Anthology pp.26–35. Use your printed **CD (file 4.2)** to record and tell each set of partners which verses to focus on.
- Tell them that Partner 1s will learn the first of their verses, Partner 2s will learn the second and they can both learn the third verse to recite together. Ensure you give children plenty of support if they need it.
- Say that there are lots of tips for memorising verse. Display **CD (file 4.3)** to show Top Tips for memorising a poem. Talk through the Top Tips. Ask the children to TTYP to share which tip they think they will find the most useful.
- Now give each child a copy of printable **CD (file 4.4)**. Ask them to write down their two verses in the space provided.
- Explain that they are going to be rehearsing and reciting their verses at the end of their next literacy lesson. Say that they are going to spend some time now, using the Top Tips printed on their sheet, and they will also take their verses home to learn and practise them. Give each child a mini-whiteboard and pen to allow them to use the technique recommended in Top Tip number 6.
- Make sure that the children take their Top Tips for memorising a poem sheet home with them. Explain that for homework, they must continue to learn their verses and practise reciting them for their next literacy lesson.

Curriculum link: recording ideas

Daily log

Purpose: for children to keep a personal log of notes, thoughts and ideas, collected from their reading and discussions. Some ideas will be used in their own writing

- Tell the children to TTYP to discuss which character from *The Bogeymen and the Troll Next Door* is their favourite. Remind them that they must be able to give reasons for their answer.
- Choose two or three sets of partners to share their choices and reasons.
- Tell them which character is your favourite and why. Model recording your choice and reasons in full sentences on the board or a flipchart under a suitable heading. Now ask them to write a few sentences in their Daily log, recording their own choice and reasons. Tell them to think of and add a suitable heading.

Curriculum link:
discussion;
develop, agree on,
and evaluate
rules for effective
discussion

Big Question

Purpose: for children to develop their skills of argument and discussion through a mini enquiry session based on a philosophical question relating to the work of the day

- Display today's Big Question on the **CD (file 4.5)**:

  Which is easier – to remember or to forget?

- Follow the process as explained on Day 1.

DAY 5

You will need to pre-arrange for someone to use a digital video camera to film the performance in the second half of this lesson.

Presenting, performing and practising

Purpose: for children to learn how to develop their presentation and performance skills

- Tell the children that they are going to get some advice from a professional presenter to help them to prepare for their recitation. Explain that she will be showing them some warm-up exercises.
- Play the video from **CD (file 5.1)**. Join in the warm-up exercises with the children when the presenter gets to that part.
- Now allow time for the children to TTYP to practise reciting their verses in turn and putting into practice the advice and techniques they have just watched.
- Make sure that you create an atmosphere of enjoyable challenge, not anxiety. It is crucial that this activity does not become daunting for less confident speakers.
- Now arrange the sets of partners in the right order to allow their recitations to follow the chronology of the story. Have one rehearsal when you orchestrate the whole performance by reading (or reciting) the verses you are going to read as a lead in to the first set of partners' recitation.

preparing
poems to read
aloud and to
perform, showing
understanding
through
intonation, tone,
volume and action

Performance **A** (teacher only)

For this activity, you may wish to book the school hall as an appropriate space for the children to perform and be filmed.

Purpose: for children to experience the tradition of reciting a verse narrative and to use their presentation and performance skills

- Tell the children that they are now going to create a class recitation of *The Bogey Men and the Trolls Next Door* as they did in their rehearsal, but this time they are going to be filmed.
- Decide how you want to organise the children, e.g. you could have them in rows or in a circle or semi-circle. You could have all of the children standing up at the same time during the whole recitation; alternatively, you could have all the children sitting down and only standing during the recitation of their verses.
- Show the children a previously agreed start signal and begin the recitation and filming with your verses. Once the children are reciting their verses, you become the 'prompt' (or arrange for someone else to be the 'prompt'), keeping an eye on the text ready to prompt children discreetly (using the Anthology text) if they get mixed up or falter.
- Be prepared to repeat the activity once more if things go awry! Celebrate the completion of the recitation even if there are hitches.

<table>
<tr><td>

Curriculum link:
discussing and
recording ideas

</td><td></td></tr>
</table>

Daily log

*Purpose: for children to keep a personal log of notes, thoughts and ideas, collected from their
reading and discussions. Some ideas will be used in their own writing*

- Tell the children that they will be able to watch the film of the recitation at a later
  date. This will allow time for checking the film and arranging a time for the whole
  class to watch it.
- Say that you would like them to reflect on the experience and evaluate how well
  they think they accomplished th
- Ask the children to write the h
  you want them to write a sente
  preparing for the recitation.
- Repeat the process with the he
  Performing.

[handwritten note:]
Tues   Day 6
Narrator's point of view

Anthology P26
Pupil Bk p27

discussion;
develop, agree on,
and evaluate
rules for effective
discussion

Big Question (CD)

Purpose: for children to develop their
enquiry session based on a ... ay

- Display today's Big Question o
  Does how we present ourselves
- Follow the process as explaine

WRITING FICTION

DAY 6

Points of view

Purpose: for children to develop an awareness of the narrator's point of view in a story

- Remind the children that all narratives have a narrator. Display **CD (file 6.1)** to
  show the *Oxford Junior Dictionary* definitions of the words *narrative* and *narrator*.
  Use MT/YT to read each word and definition.
- Explain that a writer *writes* the story or *narrative* but they can choose a character
  to *tell* or *narrate* the story. Say that this can mean that we get the narrator's point
  of view about other characters and events.
- Ask the children to turn to p.26 in their Anthology and to look at the first verse
  together. Tell them to TTYP to say who is narrating the story and how they know.
  Choose two sets of partners to share their answers. Check their understanding
  and clarify if necessary, e.g. '*Fred introduces himself to us and uses the personal
  pronoun "I", showing that Fred is going to be telling the story.*'
- Say that what Fred tells us shows us that he has some very strong views about
  people and how they should behave.
- Ask the children to TTYP and discuss how we could describe Fred's point of view
  about his own family. Collect feedback, making sure they can support their views
  with evidence from the story.
- Now ask them to TTYP and discuss how they would describe Fred's point of view
  about the Troll family before the babies go missing. Collect feedback again, making
  sure they can support their views with evidence from the story.
- Tell the children to look at the Points of view activity on p.27 of their Pupils' Book
  and TTYP to discuss the questions about characters, events and points of view.
- Use the Pupils' Book questions and the children's responses to generate further
  discussion, teasing out and developing their thoughts about stereotyping, making
  judgements, and what is or isn't acceptable behaviour.

Fiction: Narrative verse

Curriculum link:
drawing inferences;
participate in discussion about books

What if not...? PB CD

Purpose: for children to imagine other directions the story could take

- Ask the children to look at the What if not...? questions on p.27 of the Pupils' Book. Model how you consider the first question: What if not *Fred the Bogeyman narrating*? What if *someone else had narrated the story?*
- Open **CD (file 6.2)** and use your own ideas and/or the TOLs, relating your points back to the exploration of a narrator's point of view.
- Now ask them to TTYP and discuss the other What if not...? question in the Pupils' Book: What if not *Trolls*? What if *another Bogey family had moved in next door?* Use these prompts to help them:
  - The families might have been best friends from the beginning.
  - The new Bogeys could have turned out to be much worse neighbours than the Trolls.
  - Fred might have found something to complain about anyway.
- Collect feedback and encourage others to build upon thoughts and ideas. Give your opinion too.

retelling stories orally

Hear and tell a story CD

Purpose: for children to develop their awareness of stories in different forms

- Have one copy of printable **CD (file 6.3)** ready for you to read from when indicated in these notes.
- Remind the children of the ballads they looked at and heard in The story store in Week 1. Explain that hundreds of years ago, stories told in ballad form were spoken or sung and not written down.
- Say that the stories or ballads were re-told by people who had heard them and they would add their own bits to the story or miss bits out, change the words and shorten or lengthen them.
- Explain that really great stories, like Kaye Umansky's *The Bogey Men and the Trolls Next Door*, can inspire us to write our own versions, maybe using the same form (narrative verse) or some of her characters. Tell them you have a short verse narrative that was inspired by some of the characters from the Bogey and Troll families.
- Ask them to listen carefully as you read the narrative verse from your printed copy of **CD (file 6.3)** to the children, in your Storyteller voice, but do not reveal the title yet as the children will need to identify the narrator.
- Ask the children to TTYP to retell the story in their own words. Explain that Partner 1s will begin and Partner 2s will take over when you say 'Stop and swap' (at about 30 second intervals two or three times).
- Display the story on **CD (file 6.4)** and ask the children to TTYP to discuss how far their retellings matched or differed from the original. Choose two or three sets of partners to feed back and tease out which parts were easy to recall, which parts were forgotten, and why that might be.
- Ask them to Popcorn (see Introduction p.17) their answer to the question: '*Who was the narrator of the new story?*' Now tell them that the title of the verse narrative is *The Ballad of Beryl Bogey*.
- Ask the children to TTYP to recall what a ballad is. Take feedback and clarify if necessary.
- Read it out chorally with the children. Ask them to join you in using expression and intonation to show their understanding.

<table>
<tr><td>

Curriculum link:
write for a range
of real purposes
and audiences

</td><td>

Daily log

Purpose: for children to keep a personal log of notes, thoughts and ideas, collected from their reading and discussions. Some ideas will be used in their own writing

- Ask the children to TTYP to share ideas for a blurb about *The Ballad of Beryl Bogey*. Remind the children that a blurb is a short description.
- Collect examples and ideas from two or three sets of partners.
- Now ask them to write notes for a short blurb for the ballad in their Daily log.
- Tell them to use the notes to create an opening sentence and to say it to their partner before writing it down in their Daily log and then completing the blurb.

</td></tr>
</table>

discussion;
develop, agree on,
and evaluate
rules for effective
discussion

Big Question

Purpose: for children to develop their skills of argument and discussion through a mini enquiry session based on a philosophical question relating to the work of the day

- Display today's Big Question on the **CD (file 6.5)**:

  Should we judge people we haven't met by what we hear about them?

- Follow the process as explained on Day 1.

DAY 7

plan writing by
discussing writing
that is similar

Build a story 1

Purpose: for children to see the first stage of a story's development as a model for their own planning and writing

- Ask the children to look at p.30 of the Anthology. Ask Partner 1s to read verse 24. Say that this shows us that the Trolls liked music, singing and making up songs!
- Explain that this part of the story gave you an idea for a new story about the characters. (From this point on, you are in the role of the writer.)
- Display **CD (file 7.1)** and explain that these were the notes from your writer's log that helped you to plan the new story. Read them through with the children.
- Remind the children that they heard two versions of the verse narrative *The Bogey Men and the Trolls Next Door* (Story versions 1 and 2) before they heard and read the full story. It prepared them to read the full story.
- Explain that you are going to show them the first of two versions of your new story. The notes prepared you to write the bare bones/first version and the second version prepared you to write the full story.
- Now display **CD (file 7.2)** to show your bare bones version. Use MT/YT to read out each bullet point to the children. Click 'Hide' to blank the screen and ask them to TTYP to summarise what this new story will be about.
- Explain that later on you are going to show them how these bare bones were developed by adding more information and more interesting vocabulary.

composing
and rehearsing
sentences orally;
creating settings,
characters, plot

Write a story 1

Purpose: for children to develop their confidence in planning and developing a story

- Tell the children that you want them to write a story of their own involving the Trolls and Bogeys and you have some ideas to help them to get started.
- Ask them to look at the Write a story 1 activity on p.28 of their Pupils' Book. Explain that they have some jumbled notes of ideas for a new story about the band that the Trolls and Bogeys have formed.
- Tell them to TTYP and take turns to read the notes and then to discuss the order they should be in to make the bare bones of a story. The correct order is:
  - Been asked to play in front of an audience for first time.
  - Where is it taking place? Is it a party? A concert? An audition?

- Something goes wrong – could be with equipment or band member.
- Could have someone or something that comes to the rescue.

- Choose two or three sets of partners to share their order, pointing out any anomalies or illogical chronologies and talking them through. Make sure that the children realise that their story will start from the point where the band have been asked to perform (point 4 in your Build a story 1). This allows the children to develop a different part of the story to the one you will have modelled.
- Now ask them to write the bare bones in the right order, in their own words in their Daily log. Explain that they will be using it as a plan to be developed over the next few days.
- Ask the children to TTYP to start sharing ideas about what form the disaster might take, who or what could come to the rescue and how. Take as much feedback as possible, scribing ideas on a flipchart for the children to refer to on Days 8 and 9.

Daily log 🅰 ⓒⅮ 🅿🅱

Purpose: for children to keep a personal log of notes, thoughts and ideas, collected from their reading and discussions. Some ideas will be used in their own writing

Curriculum link: recognising some different forms of poetry; discussing writing that is similar to that which they are planning to write

- Remind the children of the anti-Bogey songs that the Trolls made up about the Bogey family (p.30 in the Anthology, verse 24).
- Say that song lyrics are like poems set to music. Explain that lots of songs follow a kind of pattern or set of rules that make them memorable and catchy.
- Ask the children to TTYP to say a line from any pop song that has stuck in their minds for a long time. Collect a few examples and give some of your own.
- Display **CD (file 7.3)** to show the beginning of a pop song that Beryl Bogey wrote about her love for her husband Fred. Explain that this is the first verse.
- Read it out chorally with the children. Explain that many verses in pop songs have end rhymes, a strong rhythm and repeated words or phrases. Point these out.
- Tell the children that lots of songs also have a chorus that is repeated after each verse but Beryl hasn't finished the chorus yet.
- Ask them to look at the Daily log activity on p.29 of their Pupils' Book. Explain that they have Beryl's unfinished chorus and her ideas about how to finish it.
- Ask the children to TTYP to share ideas about how the chorus could be completed, using Beryl's notes and/or their own ideas for rhyming lines.
- Tell them to write Beryl's unfinished chorus down in their Daily log and then experiment with different words and phrases to complete the chorus. Make sure they understand that song writers do a lot of evaluating and editing as they write, with lots of crossing out, re-writing and playing with words until the song sounds right.
- Say that it is sometimes easier to write the words of a song if you already have a tune in your head. Ask three or four children to share their chorus lyrics even if they haven't quite finished in the time available. Some may be happy to sing their lyrics to a tune that fits!

Big Question ⓒⅮ

discussion; develop, agree on, and evaluate rules for effective discussion

Purpose: for children to develop their skills of argument and discussion through a mini enquiry session based on a philosophical question relating to the work of the day

- Display today's Big Question on the **CD (file 7.4)**:

  Are some skills or talents more valuable than others?

- Follow the process as explained on Day 1.

DAY 8

Curriculum link:
plan writing by
discussing writing
that is similar;
recording ideas

Build a story 2

Purpose: for children to see the second stage of a story's development as a model for their own writing

- Now display **CD (file 8.1)** to show the bare bones of your new story again.
- Read it aloud to the children. Explain that you are now going to show them another version of the new story to be written. This one has additional information and words – it has been developed.
- Move to the next slide to show Build a story 2 and read it aloud to the children in full storyteller mode.
- Ask them to TTYP to share ideas about how the story has been developed. Take feedback and make sure you draw attention to the narrator and the fact that it is written in the 1st person and in the past tense. Ask the children to Popcorn an answer to the question: *'Who is narrating the story?'*
- Click 'Highlights' to show highlighted sections. Use this to clarify how the story has been developed. Whenever possible, use correct grammatical terms within their range such as verbs, adjectives, synonyms, inverted commas (speech marks) and adverbs to describe additions and changes, e.g. *'Oh yes, the adverb* awful *tells us about Daphne's singing, doesn't it?'.*
- Ask them to TTYP to say what they notice about Mol the narrator. Ask them what we find out about her character from Build a story 2 that we didn't know before, e.g. *she is very bossy, controlling, a bit unkind to Daphne, she thinks she is the singing star.*
- Leave Build a story 2 on the screen to refer to during the next activity.

Write a story 2

composing
and rehearsing
sentences orally;
creating settings,
characters, plot

Purpose: for children to gain confidence in developing and writing the second stage of a story

- Ask the children to look at their own bare bones for a new story that they wrote in their Daily log. Remind them that these begin from the point that the band have been asked to perform (point 4 in your Build a story 2).
- Explain that you are going to model the development process for them first.
- Ask one or two sets of partners to read out their first sentences. Choose one of the sentences or make up a similar one and write it on the board or flipchart.
- TOL as you model how to develop the sentence by adding some information: adjectives, adverbs and synonyms as appropriate.
- Leave Build a story 2 on the screen (**CD (file 8.1)**) to refer to as a guide and draw the children in to the process, allowing them to see how small changes can take writing in different directions. Don't make it look too easy – show them writing in action with all its crossings out, false starts, etc.
- Repeat the process with one of the children's second sentences.
- Explain that you want them to use your modelling as a support to help them to develop their first two sentences.
- Say that they can also borrow ideas for the development of the story from the notes you wrote down in the last session. These should be displayed where children can refer to them easily, but explain that you want them to think of their own ideas as well.
- Tell them that they can experiment by writing in their Daily log so that they can keep changing their sentences until they are happy with them. It is important that they know that this is writing in action, not a finished piece of work.
- Once they are happy with their developed sentences 1 and 2, they can write them out underneath their bare bones.

- Now tell the children that they are going to develop the rest of their sentences using the same methods you have modelled. Remind them to TTYP to share ideas and try sentences out orally before writing them down.
- Explain that they can experiment again with ways of developing their sentences, and then they should write them out in full when they are happy with them.
- Walk around as the children work, noting use of ambitious vocabulary, and ideas to give feedback on once they have finished writing. Choose two or three sets of partners to share their developed sentences.

<table>
<tr><td>Curriculum link:
discussing and
recording ideas</td></tr>
</table>

Daily log

Purpose: for children to keep a personal log of notes, thoughts and ideas, collected from their reading and discussions. Some ideas will be used in their own writing

- Say that when writers are developing a story, they often give it what is called a *working title*. Explain that this means it might be changed once the story is finished or even in the middle of writing it, but it is useful to have a title as it is being written.
- Ask the children to take turns to read their Write a story 2 versions to each other and then share ideas for a working title for their own and their partner's story.
- Ask them to record their best idea/s in their Daily log and to think about why it is a good title. Now tell them to Popcorn their working titles. Pick out a few children to explain their choices.

<table>
<tr><td>discussion;
develop, agree on,
and evaluate
rules for effective
discussion</td></tr>
</table>

Big Question

Purpose: for children to develop their skills of argument and discussion through a mini enquiry session based on a philosophical question relating to the work of the day

- Display today's Big Question on the **CD (file 8.2)**:

  Can you learn to be talented, or do you have to be born with a talent? *

- Follow the process as explained on Day 1.

  * *This Big Question will be revisited on Day 11 – the first day of the Non-fiction week.*

DAY 9

Grammar: adverbials

Purpose: for children to consolidate their understanding of adverbs and to widen children's awareness and use of adverbials

<table>
<tr><td>Year 4 Grammar
using fronted
adverbials; use
and understand
grammatical
terminology

NB Children will
need to know
the term 'fronted
adverbial' for the
English Grammar,
Punctuation and
Spelling test from
2016.</td></tr>
</table>

- Remind the children that adverbs are useful because they can work with other words to tell us more about when, where or how something happens or has happened.
- Display **CD (file 9.1)** to show some examples. Read the first two sentences of the first example aloud on your own and then use MT/YT to read the third sentence, giving special emphasis to the adverb as you say it and point to it.
- Explain that an adverb is a type of adverbial. Say that an adverbial doesn't just have to be a single word, it can be a phrase which gives more information about a verb, an adjective or an adverb.
- Navigate to the next slide to show an example. Use MT/YT to say the example and then use the think bubble to introduce the term *adverbial*.
- Remind them that as well as using adverbials to show *when* something happened, we can use them to show *where* and *how* something happened. Navigate to the next slide to show another example and explanation for *where* and read it aloud. Repeat this for the next slide with the example for *how*.
- Now ask the children to look at the Grammar: adverbials activity on p.30 of their Pupils' Book and to focus on the first section. Explain the activity and ask them to complete it with their partners.
- Choose two or three sets of partners to share their answers. Clarify where necessary.

- Say that in all of the examples in the first three sentences, the adverbials appear at the end of the sentence.
- Explain that sometimes adverbials can appear at the beginning of the sentence. Navigate to the next slide on the **CD (file 9.1)** to show examples of fronted adverbials. Use MT/YT to say them aloud, making sure you pause at the comma each time.
- Ask the children to TTYP to say what punctuation has been added after the adverbial and to give their answer (a comma) chorally. Click 'Punctuation' to show the sentences again with the punctuation highlighted.
- Now ask them to look at the Grammar: adverbials activity on p.30 of their Pupils' Book again and to focus on the second section. Explain the activity and ask them to complete it with their partners.
- Collect feedback and clarify where necessary.

Homework Book p.11 provides further practice on adverbials.

Build a story 3 (CD) 📄 🄰 **(teacher only)**

Purpose: for children to see the third stage of a story's development as a model for their own writing

> **Curriculum link:** understand the skills and processes that are essential for writing

- Before the lesson, print enough copies of the story from **CD (file 9.3)** for each set of partners.
- Tell the children that you have started writing the beginning of your new story. Explain that you are going to show them your first draft that was based on Build a story 2. Say that you concentrated on developing paragraphs that linked sentences and ideas together.
- Display **CD (file 9.2)** to show Build a story 3 and read it out to the children.
- Tell them that that you decided to make it a bit more interesting and funny, so you *re-drafted* it and tried to write in the style of Kaye Umansky, the writer of *The Bogey Men and the Trolls Next Door*. Explain that you like:
  - the way the author adds extra bits of information in brackets as if the narrator is telling the reader something that not everybody knows about
  - the way the author creates comical images through the characters' words and actions
  - the way the author's characters say exactly what they think and don't worry about offending people
  - the way the *narrator* (remind the children of the difference between the author and the narrator) uses dialogue to tell us what he or she has said
  - the author's made-up adjective *trollish*.
- Read out an example from Kaye Umansky's text for each of the above bullet points.
- Explain that you decided not to write in rhyming verse because sometimes, trying to make things rhyme can get in the way and ruin your ideas.
- Say that instead of rhyme, you tried to catch the writer's 'voice' and humour and use some of the phrases she used. Click 'Re-draft' to show a re-drafted version of Build a story 3. Read it to the children with enthusiasm, putting special emphasis on words and phrases where appropriate.
- Now give a copy of the story from **CD (file 9.3)** to each set of partners. Ask the children to underline or circle parts they think are written in the style of Kaye Umansky's story and parts they particularly like (or don't like), as well as powerful adjectives and verbs.
- Collect feedback, encouraging the children to share why they picked out specific parts of the story so far.
- Tell them that this is as far as you have got with the new story and you would like them to continue it using their Write a story 2 sentences.

Write a story 3

Purpose: for children to develop their confidence and ability to write a story using the sentences they have developed, teacher modelling and prompts

- Tell the children that they are now ready to write their story. Remind them that their story begins from the point that the band have been asked to perform for the first time in public (point 4 in your Build a story 2).
- Display **CD (file 9.4)** and guide the children through the composition prompts. Explain that they are going to use the sentences they have already developed and these prompts to help them to write their story.
- Click 'Next' and talk through some tips on how the children can use adverbs, adjectives and exclamation marks to enhance their writing.
- Remind them to use any useful parts of their Daily log to help them and to keep re-reading what they have written to check it makes sense.
- Encourage the children to rehearse their opening sentence in their minds before they begin to write.
- Walk around as they write, giving support and clarification where appropriate.
- Tell them that they will have some of tomorrow's lesson to complete their story.
- Expect most of the children to develop most of the points from their Write a story 2 by the end of this session, completing it during the first part of Day 10. Some will finish the whole story and Day 10's extra time can be spent refining their work. A few children may not complete the whole story. The focus should be on good quality writing, not quantity at this stage and they should be encouraged to take pride in what they have written rather than rushing to finish.

(DAY 10)

Write a story 3 (continued)

Purpose: for children to have time to complete their work, so they can see that you value the act of writing

- Allow time for the children to finish and refine their stories.

Share a story

Purpose: for children to develop their willingness to share their work with their peers, and their ability to identify qualities of others' work as well as their own

- Ask the children to read through their own story and to underline one or two favourite sentences. Now ask them to swap stories with their partners and to read each other's work. Tell them to TTYP to discuss their favourite parts and to explain their choices.
- Ask them to discuss whether they would pick the same or different favourite parts.
- Choose two or three children to share their favourite parts, either from their own story or their partner's.
- Make sure that any ambitious vocabulary or Special phrases they or you have picked out are written out and added to the Story wall.

Evaluate and edit

Purpose: for children to evaluate their own and their partner's work against specific criteria and then discuss how they could improve their work

- Display **CD (file 10.1)** and read through the evaluation points using MT/YT.
- As a model, select an example of work where the writing has met the criteria, and share this with the other children, explaining why it works well.

- Tell the children to take turns to read their partner's writing in pairs and discuss together how well each piece of writing has met the criteria.
- Ask the children to discuss at least two changes they could make to improve their work.

Curriculum link: proofread for spelling and punctuation errors

Proofread

Purpose: for children to proofread their work and make changes to improve the accuracy of their grammar, punctuation and spelling

- Now ask the children to proofread their work. If you have noticed that several children need to improve on a particular aspect of spelling, grammar or punctuation, use this as a focus for the Proofread activity. Write an example which includes common errors from the children's writing and use this as a model.
- The children should always be checking for standard use of punctuation and correct spelling of common exception words.
- The following points would be particularly relevant for this Unit:
  - checking spelling of ambitious vocabulary choices (i.e. those borrowed from the Pupils' Book or Anthology text)
  - making sure that children have used the past tense throughout
  - checking that children have consistently used the first person ('I') as the narrator.

discussion; develop, agree on, and evaluate rules for effective discussion

Very Big Question ⓒⅅ

Purpose: for children to develop their willingness to revise or broaden their opinions and ideas through the exploration of one of the Big Questions in depth

- See Unit 1 Day 10 for teaching notes on the Very Big Question (p.41).

READING AND WRITING NON-FICTION

Linked via a Big Question, the Non-fiction week looks at explanation texts. The children revise previous knowledge of the language and organisational features of explanation texts and explore examples of visual, verbal and written explanations. They create their own explanations in a variety of forms, culminating in the delivery of an explanatory lesson on how to get the 'pop star look'. See p.82 for the daily timetable for the Non-fiction week.

Non-fiction

Reading

Children will:

- consolidate their understanding of how explanation texts are structured to make information clear, using features e.g. *headings, subheadings, pictures* and *boxed text*
- read and evaluate a range of explanation texts
- understand how visual aids such as flow charts help the audience to understand complicated processes more easily.

Writing

Key writing purpose to be shared with the children:

To write about a pupil's life at stage school based on a radio interview.

Writing evaluation to be shared with the children

My explanation:

- gives clear information about life at stage school
- has a title and subheadings to organise the information
- uses quotations (direct speech) and/or reported speech to explain about life at stage school.

Grammar:

- includes reported speech and/or direct speech, which is set out and punctuated correctly.

See the Planning section of the Software ('Timetables' tab) for a printable version of the Writing purpose and evaluation.

DAY 11

Curriculum link:
thinking aloud
to explore and
collect ideas;
reading for a range
of purposes

Think and link

Purpose: for children's interest in explanation texts to be stimulated and to provide a link between the fiction and the non-fiction texts

- Remind the children that all of our Big Questions helped us to share our opinions about something.
- Display the Big Question from Day 8 on the **CD (file 8.2)**:

  Can you learn to be talented, or do you have to be born with a talent?

- Check that all the children can recall the meaning of the word *talented* and then ask them to TTYP to recall some of the opinions they shared and take feedback.
- Remind them that many people think of talent as something that comes naturally, but most people who are naturally good at something also have to be trained and practise for hours if they want to develop their talent.
- Tell the children that even if you have little natural ability for something, enthusiasm, training and practice can still help you to be good at it.
- Remind the children that in *The Bogey Men and the Trolls Next Door*, the Trolls loved to sing and play instruments and in our version of the story, the Bogey and Troll children formed a band. Say that if you were going to write a sequel to the story, you might want them to improve their voices! Ask the children to TTYP to think of ways that singers can improve their voices.
- Take feedback, and guide their responses to explore the fact that there are lots of different ways to be taught about things, e.g. *through information and explanations in books, websites, or through spoken information and explanation from friends or teachers.*
- Tell the children that one way people develop their singing talent is by attending a stage school which specialises in teaching children about music, acting and dancing.
- Ask them to imagine that one of the Bogey children, little Douggie who is only seven, has decided to apply for stage school. Tell them to TTYP and discuss two questions they think he would have about the new school, e.g. *How do I apply? How old do I need to be? Can I come and visit before I start?* Take feedback.
- Ask the children to TTYP and talk about where they might find the answers, e.g. *a school prospectus, by contacting the school, through a website.*

Context – stage school

Purpose: for children to be introduced to the context for their exploration of explanation texts

- Display **CD (file 11.1)** to show the homepage of a stage school website. Point to the text as you read it aloud.
- Ask the children to TTYP to say whether Douggie would be able to find the answers to his questions on the website, or if there is a link to where he might find the answers. Choose two sets of partners to feed back.
- Explain that when websites are designed, the person putting them together thinks about the most effective way to display information so that it is useful, easy to find and interesting to read.
- Ask the children to TTYP to discuss what features of or information from the website they found most useful and to feed back to the class, e.g. *It was useful to know straight away that the school is for children aged between 8 and 16, so we knew that Douggie wouldn't be able to apply until next year.*
- Now talk through the layout and organisation of the page, drawing attention to:
  - headings and subheadings
  - navigation buttons
  - boxed text
  - links to further information
  - pictures and graphics.

- Tell the children that the style of writing is really important too. The purpose of the website is not just to provide information and explanations – it also needs to be appealing, not just to children but to adults too, as they will be deciding whether this is the right school for their child. The language used is trying to persuade us that it's a great place to study, and also that we should follow the links to find out more. Draw attention to examples of:
  - imperatives, e.g. 'Apply now', 'Join', 'Read'.
  - powerful words and phrases, e.g. 'inspiring stories', 'achieve their dreams'.
  - the play on words in the mission statement: 'Let us have a leading role in your life'.
- Now ask them to TTYP to discuss how effective they think this homepage is. Write this list of things they need to consider on the board or a flipchart, and ask them to score each one with a mark out of five:
  - How well organised and easy to follow is it?
  - How effective is it in making the school sound like a great place to learn how to sing, dance or act?
  - Is the writing style suitable for both children and their parents or carers to read and understand?
- Read out the first question and ask them to Popcorn their marks. Choose two sets of partners with different marks and ask each of them to give a reason for their score.
- Repeat the process for each question.

Audience and purpose PB

Purpose: for children to use the Stellar Stage School website as a model for their own writing; to develop their awareness of writing for a specific purpose and audience

- Tell the children that they are going to invent a new school for talented children. Explain that it could be a performing arts (stage) school, a sports academy or a combined school where children choose whether to attend the stage classes or the sports classes. Say that they are going to work with their partner to create a homepage for a website explaining all about the new school for prospective pupils.
- Give each set of partners a piece of A3 paper (this will allow space for pictures, headings, etc.). Ask them to look at the Audience and purpose activity on p.31 of their Pupils' Book. Guide them through the discussion and planning questions and tell them to make notes and drafts in their Daily log before creating their web page on the A3 paper.
- Walk around as they work, giving support, clarification and praise as appropriate.

Daily log

Purpose: for children to keep a personal log of notes, thoughts and ideas, collected from their reading and discussions. Some ideas will be used in their own writing

- Ask the children to TTYP to say which classes they would prefer to attend – the performing arts or the sports classes – and why.
- Choose two or three sets of partners to feed back, encouraging the children to explain their choices and reasons clearly.
- Now ask them to write a couple of sentences recording their choices and reasons in their Daily log.

> **Curriculum link:** purposes and audiences should underpin decisions about the form writing should take

> discussing and recording ideas

DAY 12

Visual explanations (CD)

Purpose: for children to develop their awareness and understanding of explanatory diagrams

- Tell the children that not only are there many different places where explanations can be found, but there are many ways they can be presented, given or shown.
- Display **CD (file 12.1)** to show the definition of the term *flow chart* from the *Oxford Junior Dictionary*. Read it aloud to the children.
- Move to the next slide to show a simple flow chart. Ask the children to TTYP to discuss what the chart is explaining. Choose two sets of partners to share their interpretations and explanations.
- Say that flow charts can also be used to help us to make a decision about what actions to take because they explain the choices we have, the consequences of each choice and the end result of the path we have chosen.
- Go to the next slide to show a light-hearted flow chart. Talk through it, engaging the children with exaggerated facial expressions and intonation for 'good' and 'bad' choices and consequences.
- Explain that diagrams or flow charts can be used on their own for simple explanations but they can also be used as a visual aid alongside a written explanation to help to explain something complicated.

Deconstruction 1 A PB

Purpose: for children to develop their ability to think about audience and purpose; to develop their ability to identify different kinds of information in a text

> **Curriculum link:** discussing writing that is similar to that which they are planning to write; justifying inferences with evidence

- Ask the children to recall the discussions they had on Day 11 about their thoughts on attending a stage school or a sports academy. Say that it would not be easy to decide whether or not that kind of school would be right for them.
- Ask them to give a quick thumbs up or down to show whether they would like to attend the Stellar Stage School or not.
- Tell them to look at The Stellar Stage School chart on pp.36–37 of their Anthology. Explain that the stage school website had a link called 'Is stage school for you?' and that this is a printed copy of it.
- Ask the children to TTYP to read the flow chart, taking it in turns to read each box.
- Point out the box that tells them that anyone deciding they would like to go to the school would have to apply, explaining why they should be accepted.
- Ask them to TTYP to discuss which boxes would be the most useful to help them with their letter of application and at an interview.
- Tell them to give their answers chorally and check that they have chosen correctly. Choose two children to explain why these boxes would be helpful.
- Explain that it is just as important to think about what *not* to say if we want to give the right impression in a letter of application or an interview.
- Tell the children to turn to p.32 of their Pupils' Book and look at the Deconstruction 1 activity. Ask them to TTYP to read the speech bubbles. Now tell them to discuss why the boy's statements would not help him to get a place at the school. Choose two or three sets of partners to share their answers.
- Say that Miss Lark's responses give lots of clues about what kind of pupil she is looking for. Ask the children to TTYP to say what kind of pupil they think Miss Lark would like at the school and to give reasons for their answers. Take feedback and make sure they have picked up the main points, e.g. *someone who is willing to work hard, who understands that success is not guaranteed, is not just boasting but can perform, is willing to learn from others.*

Hotseating

Purpose: for children to role-play a scenario as preparation for their own writing

- Tell the children that they are all in role as someone who is desperate to be given a place at the Stellar Stage School. Use MT/YT to say *'I am desperate to get a place at stage school!'* adding the exclamation mark mime at the end (see the Extras section of the Software).
- Ask them to TTYP to say the sentence and do the mime again with exaggerated expression to convey meaning.
- Explain that Partner 2s are going to be first in the hotseat. Say that they are going to face their partner and begin to explain, clearly and enthusiastically, why they deserve a place at the school, using what they have read to help them.
- Tell them that when you say *'Stop and swap'*, they will stop and Partner 1s will begin their explanations.

> **Curriculum link:**
> retrieve and record information from non-fiction; write for a range of real purposes and audiences

Write 1 (CD) A

Purpose: for children to use a flow chart and their role-play as the basis for writing an explanatory letter

- Tell the children that they are going to stay in role to write a letter of application to the Stellar Stage School, explaining why they deserve a place. Display **CD (file 12.2)** to show the stage school's explanation of how to apply. Talk through the points, stopping after each one to ask the children to TTYP to share ideas about what kind of things they will write about.
- Go to the next slide to show a letter template. Use the think bubbles and/or your own ideas to explain the conventions of the layout and to ensure that the children understand the purpose of the task, the audience (the manager of the school) and the need for formal language.
- Remind them to use the Anthology flow chart to help them to compose their letter in role. Tell them to rehearse their opening sentence in their minds before writing it down.

> **recording ideas and information**

Daily log

Purpose: for children to keep a personal log of notes, thoughts and ideas, collected from their reading and discussions. Some ideas will be used in their own writing

- Share with the children one secret or surprising talent you wish you had or would like to improve on through training and practice, e.g. *juggling, dancing, drawing*.
- Tell the children to write down what secret or surprising talent they would like to have or to improve on through training and practice. Ask for feedback from any children who are willing to share their thoughts.

(DAY 13) Deconstruction 2 (CD)

> **retrieve and record information from non-fiction**

Purpose: for children to take well-organised notes from a verbal explanation

- Explain that a teenage boy who is a pupil at the stage school was interviewed by a local radio station. He explained how he got a place there, what his life is like at the school and what ambitions he has.
- Ask the children to listen carefully while you play the broadcast. Display **CD (file 13.1)** and click 'Audio' to hear the interview.
- Tell them to TTYP to share anything they can recall from Jack's interview. Collect feedback and write their contributions on the board or a flipchart in note form

under appropriate headings, e.g. *How did he get accepted? Why did he want to go to stage school? What are his ambitions for the future?*

- Now make sure they have their Daily log and a pen ready to make notes as they hear the broadcast again. Tell them that you will play a bit of the interview and then pause it while they make notes of their own.
- Begin the process of playing and pausing the interview while the children make their own notes.
- Choose two or three sets of partners to share what they have written and add them to the notes you wrote on the board or flipchart. Preserve the notes ready for the next activity.

> **Curriculum link:**
> thinking aloud
> to explore and
> collect ideas,
> drafting and
> re-reading to
> check their
> meaning is
> clear; using and
> punctuating direct
> speech

Write 2

Purpose: for children to use notes as the basis for an explanation text and to develop their ability to recognise differences between the spoken and written forms of language

- Before the lesson, print a copy of **CD (file 13.3)** for each child.
- Tell the children that they are going to help you to use notes from a verbal explanation to create a written account.
- Display **CD (file 13.2)**. Read the opening sentences, then click 'Reveal' to reveal a heading and a callout. Read them out to the children.
- Click 'TOL' to reveal a think bubble and use it to help you to model composing an opening of a sentence from the notes and rehearsing it aloud, checking it makes sense before typing it into the text box below.
- Click 'Reveal' again to show another callout that focuses on using the notes to complete the sentence. Click 'TOL' again to reveal a think bubble. Use it to involve the children in the writing process, paraphrasing and scribing their suggestion into the editable text box. It is important that they participate with you in the thinking and rehearsing process.
- Use your own TOL to model and write what Jack said in direct speech, using inverted commas.
- Now give the children a copy each of **CD (file 13.3)** and explain that they should carry on with the account, using the notes and headings and your modelling to help them.
- Remind the children to select at least one appropriate note to create a sentence and a quote from Jack with inverted commas, or in reported speech without, e.g. *Jack told the interviewer that he was lucky to get a place at the school.*
- Walk around as they work, checking they understand the task and supporting where necessary. Note points to raise and reasons for praise in your feedback at the end of the writing activity.
- Ask them to TTYP to share ideas for a title for the piece of writing. Collect a few examples and write them on the board or flipchart. Ask them to add a title.
- You may need to allocate the first part of Day 14 for the children to complete their writing.

> discussing and
> recording ideas

Daily log

Purpose: for children to keep a personal log of notes, thoughts and ideas, collected from their reading and discussions. Some ideas will be used in their own writing

- Ask the children to TTYP to discuss what kind of performer they would like to be if they had the choice to be a brilliant singer, dancer or actor.
- Collect responses and reasons from a few sets of partners and then have a show of hands for each type of performer.

- Tell them to write a couple of sentences in their Daily log recording their answer and explaining the reason for their choice.

DAY 14

Curriculum link: proofread for spelling and punctuation errors

Proofread

Purpose: for children to proofread their work and make changes to improve the accuracy of their grammar, punctuation and spelling

- Now ask the children to proofread their work. If you have noticed that several children need to improve on a particular aspect of spelling, grammar or punctuation, use this as a focus for the Proofread activity. Write an example which includes common errors from the children's writing and use this as a model.
- The children should always be checking for standard use of punctuation and correct spelling of common exception words.
- The following points would be particularly relevant for this Unit:
  - checking that any quotations have been punctuated correctly with inverted commas
  - checking that any reported speech has been used appropriately, without the use of inverted commas.

identifying how language, structure and presentation contribute to meaning

Deconstruction 3

Purpose: for children to explore an integrated visual, verbal and written explanation on a topic which they can later use as a model for their own texts and presentations

- Tell the children that pupils at the stage school have lessons where they learn about how the voice works and how to improve their singing.
- Ask them to look at the 'How the Voice Works' text on pp.38–39 of the Anthology. Explain that this is an example of a lesson delivered by voice coach and expert Miss Lark.
- Guide the children through the glossary on p.39 to make sure they can pronounce and understand the technical and scientific words. Tell them that a glossary is yet another kind of explanation text.
- Now ask them to TTYP to read alternate sections each of the text.
- Tell them to discuss the different ways the explanations were given in the lesson, e.g. *verbal*, *visual* (diagram), *written* (hand-out).
- Tell the children that Miss Lark's technical explanation of how the voice works would be hard to understand if she had not used a visual explanation as well. Explain that Miss Lark's diagram makes a complicated process easier to understand, and that they are going to see a close-up of the diagram.
- Display **CD (file 14.1)** to show the diagram. Say that you are going to be Miss Lark. Use Miss Lark's dialogue from your copy of the Anthology p.38 to explain the process, pointing to the relevant parts of the diagram.

write for a range of purposes and audiences; monitor whether their own writing makes sense

Write 3 **PB**

Purpose: for children to research a given topic and write an explanation text which includes a diagram and can be used as the basis of a formal presentation

- Tell the children that most people who go to stage school want to become well-known so that they get plenty of work throughout their careers.
- Say that they are going to work with their partners to create a special lesson, based on the structure of Miss Lark's, for pupils at the stage school who want to become famous pop stars. Tell them that the lesson will focus on explaining how to get the 'pop-star look' needed to become the next pop sensation.

- Ask them to look at the Write 3 activity on p.33 of their Pupils' Book and to use the ideas and instructions to help them to plan and prepare their lesson.
- You will need to provide sugar paper and felt pens for visual aids and diagrams. Tell them to make sure they ask for or bring in any props they might want to use.
- Explain that they will have the rest of the day's lesson and the first part of the next lesson to complete and rehearse their lesson.
- Walk round as they work, giving support, advice and encouragement where necessary and taking 'orders' for small numbers of hand-outs to be photocopied for their lessons.

Curriculum link:
building a varied and rich vocabulary

Daily log

Purpose: for children to keep a personal log of notes, thoughts and ideas, collected from their reading and discussions. Some ideas will be used in their own writing

- Ask the children to write down the name of a pop star whose image they think is very memorable. Tell them to think of and write down three or four words that describe or represent the image, e.g. *scruffy, fun and funky* or *sparkly, glam and gorgeous*.
- Say that they can create new words by joining parts of other words together (portmanteau words), e.g. *blingtastic, glamabulous*.

DAY 15

read aloud their own writing, using appropriate intonation and controlling the tone and volume so that the meaning is clear

Presentation – explanations

Purpose: for children to practise and deliver their stage school lessons in the role of experts

- Allow time in the first part of the lesson for the children to complete and practise their lessons.
- Explain that each set of partners is going to take turns to deliver their lesson to a 'class' made up of two other sets of partners.
- Now join three sets of partners together to form groups of six. Begin the carousel of lessons by asking one set of partners in each group to begin.
- Walk around as the lessons take place, noting good partner work, choice of explanatory methods and effective, confident delivery. You may also wish to film or photograph parts of the lessons in progress for display and/or material for discussion and evaluation at the end of the Unit.

assessing the effectiveness of their own and others' writing

Evaluate and edit

Purpose: for children to evaluate their presentation and another pair's presentation against specific criteria and then discuss how they could improve their work

- Display **CD (file 15.1)** and read through the evaluation points using MT/YT.
- As a model, select an example of work where the presentation met the criteria, and share this with the other children, explaining why it worked well.
- Tell the children to think back to their presentation and a presentation that they watched, and to discuss with their partner how well each presentation met the criteria.
- Ask children to discuss at least two changes they could make to improve their presentation.

Unit 4

Fiction: Playscripts
Non-fiction: Evaluating evidence

Timetable

WEEK 1   **Reading fiction**   *The Fly and the Fool*

Day 1	Day 2	Day 3	Day 4	Day 5
The script store	Word power 🖥	The language of playscripts 🖥	What do I want? How do I get it? 🖥	Most important?
Read a script version 1	Read a script version 3	Re-read a script version 3	Status game 🖥	Drama – Mr Lo on trial 🖥
Think and link	Think and link	Exploring character 🖥	Performing the play	Daily log
Read a script version 2 🖥	Daily log	Daily log	Daily log	Big Question
Daily log	Big Question	Big Question	Big Question	
Big Question				

WEEK 2   **Writing fiction**   *The Fly and the Fool*

Day 6	Day 7	Day 8	Day 9	Day 10
What if not...?	Build a script 1	Drama – in the dock 🖥	Write a script 3 🖥	Share a script
Read a folk tale 🖥	Build a script 2	Write a script 1		Evaluate and edit
Build a character 🖥	Stage directions 🖥	Write a script 2		Proofread
Show, don't tell	Build a script 3	Daily log		Very Big Question
Daily log	Daily log	Big Question		
Big Question	Big Question			

WEEK 3   **Reading and writing non-fiction**   Evaluating evidence

Day 11	Day 12	Day 13	Day 14	Day 15
Think and link	Zoom in on explanations	Deconstruction 2	Deconstruction 3	Write 3 (continued)
Word power 🖥	Deconstruction 1	Write 2 🖥	Write 3	Proofread
Explanations	Write 1 🖥	Daily log 🖥		Publish and present
Word detectives	Daily log			Evaluate and edit
Grammar: plurals, possession and apostrophes				
Daily log				

🖥: shows that a file should be printed out from the Software.

Overview of the Unit

In this Unit the children explore a playscript, *The Fly and the Fool* by Lou Kuenzler. They explore the play's setting, Vietnam. They look at the characters and explore the differences between how they see themselves and how others see them. The children then write an ending for a new play based on the traditional tale *Rumpelstiltskin*.

Linked via a Big Question, the Non-fiction week focuses on developing children's ability to evaluate evidence. For more information about the Non-fiction week and the Non-fiction writing evaluation criteria, see p.128.

Where appropriate, the children will be encouraged to develop an awareness of audience and purpose in relation to the fiction and non-fiction texts they are reading and writing.

Teacher modelling is provided in the teaching notes, Software and the Pupils' Book, supporting the children's writing at every stage in the Fiction and Non-fiction weeks.

The Homework Book provides a homework activity related to the content of this Unit for each of the three weeks.

Fiction

Reading

Children will:

- discuss the importance of specific characters and moments in *The Fly and the Fool*
- explore the characters to understand their actions, e.g. *how they see themselves, how others see them*
- explore how the flashback in the play helps the audience to understand the plot and make judgements about the motivations of the characters
- understand playscript conventions, including stage directions.

Writing

Key writing purpose to be shared with the children:

To write a playscript scene based on the characters from Rumpelstiltskin.

> ### Writing evaluation to be shared with the children
> My scene:
>
> - uses playscript conventions, e.g. *names before speech, stage directions* and *scene descriptions*
> - uses dialogue and stage directions to show how the characters think, move and speak
> - includes a final speech, where the King argues that the Judge should let him go.
>
> Grammar:
>
> - includes *-ing* endings for stage directions which are verbs, e.g. *standing, strutting*.

See the Planning section of the Software ('Timetables' tab) for a printable version of the Writing purpose and evaluation.

Fiction: Playscripts
The Fly and the Fool by Lou Kuenzler

READING FICTION

Resources

PB Pupils' Book, pp.34–43

A Anthology, pp.40–53

CD CD on Interactive whiteboard, Unit 4

GB Grammar Bank on CD

HB Homework Book, pp.13–16

DAY 1

Curriculum link:
listening to and discussing a wide range of fiction, identifying themes

The script store

Purpose: for children to see some images of Vietnam to help them visualise the setting of the play

- Display **CD (file 1.1)** to show the slideshow of images of Vietnam. Ask the children to TTYP (Turn to your partner) and discuss what their first impressions of Vietnam are. Take feedback.
- Tell the children that the play that they will be reading is set in Vietnam and is based on a folk tale. Show the slideshow again and tell the children that these images will help them to visualise the play. Stop at each slide and ask the children to TTYP to discuss words and phrases that come to mind when they look at each image. Take feedback and write some words and phrases on the board or flipchart to refer to later.
- Display the last two slides of **CD (file 1.1)** to show images from the play *The Fly and the Fool*. Draw attention to the title of the play and the illustrations. Ask the children to TTYP and talk about what they think the play will be about.

predicting

Read a script version 1 _{CD}

Purpose: for children to become familiar with Script version 1, the bare bones of the playscript

- Tell the children that they are now going to hear the bare bones of the new playscript and we are going to call it Script version 1.
- Read the bare bones of the playscript aloud to the children, one sentence at a time. You could add some actions or expressions that you think will help the children to hold the script in their minds. Do not reveal any surprises or the ending.
- After each sentence, ask the children to TTYP and repeat it. Continue in this way with each sentence from Script version 1 (below), first reading a part of the playscript with actions, then asking the children to tell each other the sentence.
  Script version 1
  1. A rich merchant demands payment of a loan from a poor family.
  2. A judge will decide what should be done.
  3. The boy from the poor family and his sister tell the judge that the merchant has already been paid back but he wants more.
  4. The merchant demands that he should be paid more so he can make a profit.
  5. The boy explains that the merchant came to their house looking for his parents.
  6. The boy told him two riddles which explained where his parents were.
  7. The merchant tried to solve the riddles but could not.
  8. The merchant was so annoyed that he agreed to let the family off paying the extra money if the boy told him the answers.
  9. The boy agreed but said he needed a witness to the bargain. The merchant saw a fly and said that the fly could witness the deal...
  10. Will the judge believe the boy?
- At the end, ask the children to tell their partner the bare bones of the play, including key characters and events. Display the bare bones on **CD (file 1.2)** and ask the children to TTYP to discuss how much they remembered.

- Ensure the children understand what *profit* is – explain that when grown-ups borrow money, the person lending it to them will often make them pay some extra money and this is their *profit*.

Curriculum link:
asking questions

Think and link

Purpose: for children to make connections between the landscape of Vietnam and the setting of the play, and to start exploring the characters

- Display **CD (file 1.1)** again to show the images of Vietnam. Link the images of the village and meeting place to Script version 1. Use the images as a stimulus for discussion about the setting of the play. Write any ideas or words that will help the children visualise and make connections with the setting on a flipchart.
- Look at the pictures of the judge and the merchant on the **CD (file 1.1)**. Ask the children to TTYP and discuss what they know about these characters so far and what they would like to know about them before they hear the full version of the play for the first time. Take feedback and write the main ideas on the flipchart.

predicting;
identifying how
language, structure
and presentation
contribute to
meaning

Read a script version 2

Purpose: for children to examine how Script version 2 provides additional information for the reader; for children to become more familiar with the play before they hear the full version

- Before the lesson, print a copy of Script version 1 and Script version 2 from **CD (file 1.3)** for each set of partners.
- Tell the children that you have managed to find out more about the characters and what happens in the play. Explain that you are going to read Script version 2 to them and they must listen carefully for new information that might change the pictures they have in their minds.
- Read Script version 2 aloud to the children with appropriate intonation, facial expressions and gestures to convey meaning, and with particular emphasis on the new information.
  Script version 2
  1. All the inhabitants of a small village in Vietnam have gathered to hear a rich but deceitful merchant called Mr Lo demand payment of a loan from a poor family.
  2. The village has a judge, whom they have chosen because he is a fair and honest man, and he will decide what should be done.
  3. The boy from the poor family, Lan, and his sister, Kym, explain that the family took a loan from Mr Lo which was just enough money to buy food until the rice was harvested. They say that once the rice was harvested the family paid back the loan but greedy Mr Lo insisted that they pay back twice as much. The family couldn't do that and a year later Mr Lo insisted that the debt was now ten times the original amount!
  4. Mr Lo explains to the Judge that he is a fair and quick-witted businessman and he should be paid more so he can make a profit. The Judge asks Lan to explain his side of the story.
  5. Lan insists that the family have been cleared of their debt by Mr Lo. He explains to the Judge that Mr Lo had come to their house the day before, when his parents were out.
  6. The merchant demanded rudely to know where Lan's 'worthless' parents were.
  7. Lan loves telling riddles, so he told Mr Lo two riddles which explained where his parents were.

8. The vain Mr Lo was sure that he was clever enough to solve a boy's riddles. He tried to solve them but could not.

9. Mr Lo was so annoyed that he agreed to let the family off paying the extra money if Lan revealed the answers.

10. Lan agreed but wanted to make sure there was a witness to the deal because he didn't trust the crafty merchant. The dishonest Mr Lo saw a fly on the gate post and said that the fly could witness the deal…

11. Mr Lo says that Lan is telling lies…

12. Will the Judge believe Lan or the merchant, Mr Lo?

- TOL (Think out loud) and use TTYP to share how the new information has changed the pictures in our minds.
- Now give each set of partners a copy of Script version 1 and Script version 2 from **CD (file 1.3)** and ask them to take turns to read a section each of the two versions of the playscript. Ask them to use a coloured pencil or highlighter pen to underline or highlight the new information in Script version 2.
- Display **CD (file 1.4)** to show the two versions of the playscript on screen. Click 'Highlights' to show the additional information and synonyms for words in Script version 2.
- Choose children to feed back on the new information they identified. Use their answers and TOL to talk through the additional information relating to plot, character and vocabulary.
- Next, remove the playscript from the screen and ask the children to hide their copies. Ask Partner 1s to begin retelling the play to Partner 2s in their own words, until you say '*Stop and swap*', when Partner 2s will take over. Repeat the *stop and swap* process until the children have finished telling the play to each other.

<table>
<tr><td>

Curriculum link:
predicting;
discussing and
recording ideas

</td></tr>
</table>

Daily log

Purpose: for children to keep a personal log of notes, thoughts and ideas, collected from their reading and discussions. Some ideas will be used in their own writing

- Ask the children to TTYP and talk about how the play could end. Who do they think will convince the Judge and why? Take feedback.
- Ask the children to imagine being the writer of the playscript and to TTYP to discuss how could they use the fly to help Lan convince the Judge that he is telling the truth. Take feedback and write some of their ideas on to a flipchart.
- Ask the children to write how they would end the play in their Daily log. Remind them to visualise the play and setting. Make sure they understand that they don't have to make a correct prediction.

<table>
<tr><td>

discussion;
develop, agree on,
and evaluate
rules for effective
discussion

</td></tr>
</table>

Big Question (CD)

Purpose: for children to develop skills of argument and discussion through a mini enquiry session based on a philosophical question relating to the work of the day

- Display today's Big Question on **CD (file 1.5)**:

  Are games always fun?

- Ask the children to TTYP to discuss this question. Collect feedback and write some responses on the board.
- Click 'Prompts' to show some statements that may help to encourage discussion.

DAY 2

Curriculum link:
discussing words
and phrases
that capture the
reader's interest
and imagination

Word power

Purpose: for children to learn the meaning of specific vocabulary used in the playscript and increase their knowledge of synonyms

deceitful   imposing   immensely   worthless

- Display **CD (file 2.1)** to show the Power words and their definitions. Look at the words and definitions with the children and then use MT/YT (My turn/Your turn) to read the sentences, putting special emphasis on the relevant words.
- Explain that the writer could have chosen different words that mean the same thing. Move to the next screen to show some examples.
- Use drag and drop to substitute synonymous words into the first sentence. Use MT/YT to read the sentence aloud after each substitution. TOL as you explain how the words subtly change the meaning of the sentence.
- Ask the children to TTYP to talk about which word they want to use and to try it in the sentence.
- Repeat the process for the other three sentences.
- The words and definitions can be printed from **CD (file 2.2)** to display on your Playscript wall for this Unit. Let the children hear you using these words in a deliberately exaggerated fashion in your conversation and teaching throughout the day, e.g. *'The character in the story was* deceitful *when he kept the truth from his friends.' 'That money is* worthless *now we are back in the UK.'*

checking that the
text makes sense,
asking questions,
drawing inferences

Read a script version 3

Purpose: for children to hear and enjoy the full version of the play for the first time

- Tell the children that they are now going to hear the whole play for the first time. TOL about which parts you can't wait to hear about.
- Ask the children to TTYP to share what they are looking forward to in the play.
- Play the audio file on **CD (file 2.3)** to hear the play being performed.
- At the end of the play, ask the children to look at the Read a script version 3 activity on p.34 of their Pupils' Book. Guide them as they TTYP to discuss the questions and feed back to the class.

asking questions
to improve their
understanding of
a text; retelling
orally

Think and link

Purpose: for children to understand the chronology and main points of the play

- Ask the children to turn to p.35 of their Pupils' Book and look at the Think and link activity. Ask them to TTYP and discuss the questions, then go through each question with the children, clarifying where necessary.
- Make sure the children know what the main events of the play are, and explain that they are going to re-tell the events to their partner, using a story map to help them.
- Ask the children to look at the story map on Pupils' Book p.35 and draw the children's attention to the *flashback* in the play, where the Judge is told of events that have already happened, and the role of the fly. Ask them to think about how they could make these parts of the play clear.
- Ask the children to use the story map to take turns to retell the events of the play to their partner.

Fiction: Playscripts

Curriculum link:
recording ideas

Daily log 📖

Purpose: for children to keep a personal log of notes, thoughts and ideas, collected from their reading and discussions. Some ideas will be used in their own writing

- Ask the children to look again at the story map from the Think and link activity on p.35 of their Pupils' Book. Tell them to write the numbers in their Daily log for each of the pictures from the story map.
- Ask the children to write notes beside each number to help them remember the main points of the play. Encourage them to include any cultural details that will add richness to the play.

discussion;
develop, agree on,
and evaluate
rules for effective
discussion

Big Question 💿

Purpose: for children to develop skills of argument and discussion through a mini enquiry session based on a philosophical question relating to the work of the day

- Display today's Big Question on **CD (file 2.4)**:

  Can two people disagree and both be right?

- Follow the process as explained on Day 1.

DAY 3

listening to a wide
range of fiction

The language of playscripts 💿

Purpose: for children to become familiar with particular words associated with playscripts

- Tell the children that they need to understand how a playscript works.
- Display **CD (file 3.1)** to show part of the playscript. Click 'TOL' to show think bubbles explaining what each part of the script is and how it helps the reader or the actors. Do the same for the second slide.
- Move to the next slide to display words related to playscripts. Ask the children to look at the first part of the playscript on pp.40–41 of their Anthology and to work with their partner to find examples of each feature in the playscript.
- You can print these words from **CD (file 3.2)** to display on your Playscript wall. Where possible, use the words in your teaching during the day and praise the children if they manage to use them too.

Re-read a script version 3 🅰 💿

Purpose: for children to gain a deeper understanding of the play and to see the full text for the first time

- Let the children follow their own copy of the text on pp.40–49 of the Anthology as they listen to the play on the **CD (file 2.3)**.

Exploring character 💿 🖨 🅰

Purpose: for children to use inference and deduction to gather information about Mr Lo from the text

- Before the lesson, print out copies of **CD (file 3.3)**, one for each set of partners.
- Ask the children to TTYP and discuss all that they know about the greedy merchant, Mr Lo. Take feedback and write some ideas on the board or a flipchart.
- Model using the text on pp.41–43 of the Anthology to find information about Mr Lo. For example, he thinks that he is an important and esteemed member of the community: "I am a respectable businessman." "I am a fine, upstanding member of the community…"
- Display **CD (file 3.3)**, showing the outline of a body, on screen or as a copy enlarged to A3. Explain that the information that you have just found is about how

Mr Lo sees *himself*, so you are going to write the quote from the playscript onto the *inside* of the body.

- Now TOL about the part of the play on p.42 in which Mr Lo edges towards the Judge and whispers to him that he is rich and can give the Judge a loan. Explain that this tells you that Mr Lo thinks he is powerful enough to talk to the Judge as an equal, so that goes on the inside of the body; and that you can also infer that Mr Lo is not as honest as he pretends to be. The Judge can see that Mr Lo is not being honest, so that goes on the *outside* of the body – it is how Mr Lo can be seen by another character in the play.
- Ask the children to TTYP to use the text to make another inference about Mr Lo. Take feedback and add the inferences to the inside or outside of the body as appropriate.
- TOL as you use Mr Lo's actions to make a deduction about how he thinks, e.g.

  I think that when Mr Lo refuses help to work out the riddle this shows that he is arrogant – he thinks Lan is inferior to him. So I would put superior to others *on the inside of the body because that is how Mr Lo sees himself.*

- Ask the children to TTYP to make a deduction about Mr Lo's character from his actions. Take feedback, noting any further ideas either inside or outside the body as appropriate.
- Give each set of partners a copy of **CD (file 3.3)**. Ask them to continue finding evidence about Mr Lo. Ask them to note on their copy of the body outline what it tells them about Mr Lo.

Daily log

Curriculum link: thinking aloud to explore and collect ideas; recording ideas

Purpose: for children to keep a personal log of notes, thoughts and ideas, collected from their reading and discussions. Some ideas will be used in their own writing

- Ask the children to TTYP and talk about their first impressions of the play, e.g. characters, setting, plot. Popcorn (see Introduction p.17) feedback.
- Tell the children that they are going to collect their initial thoughts about each of the characters. Choose one character and ask the children to TTYP to discuss their initial thoughts about them.
- Ask each set of partners to draw a mind map for each character (Lan, Kym, Mr Lo and the Judge). Ask the children to write brief notes and words about the character on to the mind map. Take feedback and discuss some of the children's ideas.
- Ask the children to write one or two sentences about each character in their Daily log.

Big Question ⓒ

discussion; develop, agree on, and evaluate rules for effective discussion

Purpose: for children to develop skills of argument and discussion through a mini enquiry session based on a philosophical question relating to the work of the day

- Display today's Big Question on the **CD (file 3.4)**:

  Which matters most – what you think about yourself or what other people think about you?

- Follow the process as explained on Day 1.

DAY 4

What do I want? How do I get it? ⓒ 🖨 🅰

Purpose: for children to explore the characters' motivations and subsequent actions

- Before the lesson, print a copy of **CD (file 4.2)** for each child.
- Tell the children that different characters want different things in the play. Some of the things they want are obvious and others less so. Explain that you are going to explore what different characters want and how they get it.

- Display **CD (file 4.1)** to show the What do I want? How do I get it? grid.
- TOL as you go through the grid (slides 1 and 2) for the first character, Mr Lo. Click 'Reveal' to show the entries in each column. Explain your thinking and ideas and then show the children how you locate the evidence in the playscript that proves your point.
- Give the children printed copies of **CD (file 4.2)**. Ask them to TTYP and fill out grids for Lan, Kym and the Judge using their Anthology pp.40–49 to locate their evidence.
- Collect feedback and give the children time to add to or amend their grids before pasting them into their Daily log.

Status game

Purpose: for children to see how your status can be shown by how you move

- Before the lesson, cut out sets of cards marked 1–4 from copies of **CD (file 4.3)**, enough sets for each child to have a card.
- Organise the children to work in groups of five.
- Give four children in each group a card, numbered 1–4. Explain that they should remember the number on their card without showing it or telling it to anyone else in their group.
- Display **CD (file 4.4)** to show the meaning of the numbers on the cards. Use MT/YT to read through the statuses, from 4, *superior*, to 1, *inferior*. Explain that the child in each group without a status card is the 'observer'.
- Ask the children to move around in role, showing their status through their movements. For example, if they are superior they might stand up straight and move with confidence; if they are inferior they might move with their head down, avoiding eye contact.
- Tell the children to watch the other members of their group. When they come close to another group member they need to act inferior to them if they think they are a lower status, or be imposing if they think they are a higher status.
- At the end of a few minutes of role-play, ask the observer to put the children in their group in status order.
- Ask the other children in each group to reveal the true order.
- Ask the children to TTYP to discuss which physical clues denoted different statuses. Take feedback and write some ideas on a flipchart.

> **Curriculum link:** preparing and rehearsing play scripts to perform

Performing the play A

Purpose: for children to read through the play taking parts, and to rehearse and perform the play

- Ask the children to get into groups of four and look at the playscript *The Fly and the Fool* on pp.40–49 of their Anthology. Ask them to share out the parts in the play.
- Remind the children of what they know about the characters: what they want, how they see themselves and how other people see them. Remind them about the Status game and how the characters might move to show their status.
- Ask the children to act out the play as a group. Give them time to work out how they want to move and to rehearse the play until they feel happy with their performance.
- Break the play down for each group to perform part of it, so that the script can be performed with all the children involved. Allow groups time to rehearse and polish their part of the play.
- You may wish to invite another class to come and watch the play.

Curriculum link: recording ideas; write for a range of purposes

Daily log

Purpose: for children to keep a personal log of notes, thoughts and ideas, collected from their reading and discussions. Some ideas will be used in their own writing

- Ask the children to write a few sentences about how it felt to perform the play. Ask them to TTYP to discuss whether they learned anything more about the characters from their performance.
- Ask the children to TTYP to discuss what advice they would give to another set of children who were thinking about performing the play.

discussion; develop, agree on, and evaluate rules for effective discussion

Big Question CD

Purpose: for children to develop their skills of argument and discussion through a mini enquiry session based on a philosophical question relating to the work of the day

- Display today's Big Question on the **CD (file 4.5)**:

  Do we always know what is fair or unfair?

- Follow the process as explained on Day 1.

DAY 5

reading for a range of purposes; justifying inferences with evidence

Most important? CD

Purpose: for children to explore the importance of individuals and events in the context of the play

- Tell the children that all the characters are important in the playscript, but they might think that some are more powerful than others.
- Display **CD (file 5.1)** showing a section of the playscript *The Fly and the Fool* over two slides. Ask the children to read the playscript aloud, chorally and with appropriate intonation and expression to convey impact.
- Click 'TOL' and use the think bubbles and/or your own ideas to discuss who seems to be the most powerful character in this part of the play. Make sure you use discursive language, e.g. *'On one hand it could be…but on the other hand…'*
- Draw the children into the TOL. Then ask them to TTYP to discuss which character they think is the most powerful and why. Take feedback and ensure the children can support their ideas.
- Ask the children to turn to their Anthology pp.48–49. Explain that you want them to TTYP to read the final part of the play (the section after the diamonds across the page) and then discuss who is the most powerful in this scene. Make sure they understand that there is not a right answer, you are just looking for their own ideas and opinions.
- Take feedback and give particular praise when the children use discursive language in the way that you modelled.
- Now ask the children to look at the Most important? activity on p.36 of their Pupils' Book. Ask them to TTYP to read the statements about what the most important moment is in the whole play. Tell them to TTYP to discuss which statement they agree with the most and which they agree with the least, and why.
- Collect feedback and lead a short whole-class discussion based on the children's responses.

inferring characters' feelings, thoughts and motives from their actions

Drama – Mr Lo on trial CD

Purpose: for children to infer a character's motives from their knowledge of the playscript

- Before the lesson, print a copy of the questions from **CD (file 5.2)**.
- Tell the children that Mr Lo is going to be put on trial for his deceitful behaviour. It will be a chance for the children to delve deeper into Mr Lo's motives and try to understand his actions.

- Ask the children to TTYP to describe to each other what Mr Lo's crime was. Take feedback and write the crime on the flipchart, e.g. *'Mr Lo, you are charged with deceitful behaviour, overcharging immensely for loans and lying in a court of law.'*
- Now ask the children to TTYP and discuss how Mr Lo could justify acting in the way he did. Encourage them to use all the information they have gathered about Mr Lo to help them. For example, we know Mr Lo thought of himself as a *businessman* so he might try to justify his remarkably huge fees as just being good at business. He says that Lan and Kym have *no respect for authority* so might feel that Lan's family have been disrespectful towards him.
- Take feedback from the children and write their ideas on the board or a flipchart. Encourage them to give their opinions and justify them.
- Organise the class into a semi-circle facing you. Tell the children that you are the Judge and they are all Mr Lo. Explain that you will ask a question and they will TTYP to prepare an answer. You will then ask a volunteer to stand up and answer your question, justifying their actions to you, the Judge. If any of the children feel they can do more to answer the question or justify their actions (as Mr Lo), they can stand up and add their voice.
- Explain that, as Judge, it is your role to keep the court in order and decide who should answer the questions. You can use the questions on printable **CD (file 5.2)** for guidance.
- At the end of the role-play, give your judgment. Has Mr Lo convinced you that he was not being deceitful and wilfully lying in court, or is he guilty of the charges?

Curriculum link:
exploring and recording ideas

Daily log

Purpose: for children to keep a personal log of notes, thoughts and ideas, collected from their reading and discussions. Some ideas will be used in their own writing

- Ask the children to reflect on how it felt to be Mr Lo. What did they find out about his character by acting in role? Take feedback.
- Ask the children to write about their findings in their Daily log.

discussion; develop, agree on, and evaluate rules for effective discussion

Big Question

Purpose: for children to develop skills of argument and discussion through a mini enquiry session based on a philosophical question relating to the work of the day

- Display today's Big Question on the **CD (file 5.3)**:

  How do we know when we have justice? *

- Follow the process as explained on Day 1.

  * This Big Question will be revisited on Day 11 – the first day of the Non-fiction week.

WRITING FICTION

DAY 6

What if not...?

Purpose: for children to understand how small changes can have big consequences in narratives

drawing inferences; participate in discussion about books

- Show a picture of Mr Lo in the dock on **CD (file 6.1)**. Then ask: *'What if not fair? What if the Judge took sides with one of the characters?'*
- TOL with some ideas to get the children started, e.g. *'If the Judge was not fair, he might have accepted Mr Lo's bribe and sided with Mr Lo. Lan's family might have had to pay back all of the money that Mr Lo was asking for.'*

- Ask the children to TTYP to discuss their own ideas about the What if not...? question. Take feedback.
- Now ask the children to TTYP and discuss the other questions in the What if not...? activity on p.37 of their Pupils' Book. Collect feedback and discuss the questions with the children, helping them to develop their ideas.

Read a folk tale

Purpose: for children to read the story on which their own playscript will be based

- Before the lesson, print copies of **CD (file 6.2)** for the whole class.
- Tell the children that you have found a traditional tale with similar themes to *The Fly and the Fool*. This tale is all about people who are greedy and who don't tell the truth. Explain that you think this tale would be a great basis for a play where a character has to explain their actions, just like the drama activity they did where Mr Lo was on trial.
- Tell the children that the traditional tale is called *Rumpelstiltskin*. Ask the children to TTYP to see if they know the story. Take feedback and make sure that the children know the main characters and the basic plot before you read it to them.
- Tell the children that you want them to look out for the themes of greed, dishonestly, riddles and the uncovering of the truth as you read the story to them.
- Give the children a copy of the story from the **CD (file 6.2)**. Ask them to follow as you read the story. Then ask them to TTYP and share any examples of the themes of the story. Take feedback and write their ideas onto a flipchart.
- Ask the children to TTYP and discuss which of the characters from the story they think should be put on trial and why. Take feedback and help the children expand their ideas. Write a crime (or crimes) on the flipchart for each of the characters they mention, e.g. *'Miller, you are charged with the crime of lying and possibly sending your daughter to her death just so you could feel important.'*

Build a character

> **Curriculum link:**
> inferring characters' feelings, thoughts and motives from their actions

Purpose: for children to be able to use details from the story to begin to build a character

- Before the lesson, print a copy of **CD (file 6.4)** for each child.
- Tell the children that you are thinking of writing a playscript in which Rumpelstiltskin is put on trial. Explain that in order to write a good playscript you really need to know the character, so you are going to build up your knowledge of Rumpelstiltskin.
- Ask the children to look at the story of *Rumpelstiltskin* on **CD (file 6.2)** and TTYP to find words and phrases that describe the character of Rumpelstiltskin. Take feedback.
- Display the **CD (file 6.3)** to show the blank Role on the wall figure, the bank of words and phrases for describing a character and the character statements.
- Use MT/YT to read the five character statements. Ask the children to help you to find one or more words that match up with each statement. Drag and drop the words into the figure, e.g. words to go with 'He is greedy' might be *selfish*, *crafty*, *grasping*, or *mercenary*.
- Give the children copies of their own Role on the wall figure from **CD (file 6.4)**. Tell them that they need to put the King on trial. Ask them to follow the instructions on the sheet to help them choose descriptions to write inside the figure.

Show, don't tell ⓒ ⒫

Purpose: for children to explore ways of developing characterisation by showing rather than telling

- Explain that the character statements in the previous activity *tell* us what the character is like or what they have done, and the words inside the figure *tell* us what kind of person they are. Say that you are now going to write some sentences that will *show* what a character is like.
- Use the **CD (file 6.5)** to display a sentence from *Rumpelstiltskin*. Use MT/YT to read it. Say that this sentence *tells* the audience that Rumpelstiltskin was planning all along to get something he wanted from Bethany. You are going to change it so that it *shows* this instead.
- Click 'Reveal' to display your *showing* ideas.
- Say the sentence: *'The goblin had a clever plan to get Bethany to give him something he really wanted, so he smiled and said, "Don't worry. I will help you spin the straw into gold."'* Using the *showing* ideas on screen, TOL and show what this might really look like:

  If I was an actor and I wanted to show that Rumpelstilskin was being devious *I might hunch my body and turn to the audience and* smile craftily *as I said "Don't worry."*
  I would make my voice sickly sweet *as I said that I would help Bethany, but I would* turn my face away *from her so she couldn't see the excited gleam in my eye because my wicked plan was working!*

- Ask the children to do their own mini-mime of Rumpelstiltskin. Tell them to freeze-frame and walk round commenting, using appropriate and varied vocabulary to describe what you see.
- Click 'Reveal' to display your completed *showing* sentences. TOL about how *telling* in the first piece of writing has been changed into *showing* in the second.
- Now ask the children to look at the Show, don't tell activity in their Pupils' Book p.37. Ask them to TTYP to decide how to turn the *telling* sentences into two or three *showing* sentences, e.g.

  In the morning, the King's eyes widened with excitement *at the huge room filled to the brim with gold. He said* furiously, *"Tomorrow you will spin another room of straw into gold and then you can be my wife, or else…you die."*

- When all the children have their sentences, ask them to choose one and write it in their Daily log.
- Collect feedback and write some good examples of *showing* sentences on the board or a flipchart.

Daily log

Curriculum link: discussing, exploring and recording ideas

Purpose: for children to keep a personal log of notes, thoughts and ideas, collected from their reading and discussions. Some ideas will be used in their own writing

- Ask the children to TTYP to discuss what the King would think if he was put on trial because of his greed. Ask: *'How would he show his feelings at first? Would he be furious and show his fury by ranting and raging? Or would he be so surprised that he would show his shock through silence?'* Take feedback and ask some children to act out how they think the King would show his feelings.
- Ask the children to write one or two sentences in their Daily log about how they imagine the King behaving.

Big Question

Purpose: for children to develop skills of argument and discussion through a mini enquiry session based on a philosophical question relating to the work of the day

Curriculum link:
discussion;
develop, agree on,
and evaluate
rules for effective
discussion

- Display today's Big Question on the **CD (file 6.6)**:

  Which is worse, greed or pride?

- Follow the process as explained on Day 1.

DAY 7

plan writing by discussing writing that is similar

Build a script 1

Purpose: for children to be able to see a script grow through three stages of development

- Remind the children that they heard two versions of *The Fly and the Fool* (Script versions 1 and 2) before they heard the whole playscript, to prepare them for reading the full script.
- Tell the children that you are going to show them two versions of your playscript, which you have called *On Trial*. Say that these versions prepared you to write the full script. Show the first version of your script on **CD (file 7.1)** and read it aloud to the children.
- Blank the screen and ask the children to TTYP to summarise the story. Ask one or two sets of partners to share their summaries and clarify where necessary.
- Explain that you are now going to show them another version with additional information, that has been developed into script form.

plan writing by discussing writing that is similar; recording ideas

Build a script 2

Purpose: for children to be able to see a script grow through three stages of development

- Open **CD (file 7.2)** to display the second version of your script over two slides. Read it aloud to the children. Ask them to TTYP to discuss how it differs from version 1, then take feedback.
- Click on 'TOL' and use this to build on the children's ideas, e.g. the script conventions you have added and how the dialogue conveys the story and more about the characters.
- Tell the children that there are no stage directions in your script and that you are going to explore how these can be added and why they are important.

Stage directions

Purpose: for children to understand how stage directions tell the actors how to move as well as how to say their dialogue

- Before the lesson, print a copy of **CD (file 7.4)** for each child.
- Display **CD (file 7.3)** and say that this is scene 1 from your script version 2. Tell the children that you are going to show them how important the stage directions are.
- Navigate to the next slide to show the same part of the playscript again, but this time with added stage directions. Click 'Highlights' to highlight the stage directions and explain that these do three things:
  - they set the scene, so we know where the characters are
  - they tell us how the characters are speaking and moving
  - they give us clues about how the characters are feeling.
- Draw the children's attention to *–ing* endings for stage directions which are verbs, e.g. *sitting, jumping, turning*.
- Navigate to the next slide to show scene 2 without any stage directions. Click on 'TOL' and use the prompts to discuss what stage directions need to be added.

- Give each child a copy of scene 2 from **CD (file 7.4)** and ask them to TTYP to read the scene. Then ask them to discuss what the setting of the scene is, how the characters are speaking and how the characters are moving. Choose one or two sets of partners to share their ideas.
- Now tell them to add stage directions to their copies of scene 2 in the spaces provided.
- Ask the children to turn to the Stage directions activity in their Pupils' Book pp.38–39 and to look at the more detailed version of scene 2. Organise the children into groups of three and ask them to act out the scene. Remind them to think carefully about the information that the stage directions give about the characters.
- Now ask the children to look at the questions in their Pupils' Book p.39. Guide them as they TTYP to discuss the questions and write their findings in their Daily log.

Curriculum link: understand the skills and processes that are essential for writing

Build a script 3 (CD)

Purpose: for children to see an example of writing that will provide a model for their own writing

- Display **CD (file 7.5)**. Explain that this is part of your final playscript, and that your purpose in writing it is to entertain and interest the audience or reader, and also to give them an insight into the motives behind Rumpelstiltskin's actions. Tell them that to do this you have added more stage directions, some extra information and some synonyms.
- Read the playscript to the children with appropriate intonation and emphasis.
- Click 'Highlights' and TOL about how the script has been developed.
- Ask the children to TTYP to discuss which part of the script is their favourite and why. Take feedback and build on their answers, drawing their attention to relevant features of the script.

justifying inferences with evidence from details stated and implied

Daily log

Purpose: for children to keep a personal log of notes, thoughts and ideas, collected from their reading and discussions. Some ideas will be used in their own writing

- Ask the children to TTYP to discuss their feelings about what the Judge said at the end of your playscript. Do they think that the King is as guilty as Rumpelstiltskin? Why? Take feedback and make sure they give a reason for their answer.
- Ask the children to write a sentence in their Daily log to say whether they think the King is guilty or not, and why.

discussion; develop, agree on, and evaluate rules for effective discussion

Big Question (CD)

Purpose: for children to develop skills of argument and discussion through a mini enquiry session based on a philosophical question relating to the work of the day

- Display today's Big Question on **CD (file 7.6)**:

  Should we forgive someone who has hurt us?
- Follow the process as explained on Day 1.

DAY 8

Curriculum link:
showing
understanding
through
intonation, tone,
volume and action

Drama – in the dock

Purpose: for children to improvise and explore ideas that they can use later in their writing

- Before the lesson, print out and cut in half the character information from **CD (file 8.1)**, one copy for each group of three.
- Organise the class into groups of three. Ask groups to nominate a leader, who in turn should choose children to represent the King, Rumpelstiltskin and the Judge.
- Tell the children that they are going to be put on trial in their role as the characters from the play and so they will need to understand their characters well. Tell them you have some information and one secret about the King and Rumpelstiltskin.
- Give each group a cut-up copy of **CD (file 8.1)**.
- Tell the children that the child in role as Judge is going to decide which of the others is the guiltiest of behaving dishonestly.
- The child in role as Judge should decide on the order in which the characters will speak. The other children, in role as their characters, should take it in turns to defend themselves, using all the information that they have. Tell them that they should justify their behaviour, and argue that the other character is guiltier than they are. When both the characters have spoken, the Judge should decide which one is the guiltiest.
- After the groups have completed their trials, gather feedback from the 'Judges' about who they felt was the guiltiest, and why.
- Ask the children to take a moment to reflect and write a few sentences in their Daily log about what they have discovered about the characters.

composing
and rehearsing
sentences orally;
creating settings,
characters, plot

Write a script 1

Purpose: for children to develop their confidence and skills in script planning and development

- Tell the children that they are going to develop scene 3 and finish your play.
- Display the start of scene 3 on **CD (file 8.2)** and read it with the children using MT/YT.
- Tell the children that the Judge is going to question the King. Click 'Reveal' and show the information and secret that they know about the King.
- Ask the children to TTYP to think of two questions that they would ask the King if they were the Judge. Take feedback and scribe the questions onto the board or a flipchart. You may need to add some of your own, e.g. *Why did you threaten to kill Bethany if she did not spin the straw into gold? What would you have done if she hadn't obeyed you? Why did you want to marry Bethany?*
- Tell the children to TTYP and think of the answers that the King might give to the Judge's questions. Take feedback and scribe their answers onto the board or a flipchart.
- Model turning one of the questions and answers into dialogue in script form.
- Ask the children to TTYP to think of some adverbs that could be added to show how things are said by the characters. Take feedback and use one or two of their ideas in your modelling.
- Now tell the children to use the questions and answers from the board or flipchart to start drafting their own continuation of scene 3, where the Judge questions the King.

composing
and rehearsing
sentences orally;
creating settings,
characters, plot

Write a script 2

Purpose: for children to use prompts to develop their scene further

- Tell the children that they are now ready to continue writing their scene. Remind them that it should be in script form and contain the Judge asking questions and the King's answers.

- Explain that they will now need to add stage directions, including adverbs to show how the characters are speaking.
- Ask the children to turn to the Write a script 2 activity in their Pupils' Book p.40 and to use the prompts to help them continue to write their scene. Remind them to use any useful notes from their Daily log and to recall the ideas they explored in their role-plays.
- Encourage the children to rehearse their opening sentence in their minds before they begin to write.
- Remind them of the dialogue you modelled but encourage them to use their own ideas.

Curriculum link:
discussing and recording ideas

Daily log

Purpose: for children to keep a personal log of notes, thoughts and ideas, collected from their reading and discussions. Some ideas will be used in their own writing

- Tell the children to TTYP and discuss what punishment they would give if they were the Judge and they found the King to be guilty. Take feedback.
- Write on the board or flipchart: *Judge: I find you, the King, guilty of being cruel and greedy. Your punishment will be…*
- Ask the children to complete the sentence in their Daily log.

discussion; develop, agree on, and evaluate rules for effective discussion

Big Question

Purpose: for children to develop skills of argument and discussion through a mini enquiry session based on a philosophical question relating to the work of the day

- Display today's Big Question on the **CD (file 8.3)**:

  Should people always be punished if they have done something wrong?

- Follow the process as explained on Day 1.

DAY 9

Write a script 3

Purpose: for children to develop their confidence and skills in script planning and development

creating settings, characters, plot; monitor whether their writing makes sense

- Before the lesson, print a copy of the TOL script from **CD (file 9.1)**.
- Tell the children that to complete the scene, both Rumpelstiltskin and the King will have the chance to give a final speech to persuade the Judge to let them go.
- Explain that you are going to write Rumpelstiltskin's final speech.
- Display **CD (file 9.2)** to show your first draft of a final speech for Rumpelstiltskin. Use MT/YT to read it with the children.
- Move through the screens and model how to develop the speech by dragging and dropping phrases into each sentence. TOL and encourage the children to offer their own ideas as you do this.
- Now expand the sentences, writing them on a flipchart and using a printed version of the TOL script on **CD (file 9.1)**. Edit the sentences further if you wish to, adding or changing words and phrases on the flipchart. Finally, write out your final versions.
- Tell the children that they are now going to write a final speech for the King. Ask them to turn to the Write a script 3 activity on p.40 of their Pupils' Book and to use the instructions to help them. Remind them that the King's secret is that he is not as rich as he pretends to be.
- Ask them to write their own developed version of the speech, including stage directions.

DAY 10

Share a script

Purpose: for children to read and share their playscripts

- Ask the children to read through their own scenes.
- Now tell them to re-read and underline their favourite or best parts. Ask them to share these with their partners and even act parts out to see how they work. Collect feedback on these best bits from partners.
- Make sure that any powerful words or phrases that the children have used are added to the Playscript wall.

Curriculum link: assessing the effectiveness of their own and others' writing

Evaluate and edit (CD)

Purpose: for children to evaluate their own and their partner's work against specific criteria and then discuss how they could improve their work

- Display **CD (file 10.1)** and read through the evaluation points using MT/YT.
- As a model, select an example of work where the writing has met the criteria, and share this with the other children, explaining why it works well.
- Tell the children to take turns to read their partner's writing in pairs and discuss together how well each piece of writing has met the criteria.
- Ask children to discuss at least two changes they could make to improve their work.

proofread for spelling and punctuation errors

Proofread

Purpose: for children to proofread their work and make changes to improve the accuracy of their grammar, punctuation and spelling

- Now ask the children to proofread their work. If you have noticed that several children need to improve on a particular aspect of spelling, grammar or punctuation, use this as a focus for the Proofread activity. Write an example which includes common errors from the children's writing and use this as a model.
- The children should always be checking for standard use of punctuation and correct spelling of common exception words.
- The following points would be particularly relevant for this Unit:
  - checking spelling of ambitious vocabulary choices (i.e. those borrowed from the Pupils' Book or Anthology text)
  - making sure the correct conventions have been used to set out the playscript.

discussion; develop, agree on, and evaluate rules for effective discussion

Very Big Question (CD)

Purpose: for children to develop a willingness to broaden or revise their opinions through exploring one of the Big Questions in more depth

- See Unit 1 Day 10 for teaching notes on the Very Big Question (p.41).

READING AND WRITING NON-FICTION

Linked via a Big Question, the Non-fiction week focuses on developing children's ability to evaluate evidence. They read an explanation about how the police use different sorts of evidence to prove who has committed a crime. Next they look at several pieces of evidence and choose two to present to a 'court'. They must weigh up which pieces of evidence will be the most useful in proving who committed the crime. See p.110 for the daily timetable for the Non-fiction week.

Non-fiction

Reading

Children will:

- understand the key features of explanation texts
- show their understanding by summarising explanations they have read
- expand their vocabulary by learning some technical language and finding the definitions of words they don't know.

Writing

Key writing purpose to be shared with the children:

To select two pieces of evidence to write about, and then present them to a 'court'.

Writing evaluation to be shared with the children

My evidence:

- has a clear introduction and is well organised, based on my plan and the notes I took
- balances the strengths and flaws carefully to show that it is reliable
- uses technical language
- includes supporting images and shares key words and phrases with my audience.

Grammar:

- includes correct use of apostrophes to show who or what something belongs to.

See the Planning section of the Software ('Timetables' tab) for a printable version of the Writing purpose and evaluation.

DAY 11

Curriculum link:
reading for a range
of purposes

Think and link

Purpose: for children's interest in evidence to be stimulated via one of the Big Questions they have explored

- Display the Big Question from Day 5 on the **CD (file 5.3)**:

  How do we know when we have justice?

- Ask the children to TTYP to recall what they discussed before. Take feedback. Write some of the children's ideas about what justice is on a flipchart. Explain to the children that sometimes justice happens in a court of law, e.g. when someone accused of a crime is brought to trial. In order to convict a person of a crime the court needs to see the evidence that proves they are guilty. There are many types of evidence that the police can find and collect.
- Ask the children to TTYP and discuss what types of evidence they have heard of that can be used by the police to track and help convict criminals. Take feedback and write their ideas on a flipchart.
- Tell the children that they will be exploring how the police use evidence to solve a crime. They will look at the different types of evidence and decide which they would use in a court of law to try to prove whether a person accused of a crime is guilty. First, they need to find out about the different types of evidence.

discussing words
and phrases
that capture the
reader's interest
and imagination

Word power

Purpose: for children to understand some technical language they will encounter when they read the text

committed	victim	reconstruction	suspect

- Tell the children that they will need to be familiar with some specialist language in order to fully understand the text they are about to read and also to help them when they are writing later on.
- Display **CD (file 11.1)**. Use MT/YT to read the words and definitions. Ask the children to TTYP and discuss which is the correct definition for the first word: *committed*. Drag the correct definition next to the word. Model using the word in a sentence, e.g. '*It was not clear who had* committed *the crime.*'
- Repeat for the remaining words.
- Ask the children to take turns to read the words and their definitions in the Word power activity on p.41 of their Pupils' Book.
- Print out the words, definitions and some example sentences from the **CD (file 11.2)** to display on the Evaluating evidence wall.

Explanations

Purpose: for children to read the explanation text for the first time

- Tell the children that they are going to read an explanation of how crimes are solved on pp.50–53 of their Anthology.
- Explain that they need to read the information, including the five tips, in order. Ask them to TTYP and summarise each tip that they have read before they move on.
- Ask them to write any words that they are unsure of in their Daily log, to be used in the next activity.
- Once they have read 'Junior Detective!', ask the children to TTYP and discuss which of the different ways of gathering evidence they found most interesting and why. Take feedback and write the main ideas on the board or a flipchart.

- Ask the children to TTYP and see if they can find anything in the text that made them think that one type of evidence was more reliable than any other. Take feedback.

Word detectives

Dictionaries will be required in this part of the lesson.

Purpose: for children to increase their vocabulary by identifying and understanding words they are unsure of

- Ask the children to look in their Daily log at the words that they were unsure of in the previous activity. Explain to the children that if we are unsure of what a word means we can look at the rest of the sentence to help us to work it out.
- Ask them to TTYP and see if they can help their partner understand any of their words. Take feedback, choose a word and model writing a simple definition.
- Tell the children that they are going to work in pairs to write simple definitions for up to four of the words that they have written down. Ask them to see if they can work out what they mean by looking at the word in context in their Anthology. Once they have come up with a definition for a word they can use a dictionary to check it, then write the definition in their Daily log. Point out that sometimes the context doesn't help much and so we *have* to look up a word in the dictionary to understand its meaning.
- When they are happy with their definition for a word, ask them to add a short sentence to their Daily log which uses the word. Take feedback and allow two or three sets of partners to share their sentences with the class.

Grammar: plurals, possession and apostrophes ⓒⒹ Ⓐ ⓅⒷ ⒽⒷ

Curriculum link:
Year 4 Grammar
indicating
possession by using
the possessive
apostrophe with
singular and plural
nouns

Purpose: for children to develop their understanding of the grammatical difference between plural and possessive 's' and the correct use of apostrophes to mark plural and singular possession

- Remind the children that *singular* words are used when we are talking or writing about only one of something and *plural* words are used when we are talking or writing about more than one of something.
- Display **CD (file 11.3)** to show a chart. Use MT/YT to read each word in *singular* and *plural* form. Say that all of these words can be made into plurals just by adding 's' to the end.
- Ask the children to write the heading *Singular and plural forms of words* in their Daily log and then to look at the first paragraph of the 'Junior Detective!' text on p.50 of the Anthology. Tell them to TTYP to find the plural form of these words as you call them out, and to write them under the heading in their log in both the singular and plural forms: *thousand, step, system, criminal, pound, diamond.*
- Explain there is another reason for adding an 's' to some words and that it is called the *possessive 's'*. Use MT/YT and TTYP to say the term *possessive 's'*.
- Tell the children that here the word *possess* means to belong to someone, so the 's' is showing who or what something or someone belongs to. Navigate to the next slide on **CD (file 11.3)** to show a chart with examples. Read it out chorally with the children and then ask them to TTYP to share what kind of punctuation mark they have noticed in the examples. Ask for a choral response and check that they have picked out the *apostrophe*.
- Move to the next slide to show the *Oxford Junior Dictionary* entry for the word *apostrophe* and its pronunciation. Explain that the apostrophe before the 's' shows us that something belongs to someone.

- Navigate to the next slide to show a highlighted passage from the 'Junior Detective!' text. Point out the words with possessive apostrophes and the words that tell us what it is that belongs to someone.
- Tell the children that there is one example of a word with a possessive apostrophe in the Tip 2 section of the 'Junior Detective!' text on p.51 of their Anthology. Ask them to TTYP to find the example (*people's*). Choose two sets of partners to share their answer and question them further to make sure they understand what it describes as belonging to the people (*memories*).
- Remind them that the apostrophe is always placed *before* the 's' when the proper noun or noun is singular. Explain that if the proper noun or noun is plural, we put the apostrophe *after* the 's'. Move to the next slide to show some examples.
- Now ask them to look at the Grammar: plurals, possession and apostrophes activity on p.42 of their Pupils' Book. Explain the activity and ask them to complete it with their partners.
- Choose a set of partners to share their choice for the first sentence and their reasons. Check their understanding and clarify if necessary. Repeat the process for each sentence.

Homework Book pp.15–16 provides further practice on plurals, possession and apostrophes.

Curriculum link: use and understand grammatical terminology

Daily log 🅿️🅱️

Purpose: for children to keep a personal log of notes, thoughts and ideas, collected from their reading and discussions. Some ideas will be used in their own writing

- Ask the children to write the heading *Apostrophes for possession* in their Daily log. Display **CD (file 11.4)** and ask them to TTYP to decide how to complete the sentence to give clear, correct information. Ask them to copy it down and complete it in their Daily log.
- Ask them to find an example of this from the activity they have just completed on p.42 of their Pupils' Book and to write it underneath their completed sentence.
- Click 'Reveal' and repeat the process using the second sentence.
- Choose different sets of partners to share their answers and the examples they have chosen. Make sure they have understood where to place the possessive apostrophe for singular and plural proper nouns and nouns.

DAY 12

learn the conventions of different types of writing

Zoom in on explanations 💿 🅰️

Purpose: for children to become familiar with some of the key language features associated with explanations

- Display **CD (file 12.1)**. Talk through the key features one at a time. For each feature, explain it to the children and then ask them to TTYP to find an example in the Anthology text pp.50–53. Take feedback, then move on to the next key feature.
- Clear up any misconceptions and make sure they understand what each key feature does.
- Now display **CD (file 12.2)**. Show the children how the author has made a text box to explain a technical term (*CSI*) in greater detail, and click 'Highlights' to show the technical language. Ask them to TTYP to find the next text box in their Anthology on p.53 and to work out which technical term it is explaining. Take feedback.

Non-fiction: Evaluating evidence

Curriculum link:
understand,
through being
shown these,
the skills and
processes that
are essential
for writing for
different purposes
and audiences

Deconstruction 1

Purpose: for children to learn how to take notes from a variety of source materials

- Tell the children that they have been asked to be expert witnesses in a court case. They have been given some pieces of evidence and they need to decide which piece it would be best to use in court and why.
- Display the evidence on the **CD (file 12.3)**. Go through each slide and discuss the type of evidence presented. Ask the children to use their Anthology pp.50–53 and TTYP to decide which type of evidence is presented on each slide. Take feedback.
- Explain to the children that they can't keep the evidence. It has to stay in the central evidence office, so they will have to take notes which are good enough for them to refer to and build on later. Tell them that you are going to show them how to take notes from one of the sources.
- Show screen 2, the evidence given by a witness, and TOL as you go through the process of taking notes, writing on a flipchart. Make sure you show the children how to include the facts in full, where needed, and when they can shorten words or even use acronyms.

write for a range
of real purposes
and audiences;
using simple
organisational
devices

Write 1

Purpose: for children to assess the source materials and make notes

- Before the lesson, print a copy of **CD (file 12.4)** for each child.
- Tell the children that they need to choose the two most reliable pieces of evidence to take notes from. Explain that if they choose wisely the two pieces of evidence should be enough to prove whether the accused is guilty. Ask the children to TTYP to make their choices. Remind them that they can make different choices from their partners.
- Give the children the source material printed out from **CD (file 12.4)** to use for note-taking. Those children who have chosen to use the audio interview can listen to it again on **CD (file 12.3)**, slide 1.
- When the children have finished their note-taking, ask them to swap notes with their partner. Ask them to check that they can understand their partner's notes. Make sure that the writer can explain any acronyms they have used and that they have provided enough information.

recording ideas

Daily log

Purpose: for children to keep a personal log of notes, thoughts and ideas, collected from their reading and discussions. Some ideas will be used in their own writing

- Tell the children that when a police artist sketches a suspect, it's called an artist's impression. Say that they are going to write a description of someone which could be used to make an artist's impression.
- Tell them to choose a famous person but not to tell anyone who it is. Ask the children to write some sentences in their Daily log to describe the appearance of their famous person.
- Tell the children to TTYP and to read their description to their partner, who should try and guess which famous person it is. Partners should then swap over.
- Choose two or three children to share their descriptions with the whole class.

DAY 13

Curriculum link:
retrieve and
record information
from non-fiction;
participate in
discussion,
listening to what
others say

Deconstruction 2

Purpose: for children to understand how to structure their evidence

- Display your plan on **CD (file 13.1)** based on the evidence you have chosen. TOL as you decide which order you are going to put your notes into so that the strongest features of the evidence go first and the weaknesses are explained at the end. Drag and drop your notes onto the table. TOL as you drop the note 'The statement was taken soon after the robbery' next to the question 'Why is it reliable?', explaining the importance of taking witness statements while the event is still fresh in the witness's mind.
- Point out the flaws section on the table and TOL as you drop the note 'She tried to write down what she had seen but was too shaken up' into the box, explaining why this could be a possible flaw.
- Ask the children to TTYP and look at their own notes to decide which their strongest piece of evidence is. Take feedback.

using non-fiction,
know what
information they
need to look for
and be clear about
the task

Write 2   **PB** **A**

Purpose: for children to assess the evidence in order to plan their writing

- Before the lesson, print a copy of **CD (file 13.3)** for each child.
- Tell the children that they are going to hear some additional evidence that has come to light. Explain that they will need to make notes in their Daily log about what the evidence is, why it might be reliable, and any flaws in the evidence. Write these prompts on the board or a flipchart for children to refer to as they listen to the evidence. Play the audio on **CD (file 13.2)** twice to give them a chance to complete their notes.
- Tell they children that they can decide whether or not they want to use this new evidence. Remind them they can only use two pieces of evidence, so the new evidence would have to replace one of their current choices.
- Give out copies of the evidence planner from **CD (file 13.3)**. Ask the children to use it and the prompts on p.43 of their Pupils' Book to help them plan their assessment of the evidence.
- Remind them to look at the original explanation in their Anthology pp.50–53 to help them make notes about how the evidence is collected and what the flaws in it might be.

building a rich and
varied vocabulary

Daily log

Purpose: for children to keep a personal log of notes, thoughts and ideas, collected from their reading and discussions. Some ideas will be used in their own writing

- Before the lesson, print a copy of **CD (file 13.5)** for each child.
- Show the children the technical words on **CD (file 13.4)**.
- Give out the printed copies of **CD (file 13.5)**. Tell the children that they have to TTYP to match the words and their definitions, drawing a line between them.
- At the end of the activity ask the children to feed back. Click 'Reveal' on the **CD (file 13.4)** to show the correct definitions for the children to check their work.
- Tell the children to choose two or three of the technical words that they think will be most useful when writing about their evidence. Tell them to write the definitions for the technical words that they have chosen into their Daily log, and to include the words in their plan.

DAY 14

Curriculum link:
discussing writing similar to that which they are planning to write in order to understand and learn from its structure, grammar and vocabulary

Deconstruction 3

Purpose: for children to see an example of written evidence and to understand the writing process

- Tell the children that you are ready to begin writing, based on your strongest piece of evidence. Say that your aim is to explain to the court why your evidence should be included in the trial. Your job is to make sure that the court understands how the evidence was collected and why it is reliable. Explain that it is also important to explain why your evidence may be flawed. Remind the children that, as they have two pieces of evidence, they may be able to show how their second piece of evidence fills in any 'gaps' left by the first.
- Use the TOL script on the **CD (file 14.1)** to model writing about your evidence. Draw the children's attention to the way you have used apostrophes to show plural and singular possession in the words *witness'* and *man's*.

Write 3

organising paragraphs around a theme

Purpose: for children to write about their evidence, including an introduction and a conclusion

- Tell the children that they are now ready to present their evidence to the court.
- Remind them to write a short introduction that explains who, where and what their evidence is about.
- Remind them that they should write about the piece of evidence that they think is strongest first, and structure their paragraph following the plan they created earlier. They should then do the same with their second piece of evidence. The final paragraph should sum up what they have found.
- Remind the children to have their plan and notes to hand as they write.

DAY 15

Write 3 (continued)

Purpose: for children to write about their evidence as independently as possible

- Continue the writing process from Day 14.
- Once the children have written about their evidence, ask them to TTYP to read it aloud to their partner.
- Encourage the children to make any changes they feel are necessary at this time.

Proofread

proofread for spelling and punctuation errors

Purpose: for children to proofread their work and make changes to improve the accuracy of their grammar, punctuation and spelling

- Now ask the children to proofread their work. If you have noticed that several children need to improve on a particular aspect of spelling, grammar or punctuation, use this as a focus for the Proofread activity. Write an example which includes common errors from the children's writing and use this as a model.
- The children should always be checking for standard use of punctuation and correct spelling of common exception words.
- The following points would be particularly relevant for this Unit:
    - checking spelling of ambitious vocabulary choices
    - checking that any apostrophes have been used correctly to show possession
    - checking that technical language has been spelled correctly.

Publish and present

Purpose: for children to present their evidence to the 'court'

- Tell the children that they are going to present their evidence. If presentation software is available, the children could use computers to create a slideshow. If not, they should work on a poster instead.
- Tell them that their presentation poster or slides should show only keywords and phrases, along with supporting images, to help them get their ideas across to the audience. Show the children your slideshow on the **CD (file 15.1)**. Present your evidence using the slideshow.
- Emphasise to the children that their presentation should only have key words and phrases and not every word of their written evidence.
- Give the children time to create their final slideshow or presentation.
- Children should then deliver their presentations to their partners or to small groups.

Evaluate and edit

Purpose: for children to evaluate their own and their partner's work against specific criteria and then discuss how they could improve their work

- Display **CD (file 15.2)** and read through the evaluation points using MT/YT.
- As a model, select an example of work where the written evidence and presentation met the criteria, and share this with the other children, explaining why it worked well.
- Tell the children to take turns to read their partner's evidence and discuss in pairs how well each piece of writing and presentation met the criteria.
- Ask children to discuss at least two changes they could make to improve their work.

Fiction: Stories with a historical setting
Non-fiction: Newspapers

Timetable

WEEK 1 Reading fiction *Runaways!*

Day 1	Day 2	Day 3	Day 4	Day 5
The story store	Word power 🖶	Special phrases 🖶	Re-read a story version 3	Retell the story
Read a story version 1	Read a story version 3	Re-read a story version 3	Character	Summarising the story 🖶
Context 🖶	Historical detectives	Forum theatre	Dramatic reconstruction 🖶	Daily log
Read a story version 2	Grammar: standard English	Daily log	Daily log	Big Question
Daily log	Daily log	Big Question	Big Question	
Big Question	Big Question			

WEEK 2 Writing fiction *Runaways!*

Day 6	Day 7	Day 8	Day 9	Day 10
What if not...?	Build a story 1	Role-play	Write a story 3	Evaluate and edit
Build a character	Build a story 2	Write a story 1 🖶		Proofread
Daily log	Build a story 3	Write a story 2		Very Big Question
Big Question	Daily log	Daily log 🖶		
	Big Question	Big Question		

WEEK 3 Reading and writing non-fiction Newspapers

Day 11	Day 12	Day 13	Day 14	Day 15
Think and link	Key features	Deconstruction 2 🖶	Deconstruction 3	Write 3 (continued)
Introduction	Deconstruction 1 🖶	Complex sentences 🖶	Write 3 🖶	Evaluate and edit
Word power 🖶	Write 1 🖶	Write 2	Daily log	Proofread
Newspapers	Daily log			Publish and present
Daily log				

🖶: shows that a file should be printed out from the Software.

136

Overview of the Unit

In this Unit, the children are introduced to a story with a historical setting: *Runaways!* by Jim Eldridge. They will explore the setting and use it to immerse themselves in the story. The setting and period will then provide inspiration for their own writing.

In the Non-fiction week, the children will broaden their knowledge of the Victorian period by looking through journalistic texts that are typical of the period. For more information about the Non-fiction week and the Non-fiction writing evaluation criteria, see p.155.

Where appropriate, the children will be encouraged to develop an awareness of audience and purpose in relation to the fiction and non-fiction texts they are reading and writing.

Teacher modelling is provided in the teaching notes, Software and the Pupils' Book, supporting the children's writing at every stage in the Fiction and Non-fiction weeks.

The Homework Book provides a homework activity related to the content of this Unit for each of the three weeks.

Fiction

Reading

Children will:

- engage with the historical context of *Runaways!* to develop their understanding of the plot, setting and characters
- explore how Jim Eldridge uses *showing* not *telling* to give the reader clues about the characters through their dialogue, actions and reactions
- develop their understanding of plot by summarising the most important moments in the story
- look in detail at a section of the story to explore a character's thoughts.

Writing

Key writing purpose to be shared with the children:

To use the historical setting and characters from Runaways! *to write a new part of the story from one character's point of view.*

Writing evaluation to be shared with the children

My story:

- is written from John's or Hannah's point of view
- has characters that seem real because I have used their speech and actions to *show* (rather than *tell*) the reader what they are thinking and feeling
- has historical references to describe the setting.

Grammar:

- uses the first person and past tense, because I am writing in role as a character
- may include standard and non-standard English for dialogue, depending on which character is speaking.

See the Planning section of the Software ('Timetables' tab) for a printable version of the Writing purpose and evaluation.

Fiction: Stories with a historical setting
Runaways! by Jim Eldridge

READING FICTION

Resources

PB Pupils' Book, pp.44–53

A Anthology, pp.54–67

CD CD on Interactive whiteboard, Unit 5

GB Grammar Bank on CD

HB Homework Book, pp.17–20

DAY 1

Curriculum link: listening to and discussing a wide range of fiction, identifying themes

The story store   (CD)

Background information: In 1867, Thomas Barnardo set up a 'Ragged School' in the East End of London, where poor children could get shelter and a basic education. In Victorian times he was known as Dr Barnardo, so he is referred to as such throughout this Unit. Today, Barnardo's is active in every region of the UK, helping children in distress. There are plenty of sources of further information about Barnado's on the internet.

Purpose: for children to become familiar with the historical setting of the story

- Ask the children to TTYP (Turn to your partner) and share what they know about the Victorians. Take feedback and record some answers on the board or flipchart.
- Ask the children to TTYP to discuss what they know about what happened to some children during Victorian times. Prompt discussion by asking: '*What makes someone an orphan?*' Take feedback, clarifying where necessary. Record some of their responses on the board or a flipchart.
- Display **CD (file 1.1)** to show some pictures from Victorian times. Read the captions aloud to the children. Pause after each slide and ask the children to TTYP to discuss what they have learned about the Victorians. Explain any words that the children may not be familiar with, e.g. *sanitation*.
- At the end of the slideshow add these ideas to the board or a flipchart and review all the information gathered so far. Draw attention to the setting and to the orphans. Explain that they are going to hear a story about orphans that is set in London.

predicting

Read a story version 1   (CD)

Before the lesson, you may wish to watch the video demonstrating Read a story version 1 (with a Year 5 story). This can be found in the Extras section of the software.

Purpose: for children to become familiar with Story version 1, the bare bones of Runaways!

- Read Story version 1 aloud all the way through to the children but do not reveal the ending.

Story version 1
1. A girl and her little brother have to escape from the workhouse.
2. They run away just before the gates are locked for the night.
3. They spend the first night hiding in a doorway.
4. The little brother is ill.
5. The big sister needs to make some money so that they can eat.
6. She asks for help from another street child.
7. The street child tells them to search for coins and metal in the mud by the river.
8. The sister tries this but does not find any coins.
9. They have no money to eat and the little brother is getting weaker.
10. They huddle in a shop doorway for the night.
11. Suddenly, an adult's voice addresses them.

- Use MT/YT (My turn/Your turn) and TTYP for each point. Use special emphasis to make the sentences memorable and to convey meaning. This will help the children to 'hold' the basic story in their minds.
- Ask the children to TTYP to share what happens in the story.
- Now display Story version 1 on **CD (file 1.2)** so the children can see the text and note how much of it they have remembered.

Context

Purpose: for children to make connections between the story and its historical setting

- Tell the children that things were very different for children in Victorian times. Explain that the children in the story were orphans, which means that they had no mother, father or other close family to look after them, so they were looked after in a workhouse. People feared the workhouse as it was a terrible place to live.

- Ask the children to TTYP to recall what they remember about workhouses from the slideshow. Take feedback and expand on the children's responses, making links to how the people living during the time must have felt, e.g. '*Yes, there were lots of rules, and harsh punishments for breaking them. It must have been very frightening, especially if you didn't have any parents to protect or comfort you.*'

- Display **CD (file 1.3)** to show a short slideshow. Explain that they are going to look at some jobs that are mentioned in the story. Navigate through the slides and read each caption aloud. Pause after each slide and ask the children to TTYP to discuss what they think about each job. Take feedback and encourage class discussion.

- You may wish to print the pictures from **CD (file 1.4)** to display on your Story wall for this Unit.

Read a story version 2

Curriculum link: predicting; identifying how language, structure and presentation contribute to meaning

Purpose: for children to examine how Story version 2 provides additional information for the reader and to become more familiar with the story before they hear the full version

- Read Story version 2 aloud to the children. Explain that it has been developed.

Story version 2

1. Hannah overhears the Master of the Workhouse trying to sell her brother, John, to a chimney sweep. She knows her brother is too weak to survive going up chimneys, so she decides they have to escape from the workhouse.
2. They run away by stealing out of the workhouse just before the gates are locked for the night.
3. They spend the first night hiding in a doorway, sheltering from the harsh wind and rain.
4. The cold and rain make John cough so much that his body shakes.
5. The next morning, Hannah goes out in search of money so that they can eat. They can't beg as they might be spotted and returned to the workhouse.
6. They arrive at Regent Street and Hannah watches a girl earn money sweeping the road for a rich man. Hannah asks if she can borrow the girl's broom and be a crossing-sweeper.
7. The girl says no but tells them about mudlarks.
8. Hannah and John search for coins in the oozing mud of the River Thames but don't find any coins.
9. John is starving hungry and becoming weaker.
10. They find refuge in a shop doorway for the night.
11. Suddenly, out of the gloom an adult's voice says, "So. What have we here?"

- Display **CD (file 1.5)** to show Story version 2 across two slides.
- Click 'Highlights' to highlight the parts of the story that have changed. The yellow highlighting shows the areas that give us more information, including why the children had to escape the workhouse, their names, the passage of time, names of the places in the story and what the mysterious adult says to the children. The blue highlighting shows us new vocabulary, which gives us a clearer picture of what is happening in the story.

- TOL (Think out loud) and use TTYP to share how this extra information changes the pictures in our minds as we hear the story. Link what they have read and heard so far with their knowledge about the workhouse, Victorian London and the jobs that children had.
- Remove Story version 2 from the board and ask the children to TTYP to take turns to tell the story to their partner. Challenge them to include as much of the new information and vocabulary as possible.
- Now display Story version 2 on the **CD (file 1.5)** again so the children can see the text and note how much of it they have remembered.

Curriculum link: discussing ideas and predicting

Daily log (CD)

Purpose: for children to keep a personal log of notes, thoughts and ideas, collected from their reading and discussions. Some ideas will be used in their own writing

- Display **CD (file 1.6)**. Ask the children to TTYP to discuss the questions and then write down their prediction for the story ending in their Daily log.

discussion; develop, agree on, and evaluate rules for effective discussion

Big Question (CD)

Purpose: for children to develop their skills of argument and discussion through a mini enquiry session based on a philosophical question relating to the work of the day

- Display today's Big Question on **CD (file 1.7)**:

  Is it everyone's responsibility to help those in need? *

- Ask the children to TTYP to talk about this question. Collect feedback and write some responses on the board.
- Click 'Prompts' to show some statements that may help to encourage discussion.

  * This Big Question will be revisited on Day 11 – the first day of the Non-fiction week.

DAY 2

discussing words and phrases that capture the reader's interest and imagination

Word power

Purpose: for children to encounter strong descriptive words and phrases and think about how they help the reader to engage with a story

steal out   fury   despondently   trudged   refuge   wary   awed

- Explain to the children that some of the words and phrases that the writer uses in the story are powerful because they help us to create clear pictures in our minds.
- Display **CD (file 2.1)** to show the Power words. Read the words and their definitions aloud using MT/YT.
- Navigate to the next screen and drag the words into the box, one at a time. TOL to describe the images these words and phrases create for you as a reader, e.g.

  When I see the word fury I make a link to the word angry, but I know that fury is far stronger that anger so I imagine someone feeling a deep rage. I can see them clenching their fists and their body going stiff as if ready to attack ... I wonder if Hannah feels fury when she overhears the Master of the Workhouse selling her brother? I could use that idea to create a sentence: Hannah felt the fury build up inside her as she heard the Master of the Workhouse selling her brother to the chimney sweep.

- After you have done this for each word, ask the children to TTYP to try to use each of the words in a sentence. Take feedback.
- Print the words and their definitions from **CD (file 2.2)** to display on your Story wall for this Unit.

Curriculum link: checking that the text makes sense, asking questions, drawing inferences

Read a story version 3 🄰 (teacher only)

Purpose: for children to hear and enjoy the full version of the story for the first time

- Tell the children that they are now going to hear the whole story for the very first time. TOL about which parts you are looking forward to.
- Turn to pp.54–63 in the Anthology and read the story *Runaways!* to the children with great enjoyment and appropriate intonation. Perform the story by using different voices etc. where appropriate.
- Make links to the predictions the children made in their Daily log and ask them to TTYP to share their predictions and discuss what they think will happen when Hannah and John go to the shelter in Stepney Causeway. Take feedback.

Historical detectives ⓒⅅ

Purpose: for children to identify and explore words and phrases that help create the historical setting of the story

- Tell the children that the author, Jim Eldridge, does not *tell* us that this story is set in the past. Instead he gives us information to *show* us that the story isn't set in the present. Remind the children of the information that they have learned about Victorian London, such as the jobs that children did.
- Ask them to TTYP to share any jobs mentioned in the story that would tell the reader that the story was set in the past. Take feedback and write the children's ideas on the board or a flipchart under the heading *Jobs*.
- Display slide 1 of **CD (file 2.3)** to show an extract from the story and read it aloud.
- Now read the extract again, pausing to TOL about the images that appear in your mind as you read each sentence. Say that in the first three sentences Regent Street is described in such a way that it could be Regent Street today.
- As you TOL point out to the children that the third sentence of the second paragraph has some information in it that makes you think the story is set in the past: *With so much horse-drawn traffic in London…*
- Ask the children to TTYP to see if they can find any other words, phrases or sentences that tell them that the story is set in the past. Take feedback and write the children's ideas onto the board or a flipchart.
- Navigate to the next slide to show the second extract. Point out that this extract contains some dialogue and read it aloud (the extract is spread across two slides).
- Explain to the children that the first sentence gives two big clues about the historical setting of the story: the *Master of the Workhouse* and the *chimney sweep*.
- Ask the children to TTYP to see if they can find any other words, phrases or sentences that tell them that the story is set in the past. Take feedback and write the children's ideas onto the board or a flipchart.
- Use the notes you have recorded on the board or flipchart to summarise what you have found out about the historical setting of the story. Ask the children to TTYP to talk about which of the clues in the text gave them the strongest image of the Victorian setting and why. Take feedback.

Year 4 Grammar learn about some of the differences between standard and non-standard English, e.g. in dialogue for characters

Grammar: standard English ⓒⅅ 🄿🄱 🄷🄱

Purpose: for children to become aware of standard and non-standard forms of English

- Display **CD (file 2.4)**. Explain to the children that it is an extract from *Oliver Twist* by Charles Dickens, who was a famous Victorian writer. Tell them that this extract is about the meals in the workhouse and it helps to show them how hungry the children in the story were. Read it aloud to the children (it goes over two slides).

- Tell the children that whenever writers create dialogue, they have to try to make it sound realistic and as close to how people really speak to each other as possible. Say that this means they might include ways of speaking that are *non-standard English*.
- Explain that standard English is a way of speaking and writing that follows a set of rules – but that sometimes the rules are broken for effect.
- Tell them that in the story *Oliver Twist*, there are lots of examples of characters speaking in ways that break the usual grammar rules because the writer, Charles Dickens, wanted to portray how some people in that area of London spoke.
- Explain that you have a piece of dialogue that Charles Dickens wrote for a character in the story called Mr Gamfield, a cruel chimney sweep. Move to the next slide of the **CD (file 2.4)** to display the extract. Read the dialogue aloud, with appropriate intonation and slight exaggeration to show it is a 'larger than life' character speaking. (The original spelling has been preserved in the extract.)
- Ask the children to TTYP to share ideas about what they think about Mr Gamfield's dialogue. Choose two or three sets of partners to feed back briefly. Say that you are now going to read Mr Gamfield's speech as if it was written in standard English, following the rules of grammar.
- Click 'Reveal' on the CD screen to display the extract in standard English and read it aloud. Point to the relevant words as you explain that the noun *boys* is plural and we use *are* as the correct present tense verb.
- Now remind them that the story *Runaways!* is set during the same time and in the same place as *Oliver Twist*. Say that *Runaways!* also has some dialogue that shows characters breaking the rules of grammar when they are speaking, just like many people do when they are speaking informally among themselves.
- Navigate to the next slide to show two examples from *Runaways!* Use MT/YT to read each example with appropriate intonation and special emphasis.
- Point out the pronouns (*she* and *we*) and the verbs (*were* and *was*). Explain that the verb has to agree with the pronoun (*she was, we were*) but in the dialogue, the speakers have got them the wrong way round.
- Now ask them to TTYP to say the first piece of dialogue and then ask them to say the changed version of the first speech, chorally (*she was only two*). Check that they have used the standard English form. Repeat using the second speech (*we were hungry*). Click 'Reveal' to show the altered versions.
- Tell the children that you have another example of dialogue where a verb is used in the non-standard form. Navigate to the next slide to show the example which uses *done* in non-standard form. Use MT/YT to say the dialogue.
- Explain that there are two ways that this could be changed to fit the rules of grammar. Click 'Reveal' to show the first version and TOL to explain the change. Repeat for the second version.
- Navigate to the next slide to show all three versions and ask the children to TTYP to say which version they would be most likely to use when speaking to a friend. Make sure they understand that there is not a right answer to this question, you are just looking for their own opinions. Take feedback.
- Ask the children to turn to p.44 in their Pupils' Book and look at the Grammar: standard English activity. Explain that you want them to TTYP to take turns to read the sentences and then complete them so that they are written in standard English. This is just an oral activity, they don't need to write anything down.
- Choose two or three to share their answers. Clarify where necessary.

Homework Book p.17 provides further practice on Standard English.

Curriculum link:
building a
varied and rich
vocabulary;
composing,
rehearsing
and recording
sentences

Daily log (CD)

*Purpose: for children to keep a personal log of notes, thoughts and ideas, collected from their
reading and discussions. Some ideas will be used in their own writing*

- Display the first two slides of **CD (file 2.4)** to show the extract from *Oliver Twist*
  again. Read it aloud and ask the children to TTYP to share any words or phrases that
  helped to emphasise how hungry the children in *Oliver Twist* were. Take feedback.
- Ask the children to TTYP to discuss how hungry Hannah and John would be in
  Runaways! if they had only eaten workhouse food and then had not eaten for
  another two days. Take feedback.
- Model taking some of the children's ideas and putting them into sentences, e.g.
  *'I think the children were so hungry that all they dreamed of was food. I think the children
  were so hungry that their stomachs were constantly rumbling.'*
- Tell the children to write a few sentences in their Daily log, using the ideas they
  have discussed, to describe how hungry Hannah and John felt.

discussion;
develop, agree on,
and evaluate
rules for effective
discussion

Big Question (CD)

*Purpose: for children to develop their skills of argument and discussion through a mini
enquiry session based on a philosophical question relating to the work of the day*

- Display today's Big Question on **CD (file 2.5)**:

  Does hunger mean the same thing to everyone?

- Follow the process as explained on Day 1.

DAY 3

discussing words
and phrases
that capture the
reader's interest
and imagination

Special phrases

Purpose: for children to be introduced to some Special phrases used in the story

> *his body shaking distressingly   looked at her suspiciously   a bolt of fear   questioning look*

- Explain that you have chosen some phrases from the story that you think are
  important. Say that you have chosen them because they are *showing* you how the
  characters in the story feel rather than *telling* you how they feel.
- Display **CD (file 3.1)** to show the first Special phrase. Click 'TOL' and use the
  think bubble to explore the phrase. Say that your mind shows you much more
  than if the author had simply said that John was very cold and ill.
- Click 'Story' to show the phrase in the story. Ask the children to close their
  eyes as you read the extract aloud and to think about the images that appear in
  their minds.
- Navigate through the slides and repeat the process for the remaining phrases.
- Now ask the children to turn to p.44 in their Pupils' Book and look at the Special
  phrases activity. Ask them to TTYP to discuss each of the phrases and share what
  images appear in their minds as they read them.
- Now ask them to TTYP to discuss which phrase they thought was the most
  powerful. Ask them to write some short sentences, to describe what images
  this phrase created in their minds, in their Daily log.
- Print the Special phrases from **CD (file 3.2)** to display on your Story wall for
  this Unit.

Curriculum link:
read aloud
showing
understanding
through
intonation, tone
and volume

Re-read a story version 3 🅰

Purpose: for children to gain a deeper understanding of the story and to see the text for the first time

- Ask the children to read the story on Anthology pp.54–63 aloud with their partners. They should read alternate pages each, and ensure they use expression and intonation to convey meaning and impact to their partner. Explain that you will be listening in and looking out for particularly good reading.
- For some groups, you may wish to read aloud to the children first as they follow the text in their own copy so that they can Jump in (see Introduction p.13) to say the Power words and Special phrases.

inferring
characters'
feelings, thoughts
and motives from
their actions

Forum theatre ⓒⒹ

Purpose: for children to investigate how characters' actions are affected by setting

- Explain that you are going to set up a piece of *forum theatre*, which is when an audience is shown a short play in which the central character encounters an obstacle, which they are unable to overcome. Say that you are going to use the section of the story where Hannah is searching for a way to earn some money to get food for herself and John. Explain that the obstacle is that no one will help her and that she can't beg in case she is found and sent back to the workhouse.
- Say that the scene is played out, then they will get the opportunity to give the character advice, then the play is re-run. If a member of the audience feels the main character might usefully have tried a different strategy, they can stop the action, take the character's place, and try out their idea.
- Choose one child to play Hannah and one to play the crossing-sweeper. Agree a signal to stop the action during the performance.
- Ask the child playing Hannah to watch the crossing-sweeper and then to walk over to ask for help. Freeze the action at this point and ask the children to TTYP to discuss their ideas about what Hannah could say to the crossing-sweeper to get them to help her. Take feedback and re-run the action using the audience participation to change the action as you see fit.
- Now display **CD (file 3.3)** and show the children one of the alternative settings (a market place, a park, a rubbish heap). Choose children to play any new characters that are appropriate to the setting, e.g. market traders, street children, barrow boys, and ask the actors to act out the scene as before. Explain that Hannah needs to be asking various characters for help.
- Discuss how the action should change and re-run the scene based on this.

discussing words
and phrases
that capture the
reader's interest
and imagination;
building a
varied and rich
vocabulary

Daily log ⓒⒹ

Purpose: for children to keep a personal log of notes, thoughts and ideas, collected from their reading and discussions. Some ideas will be used in their own writing

- Leave **CD (file 3.3)** displayed on the board. Choose one of the settings and tell the children that they are going to write a few sentences in their Daily log to show how Hannah might be able to find help in that particular setting.
- Remind the children of the Power words *despondently, trudged* and *wary* and the Special phrases *looked at her suspiciously,* and *a bolt of fear.* Say that these words and phrases *show* us how the characters in the story are feeling rather than *telling* us how they feel.

- Encourage the children to try to use these ideas to *show* rather than *tell* how Hannah is feeling in their chosen setting. Model composing a *showing* sentence using one of the Power words, and write it on the board or a flipchart so that they can borrow it if they want to.

Curriculum link: discussion; develop, agree on, and evaluate rules for effective discussion

Big Question (CD)

Purpose: for children to develop their skills of argument and discussion through a mini enquiry session based on a philosophical question relating to the work of the day

- Display today's Big Question on **CD (file 3.4)**:

Can you tell how another person is feeling by the way they behave?

- Follow the process as explained on Day 1.

DAY 4

asking questions to improve their understanding of a text

Re-read a story version 3 A

Purpose: for children to deepen their understanding of the story by increasing familiarity with the text

- Ask the children to turn to pp.54–63 in the Anthology and read the whole story *Runaways!* silently to themselves. Tell them they can pause to record any thoughts, ideas or questions in their Daily log as they read the text.
- Explain that it is more important for them to think about what they are reading than to finish first and, as they know the story, it doesn't matter if they don't finish it this time.

Character CD PB

Purpose: for children to understand how the author builds up a character through dialogue and actions

- Ask the children to TTYP to discuss what they think of Mr Patch the Workhouse Master, e.g. '*Is he a kind man? How does he treat the children in the workhouse?*' Take feedback.
- Ask them to TTYP to share ideas about how he behaves and what this says about his character. Take feedback and write up their ideas on the board or a flipchart.
- Tell the children that although there is an illustration of Mr Patch in the Anthology he has not been described to them in any way in the story except through a piece of dialogue, where is trying to sell John to the chimney sweep.
- Display **CD (file 4.1)** to show an extract from the story and read it aloud to the children. Ask them to TTYP to draw out the facts about Mr Patch and John from this part of the story. Take feedback.
- Click 'Facts' to reveal the facts and TOL as you link them together to create images of each of the characters, e.g.

So John is an orphan, he has been at the workhouse since he was a baby. He is now eight years old and very thin. Mr Patch is the Master of the Workhouse and he wants to sell John to the chimney sweep. He has known John since he was a baby.

- Ask the children to TTYP to discuss if the facts help them to know or understand the character of Mr Patch any better. Take feedback.
- Click 'Opinions' to reveal Mr Patch's opinions about John. Ask the children to TTYP to discuss what these opinions tell us about Mr Patch. Take feedback.

- TOL as you read each opinion aloud, e.g.

  "I've got the perfect boy for you, Mr Parker." When I read this it makes me think Mr Patch is selling John as if he were an object. He says: "I've got the perfect boy for you…" in the same way someone might say 'I have the perfect shoes for you'. It makes me think that Mr Patch does not see John as a human being at all. I can imagine Mr Patch making his voice sound persuasive to entice the chimney sweep into buying John. It makes me dislike Mr Patch.

- Ask the children to TTYP to discuss how the different opinions changed their perception of Mr Patch. Ask: *'How do you think he will say the dialogue? How do you think he will move? What other ideas have you got about Mr Patch from his opinions in the extract?'* Take feedback, referring to the children's initial ideas about Mr Patch where appropriate.

- Ask the children to turn to p.45 in their Pupils' Book and look at the Character activity. Ask them to TTYP to discuss the questions and create their own description of Mr Patch. Ask them to record their description in their Daily log.

Dramatic reconstruction

Purpose: for children to gain an understanding of the characters' feelings and motivations

Curriculum link: preparing play scripts to read aloud and to perform, showing understanding through intonation, tone, volume and action

- Before the lesson, print a copy of the script from **CD (file 4.2)** for each child.
- Tell the children that Hannah is in an awful position. She is only a child herself but she is the only person who can protect her brother. Ask the children to TTYP to recall how Hannah finds out that John will leave the workhouse to become a climbing boy. Take feedback.
- Give each child a copy of the script from **CD (file 4.2)** and tell them that it shows an extract from the story written out as a script. Explain that you have added Hannah to the scene but at the moment she doesn't have any lines.
- Join sets of partners together to create groups of four. Tell them that three children will take on the roles of Mr Patch, Mr Parker and Hannah and one child will direct the action. Explain that they will need to freeze the action after each character has read their lines, allowing for each of the characters to describe their feelings.
- Ask the children to first read the script through once without acting it out. Encourage them to use some of what they know about Mr Patch and Mr Parker to give their lines expression in order to convey meaning. At the end of the reading ask the children to look at where Hannah's lines should be in the script and talk as a group about how they think Hannah might react at each point. Take feedback and write some of the children's ideas on to the board or a flipchart.
- Now ask the children to act out the script. Make sure the director understands that their role is to freeze the action whenever a character has spoken a line. The director should then ask each character to say how they are feeling. At the end of this activity take feedback from the children about how each character feels at the freeze points in the script.
- Tell the children that Hannah isn't going to actually speak to the other characters but she is going to say how she is feeling, and describe her reactions to what the other characters are saying. Explain that this is called *soliloquy* because Hannah is either speaking to herself or the audience and not to another character in the play.
- Ask the group to have a discussion, led by the director, to decide what Hannah's lines should be. The children should now add Hannah's lines to their script.
- Ask the director to rehearse the play with their group. Tell the children that they should talk about any changes they'd like to make before they act out the play a final time. You may wish to ask the groups to perform their plays to each other.
- Finally, ask the children to TTYP to reflect on how it felt to act in role and whether they have learned anything new about the characters.

Daily log

Curriculum link:
discuss and record
ideas; learn the
conventions of
different types of
writing such as a
diary written in
the first person

*Purpose: for children to keep a personal log of notes, thoughts and ideas, collected from their
reading and discussions. Some ideas will be used in their own writing*

- Ask the children to TTYP to share what they know about Hannah. Ask: '*How does
she feel about Mr Patch and the workhouse? How does she feel about John? What does
she hope will happen when they escape the workhouse?*'
- Now ask them to write a short diary entry of three sentences in their Daily log, in
role as Hannah the night she finds out that Mr Patch is planning on selling John to
the chimney sweep. Explain that as this is Hannah's diary entry, it should be in the
first person and include information about how Hannah feels.
- Model writing a sentence for them, beginning *I felt…* Write it on the board or a
flipchart for the children to refer to when they write their diary entry.

Big Question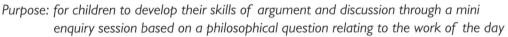

discussion;
develop, agree on,
and evaluate
rules for effective
discussion

*Purpose: for children to develop their skills of argument and discussion through a mini
enquiry session based on a philosophical question relating to the work of the day*

- Display today's Big Question on **CD (file 4.3)**:

  How much do we need to know about someone before we can trust them?

- Follow the process as explained on Day 1.

DAY 5

Retell the story

Purpose: for children to break up the story into sections to help them to retell the story

- Ask the children to turn to p.54 in the Anthology and look at the beginning of the
story. Tell them that they are going to work together to break the story into four
sections to show where the new pieces of action start.
- Model finding the first section, which is from the beginning of the story until the
sentence: 'If he was sent up chimneys every day, it could kill him.' on p.56. Tell the
children that this part of the story is where Hannah overhears Mr Patch trying to
sell John to the chimney sweep and decides that they must escape.
- Ask the children to read the rest of the story and TTYP to discuss where the next
piece of action starts and ends. Tell them to look out for sentence openings that
show time has passed or the action has moved to a new location, e.g. *That night…* ,
They trudged on until they came to…
- Complete this for each of the four sections, making sure you all agree. Take
feedback and check that the children can sum up the main action of each section.
Draw four numbered boxes on the board or a flipchart and use the children's
ideas to write a short summary of each section in the boxes.
- Join sets of partners together to create groups of four. Allocate a section to each
group (some groups may have the same sections depending on the class size).
Ask them to act out their allocated section and move around observing how they
work together. At the end of the activity feed back to the children about ideas you
liked or groups that worked well together.
- Ask the children to discuss how each of the characters was feeling in the section
that they acted out. Take feedback and add ideas to the relevant boxes on the
board or flipchart. TOL as you compare how the characters' feelings change
throughout the story, e.g. '*In the first section Hannah is worried about John and feels
frightened but in the last section she is hopeful.*'
- Now ask the children to TTYP to think of a title for each box that sums up the
most important feeling for each section, e.g. Box 1 could be *Fearing the future*.
Take feedback and write your favourite titles at the top of each box.

- Tell the children that you want them to use the notes you have made on the board or flipchart to retell the story to their partner. Explain that Partner 1s should retell the story and Partner 2's job is to listen carefully and give feedback on how well they have done. Ask Partner 2s to consider how well Partner 1s described how the characters were feeling in the different parts of the story and whether they used an effective Storyteller voice.
- Now ask Partner 2s to retell the story and Partner 1s to listen and give feedback.
- Ask the children to TTYP to discuss how acting out the story helped them to remember what happened. Take feedback.
- Finally ask the children to TTYP to reflect on what they have learned about the characters' feelings by acting out and retelling the story.

> **Curriculum link:** identifying ideas drawn from more than one paragraph

Summarising the story

Purpose: for children to summarise the main ideas and plot of the story

- Before the lesson, print a copy of **CD (file 5.2)** for each child.
- Tell the children that a book of the story *Runaways!* is being published. Say that they have been asked to create a trailer to publicise the book on the Internet.
- Say that they will need to sum up the most important ideas in the story, select the important moments and leave the audience with a cliff-hanger to entice them to read the story and find out what happens.
- Play a book trailer from the Internet, such as the one at **www.oup.com/oxed/primary/projectx/alien-adventures**. Ask the children to watch it carefully.
- Tell the children to TTYP to share three things they liked about the trailer. Take feedback and write some of their ideas on the board or a flipchart.
- Ask the children to turn to p.45 of their Pupils' Book and use the questions to help them plan their own trailer in their Daily log.
- Tell the children that they now need to translate their ideas into a storyboard. Display **CD (file 5.1)** and TOL about how you could use some of their ideas from the Retell the story activity to complete the storyboard, e.g. *'You could choose Hannah overhearing Mr Patch selling John to the chimney sweep as the first important moment, so that would go in the first storyboard square. Then you could use the second square to say what happens next.'*
- Explain that you are going to write a description of the action in the square and then add any appropriate voice-over dialogue in the box underneath it.
- Click 'Reveal' to show your ideas added to your first two storyboard squares.
- Model how to complete the third part of the storyboard by typing your ideas into the boxes provided. Draw children into this process using MT/YT and TTYP.
- Give each child a copy of the storyboard template from **CD (file 5.2)** and ask them to create their own storyboard. Choose some children to share their storyboards with the rest of the class.

> discussing and recording ideas

Daily log

Purpose: for children to keep a personal log of notes, thoughts and ideas, collected from their reading and discussions. Some ideas will be used in their own writing

- Ask the children TTYP to discuss what they have learned about the story, e.g. the historical context, the characters' feelings and the most important moments.
- Tell the children to write a short paragraph in their Daily log to explain their own personal feelings about the story, including what they enjoyed and why, and which parts of the story they feel are the most important and why.

Curriculum link:
discussion;
develop, agree on,
and evaluate
rules for effective
discussion

Big Question

*Purpose: for children to develop their skills of argument and discussion through a mini
enquiry session based on a philosophical question relating to the work of the day*

- Display today's Big Question on **CD (file 5.4)**:

  What are the most important moments in a lifetime?

- Follow the process as explained on Day 1.

WRITING FICTION

DAY 6

drawing
inferences;
participate in
discussion about
books

What if not...?

Purpose: for children to imagine other directions that the story could take

- Display **CD (file 6.1)** to show a What if not...? question: What if not *mean
spirited*? What if *Mr Patch had been a caring workhouse master*?
- Use the TOL points below and/or your own ideas to explore the question.

  *If Mr Patch had been kind perhaps he might have found some help for the children. He
knew that John was unwell so he could have tried to find work for Hannah instead so that
she could support her brother. It would still have been a hard life for Hannah and John but it
would have been safer.*

- Ask the children to TTYP to discuss the question. Take feedback and write some
of their ideas on the board or a flipchart.
- Now ask the children to turn to p.46 in their Pupils' Book and look at the What if
not...? activity. Ask them to TTYP to discuss the other What if not...? questions.
Take feedback and build on some of their ideas.

Build a character

inferring
characters'
feelings, thoughts
and motives from
their actions, from
what is stated and
implied

*Purpose: for children to use textual evidence to understand a new character and use dialogue
to tell the reader about them*

- Tell the children to imagine that Hannah and John did go to the shelter and that
the first person that they met was Matron.
- Display **CD (file 6.2)** to show a picture of Matron. Ask the children to TTYP to
discuss their first impressions of her. Take feedback.
- Click 'TOL' and use the think bubbles to explore this new character.
- Ask the children to TTYP to discuss what kind of person Matron will be. Collect
feedback and write some of the children's ideas on the board or a flipchart.
- Tell the children that you have discovered some records which contain descriptions
of Hannah and John that were written by the Matron of Dr Barnardo's shelter
in Stepney Causeway.
- Ask the children to turn to pp.46–47 in their Pupils' Book and look at the Build a
character activity. Ask them to take turns to read the records and then TTYP to
discuss any more thoughts that they have about Matron's character. Take feedback
and write their ideas on the board or a flipchart.
- Navigate to the next slide of **CD (file 6.2)** to show how Matron might describe
John (taken from the records on pp.46–47 of the Pupils' Book).
- Remind the children that they learned about the character Mr Patch through what
he said to the chimney sweep. Explain you are now going to write some dialogue
for Matron as she tells Dr Barnardo about John. TOL as you write the dialogue
below on the board or a flipchart:

"'I've got a tiny young boy for us to care for, Dr Barnardo," said Matron. "His name is John Williams, he is very unwell. When he arrived he was caked in mud. We need to give him constant care and help him to build up his strength."'

- Ask the children to TTYP to discuss what these sentences tell us about Matron. Take feedback.
- Model altering the dialogue using some of the children's ideas that you wrote on the board earlier, changing how Matron describes John, e.g. 'If I said a *desperately weak young boy rather than* tiny young boy *it would show how anxious Matron feels about John.*'
- Remind the children of when Mr Patch refers to the absence of the children's parents: '"No parents to worry about," said Patch. "He's an orphan."'
- Now model using this information to write some more dialogue for Matron as she speaks to Dr Barnardo about the children, discussing the punctuation you are using as you write:

"'Poor child, no parents to worry for him," said Matron. "His sister has been caring for him. She has hardly left his side. We are the only family they have now."'

- Ask the children to TTYP to discuss what these sentences tell us about Matron. Take feedback.
- Tell the children that they are going to continue the dialogue but this time they are going to write dialogue for Matron as she tells Dr Barnardo about Hannah. Tell the children to use the record on p.47 of their Pupils' Book and the prompts underneath to help them.
- At the end of this session give the children time to share the dialogue they have written and reflect on what they have learned about Matron.

Curriculum link: discussing and recording ideas

Daily log 🔲

Purpose: for children to keep a personal log of notes, thoughts and ideas, collected from their reading and discussions. Some ideas will be used in their own writing

- Tell the children to return to the What if not…? activity on p.46 of their Pupils' Book and choose one What if not…? question to discuss further.
- Ask them to think about a new ending for the story based on their chosen question. Tell them to TTYP to share their ideas and then write them into their Daily log.

discussion; develop, agree on, and evaluate rules for effective discussion

Big Question ⓒⒹ

Purpose: for children to develop their skills of argument and discussion through a mini enquiry session based on a philosophical question relating to the work of the day

- Display today's Big Question on **CD (file 6.3):**

  What is family?

- Follow the process as explained on Day 1.

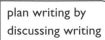

plan writing by discussing writing that is similar

Build a story 1 ⓒⒹ

Purpose: for children to see a story grow through three stages of development

- Tell the children that you have discovered some more artefacts from Dr Barnardo's shelter in Stepney Causeway.
- Display **CD (file 7.1)** to show a photograph of the sign at the entrance to Dr Barnardo's shelter. Ask the children to imagine that they are Hannah or John walking down the street, spotting the sign to the shelter and going to the door. Tell them to TTYP to discuss their thoughts.
- Draw some think bubbles on the board or a flipchart. Collect feedback and use some of the children's ideas to fill in the think bubbles.

- Navigate to the next slide to show an image of Matron. Ask the children to imagine that they are seeing her for the first time. Tell them to TTYP to discuss their thoughts about her.
- Draw some more think bubbles on the board or a flipchart. Collect feedback and use some of the children's ideas to fill them in.
- Repeat the process for the next slide which shows the inside of the shelter.
- Say that you are going to write a new story, which leads on from *Runaways!*, about what happened when Hannah and John reached the shelter in Stepney Causeway.
- Display **CD (file 7.2)** to show Build a story 1 (across two slides). Explain that this is a plan for your new story. Read it with the children using MT/YT.
- Ask the children to TTYP to discuss what they think Hannah has heard. Take feedback, then ask the children to note down their ideas about the ending of the story in their Daily log.

Curriculum link:
plan writing by discussing writing that is similar; recording ideas

Build a story 2

Purpose: for children to see a story grow through three stages of development

- Display **CD (file 7.3)** to show Build a story 2 (across two slides). Say that you have added some more detail to the story and read it aloud using MT/YT.
- Use the TOL points below and/or your own ideas as you compare this version with Build a story 1.

The description that has been used in the first paragraph, 'Hannah kept muttering to herself and John held on to her tightly, wheezing as he walked.' helps to show rather than tell us how anxious Hannah and John must have felt as they headed for the shelter.

The historical references such as '…a huge railway bridge, dark and sooty from the steam trains' help the reader to imagine the setting and put themselves in Hannah and John's position.

In the final paragraph it says, 'She tossed and turned, thoughts and ideas rushing through her head.' This shows me that Hannah is finding it really difficult to sleep. I think she might be thinking about what the future holds for her and John.

- Ask the children to TTYP to find other examples of historical references and *showing* not *telling*. Take feedback, clarifying where necessary.
- Click 'Highlights' to highlight the dialogue and examples of the use of past tense. Explain to the children that when they write their extension of the story they should consistently write in the past tense and use dialogue where appropriate.
- Ask the children to TTYP to think of words they could use to describe how Hannah might be feeling. Ask them to note down the words in their Daily log.

understand the skills and processes that are essential for writing

Build a story 3 CD PB

Purpose: for children to see an example of writing that will provide a model for their own writing

- You are in the role of the writer during this activity. Say that you have developed your story further and you want to know what the children think of it.
- Display **CD (file 7.4)** to show Build a story 3 (across three slides). Read it aloud.
- Remind the children that this is a work of fiction, and explain that in real life it is not safe to knock on strangers' doors.
- Now ask the children to turn to pp.48–49 in their Pupils' Book and to TTYP to read alternate sections of Build a story 3. Ask them to TTYP to discuss what they thought of the story.
- Ask the children to read the questions on p.49 of their Pupils' Book and to TTYP to evaluate your writing.

Daily log

Purpose: for children to keep a personal log of notes, thoughts and ideas, collected from their reading and discussions. Some ideas will be used in their own writing

- Ask the children to TTYP to share ideas for a title for the story they have just read about the children arriving at the shelter and starting their new lives. Ask them to record their best idea in their Daily log and explain why they think it is a good title.
- Choose some children to share their ideas with the class.

discussion;
develop, agree on,
and evaluate
rules for effective
discussion

Big Question

Purpose: for children to develop their skills of argument and discussion through a mini enquiry session based on a philosophical question relating to the work of the day

- Display today's Big Question on **CD (file 7.5)**:

  How do we know we are safe?

- Follow the process as explained on Day 1.

DAY 8

inferring
characters'
feelings, thoughts
and motives from
their actions, from
what is stated and
implied

Role-play

Purpose: for children to explore a stimulus for their own story

- Remind the children that your story ended with Hannah overhearing a conversation. Say that the conversation was between Dr Barnardo and Matron and that you are going to let them hear the conversation now.
- Play the audio on **CD (file 8.1)** and ask the children to TTYP to discuss their initial responses to what they heard. Take feedback and write some of the children's ideas on the board or a flipchart.
- Tell the children to imagine that they are Hannah listening to the conversation. Ask them to TTYP to discuss how they would have moved to make sure they could hear the whole conversation, and where they might be hiding. Take feedback.
- Tell them to imagine they are getting into their hiding places to listen to the conversation again. Re-play the audio on **CD (file 8.1)**.
- Ask the children to TTYP to discuss how they felt by the end of the conversation. Take feedback and write some of their ideas on the board or a flipchart.
- Ask the children to TTYP to discuss what they think Hannah should do next. Take feedback and write some of their ideas on the board or a flipchart.
- Now tell the children that they are going to role-play the situation between Hannah and John as she tells him what she overheard. Say that Partner 1s are going to take on the role of Hannah and Partner 2s are going to take on the role of John. Ask them to use this role-play to work out what the characters are going to do next. Take feedback and TOL as you expand on some of their ideas.
- Talk through the different scenarios that the children have explored and highlight any possible pitfalls. Write notes summarising the main ideas on the board or a flipchart.

composing
and rehearsing
sentences orally;
creating settings,
characters, plot

Write a story 1

Purpose: for children to create a plan for their own story

- Before the lesson, print a copy of the story plan from **CD (file 8.3)** for each child.
- Tell the children that Hannah sneaked into Matron's room later that night to see if she could find any clues about the list that she overheard Matron and Dr Barnardo talking about. Say that she found a list of names and some boat tickets to Canada in the top drawer of the desk in Matron's room. Ask the children to TTYP to discuss how this might change the ideas that they had for the story ending.

- Tell the children that they are going to write their own version of what happens next in the story.
- Display **CD (file 8.2)** to show notes for a plan for the rest of the story. Say that you have chosen to write this from Hannah's point of view but they can write their story from John's point of view if they want to.
- Read the plan using MT/YT and TOL about the information that it is useful to include in a plan, e.g. important information, questions, motivations.
- Remind the children of the ideas they had when you completed the Role-play activity.
- Give each child a copy of the plan from **CD (file 8.3)**.
- Ask them to turn to p.50 in their Pupils' Book and TTYP to read the prompts. Say that they should use these prompts and the copied plan to help them to plan their own story. Remind them that they should use the ideas from your plan but they can also add any of their own ideas.

Curriculum link:
composing
and rehearsing
sentences orally;
creating settings,
characters, plot

Write a story 2

Purpose: for children to develop their story plan by adding detail, dialogue and action

- Tell the children that you need to decide where to add detail, dialogue and action to your plan.
- Display **CD (file 8.4)** to show the plan. Read through each point and click 'TOL' to show how you might add detail to improve the story.
- After each point ask the children to TTYP to discuss what they might add to their plan. As they do this, tell them to make simple notes on their plan.

write for a range
of different
purposes

Daily log

Purpose: for children to keep a personal log of notes, thoughts and ideas, collected from their reading and discussions. Some ideas will be used in their own writing

- Before the lesson, print a copy of the map from **CD (file 8.5)** for each child.
- Display **CD (file 8.5)** to show children a map of what the shelter in Stepney Causeway might have looked like. Talk through the story so far, showing the children where different parts of it happened on the map.
- Ask the children to TTYP to look at the map and use it to summarise their story.
- Tell the children how they can use the map to add detail to their story, e.g. *'Hannah hid in the shadows of the alcove on the stairs to listen to Matron and Dr Barnardo. Hannah turned left to go into Matron's office, which had a heavy curtain across the door.'*
- Give each child a copy of the map from **CD (file 8.5)**. Ask the children to annotate their map to show the details they could use in their story.

discussion;
develop, agree on,
and evaluate
rules for effective
discussion

Big Question

Purpose: for children to develop their skills of argument and discussion through a mini enquiry session based on a philosophical question relating to the work of the day

- Display today's Big Question on **CD (file 8.6)**:

  Is it ever right to keep secrets from people?

- Follow the process as explained on Day 1.

DAY 9

Curriculum link:
creating settings,
characters, plot;
monitor whether
their writing
makes sense

Write a story 3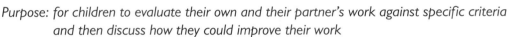

Purpose: for children to write their own version of the story

- Tell the children that they are now ready to write their own story about what happened when John and Hannah arrived at the shelter in Stepney Causeway.
- Remind them that they should use their plan to help them to structure their story.
- Ask them to turn to p.51 in their Pupils' Book and TTYP to read the prompts. Say that they should use these prompts and the words in the Word bank to help them when writing their stories.
- Remind the children that some characters will use standard English (e.g. Dr Barnardo) but others might use non-standard English (e.g. Hannah and John). They could use these different forms to make the characters' dialogue more realistic.
- Tell them that they can also look at the Story wall for useful words and phrases and say that they could use a thesaurus to look for synonyms to describe the children's thoughts and feelings.

DAY 10

assessing the
effectiveness of
their own and
others' writing

Evaluate and edit

Purpose: for children to evaluate their own and their partner's work against specific criteria and then discuss how they could improve their work

- Display **CD (file 10.1)** and read through the evaluation points using MT/YT.
- As a model, select an example of work where the writing has met the criteria, and share this with the other children, explaining why it works well.
- Tell the children to take turns to read their partner's writing in pairs and discuss together how well each piece of writing has met the criteria.
- Ask the children to discuss at least two changes they could make to improve their work.

proofread for
spelling and
punctuation errors

Proofread

Purpose: for children to proofread their work and make changes to improve the accuracy of their grammar, punctuation and spelling

- Now ask the children to proofread their work. If you have noticed that several children need to improve on a particular aspect of spelling, grammar or punctuation, use this as a focus for the Proofread activity. Write an example which includes common errors from the children's writing and use this as a model.
- The children should always be checking for standard use of punctuation and correct spelling of common exception words.
- The following points would be particularly relevant for this Unit:
  - checking for consistent use of the first person and past tense
  - making sure that speech is punctuated correctly
  - checking spelling of ambitious vocabulary choices.

discussion;
develop, agree on,
and evaluate
rules for effective
discussion

Very Big Question

Purpose: for children to explore one of the Big Questions in more depth

- See Unit 1 Day 10 for teaching notes on the Very Big Question (p.41).

READING AND WRITING NON-FICTION

Linked via a Big Question, in the Non-fiction week the children will broaden their knowledge of Victorian times by looking through journalistic texts that are typical of the period. They will learn about the features of newspaper articles and entries and be given the opportunity to write their own entry for a class newspaper set during the Victorian era. See p.136 for the daily timetable for the Non-fiction week.

Non-fiction

Reading

Children will:

- explore how different parts of a newspaper can have different purposes e.g. *to entertain*, *to inform*
- discover how newspaper articles have key features to make them easy to read, e.g. *headline*, *standfirst*, *lead paragraph* and *captions*
- understand that adverts have a main message and use attention-grabbing language to interest the reader.

Writing

Key writing purpose to be shared with the children:

To write an entry for a class newspaper that is set during Victorian times.

Writing evaluation to be shared with the children

My newspaper entry:

- includes interesting source material from Victorian times
- has attention-grabbing language, e.g. use of *synonyms* to avoid repeating words
- is well organised and includes at least one of the key features of newspaper articles, e.g. *headline*, *caption*, *columns*.

Grammar:

- uses paragraphs to organise information in longer articles
- may include subordinate clauses to give extra information.

See the Planning section of the Software ('Timetables' tab) for a printable version of the Writing purpose and evaluation.

Non-fiction: Newspapers

 DAY 11

Curriculum link:
thinking aloud
to explore and
collect ideas

Think and link (CD)

Purpose: for children's interest in journalistic texts to be stimulated via one of the Big Questions they have explored

- Display the Big Question from Day 1 on **CD (file 1.7)**:

  Is it everyone's responsibility to help those in need?

- Ask the children to TTYP to recall some of the ideas they discussed when they looked at this question in Week 1.

- Explain that in Victorian times there wasn't anywhere for the poor, orphaned or weak to go except for the workhouse, but that pioneers such as Dr Barnardo were determined to do something about this.

listening to and
discussing a
wide range of
non-fiction

Introduction

Bring in a selection of newspapers. You can also access newspapers online. Check that all the content of the newspapers and websites is suitable for the age group.

Purpose: for children to understand why we read newspapers

- Tell the children that newspapers can tell us about current news and events through articles, adverts and notices.

- Give the children some newspapers to look at or allow them to view some online. Ask them to TTYP to discuss what some of the articles are about and to note this down in their Daily log. Take feedback and write some of their ideas on the board or a flipchart.

- Ask the children to TTYP to discuss what the newspapers tell us about the time they were written. Take feedback and draw together the children's ideas.

- Ask the children to TTYP to discuss why they think people read newspapers. Take feedback. Show the children the cartoon and puzzle sections of one of the newspapers and explain that newspapers can be used for entertainment as well as a source of information.

discussing words
and phrases
that capture the
reader's interest
and imagination

Word power (CD)

Purpose: for children to understand language used in the Victorian newspaper before they read it for the first time

> feat   seething   sanitation   endure   representing   hailed

- Tell the children you have found a page from a newspaper from the year that Dr Barnardo set up the shelter in Stepney Causeway. Explain that you want them to enjoy reading the newspaper, so you have chosen some words that they might not be familiar with to learn beforehand.

- Display **CD (file 11.1)** to show the list of Power words from the newspaper that the children will look at later. Read the words using MT/YT. Say that these words are powerful because we don't often use them.

- Click 'Definition' to show a definition for each word (one at a time). Read the words and their definitions using MT/YT.

- Navigate to the next slide to show each of the words in the context of a sentence. Read the sentences using MT/YT.

- Navigate to the final slide to show the first word again. Ask the children to TTYP to say what the word means. After a short time, click 'Reveal' to show the next word and repeat the process. Complete this for all six words.

- Print the words, definitions and sentences from **CD (file 11.2)** to display on your Newspapers wall.

Newspapers

Purpose: for children to read the Victorian newspaper extract for the first time

- Ask the children to turn to pp.64–66 of the Anthology to read the article about how Dr Barnardo set up the shelter in Stepney Causeway, the entries for the 'Social Diary', and the 'This Summer in History' section of the newspaper.
- Tell the children that they can read the information in any order. Ask them to TTYP to summarise each part before they move on.
- Ask them to write any unfamiliar words in their Daily log (to be used in the next activity).
- Once they have read the newspaper extract ask the children to TTYP to discuss what ideas and events the articles suggest interested the Victorian people. Take feedback and write their ideas on the board or a flipchart.
- Ask the children to TTYP to discuss whether they found anything in the newspaper that was entertaining as well as things that were informative. Take feedback.

> **Curriculum link:** using dictionaries to check the meaning of words that they have read

Daily log

Dictionaries will be required in this part of the lesson.

Purpose: for children to keep a personal log of notes, thoughts and ideas, collected from their reading and discussions. Some ideas will be used in their own writing

- Ask the children to look back in their Daily log at the unfamiliar words they noted down when reading the newspaper extract.
- Ask them to TTYP to see if they can help their partner to understand any of the words they have written down. Take some feedback and model writing a simple definition for some of the words on the board or a flipchart.
- Tell the children that they are going to work with their partners to write simple definitions for some of the words they have written in their Daily log. Ask them to choose up to four words and see if they can work out what each one means. Once they have come up with a definition for each word, ask them to use a dictionary to check it and then to write the definition beside the word in their Daily log.
- When the children are happy with their definitions they can write short sentences in their Daily log using the words in context.

> **DAY 12**

> learn the conventions of different types of writing

Key features (CD) A

Purpose: for children to become familiar with some of the key organisational features of newspapers

- Display **CD (file 12.1)** to show the Key features grid. Read through each key feature and its definition using MT/YT.
- Navigate to the next slide to show a text extract from the article in the Anthology. Explain that the *lead paragraph* has a special job which is to answer the 5Ws: *Who? What? When? Where?* and *Why?* Read the lead paragraph aloud and ask the children to TTYP and work out where these questions are answered. Take feedback and click 'Reveal' to show the answers.
- Turn to pp.64–65 in the Anthology and read the whole article aloud.
- Now display the Key features grid again from **CD (file 12.1)**.

- Ask the children to turn to pp.64–65 in the Anthology and TTYP to see how many key features they can find examples of in the article 'Building Work Completed on Barnardo's Home for the City's Street Children'.
- Take feedback from the children, clarifying where necessary.
- Ask the children to read the rest of the newspaper and TTYP to decide the purpose of the other parts of the paper. Take feedback.

Deconstruction 1

Purpose: for children to look at adverts printed in a newspaper to prepare them to create a new advert

- Before the lesson, print a copy of the advert grid from **CD (file 12.3)** for each child.
- Ask the children to turn to p.67 in the Anthology and read the advert for 'The Marvel'. Ask them to TTYP to decide what the main message of the advert is. Take feedback.
- Display **CD (file 12.2)** to show a grid and click 'Reveal' to display the main message.
- Ask the children to look for language that grabs their attention in the advert. Take feedback and then click 'Reveal' to display some examples.
- Repeat the process for the other headings listed in the grid and TOL to show how you found the answers.
- Now ask the children to TTYP to read the adverts for 'Toghill's Clockwork Train' and 'Boyle's Chocolate Peppermint Bar' on p.67 of the Anthology.
- Give each child a copy of the advert grid from **CD (file 12.3)** and ask them to TTYP to complete the grid for 'Boyle's Chocolate Peppermint Bar' or 'Toghill's Clockwork Train'. Tell the children that they may not be able to find all of the features but they should complete the grid for the features they can find. Take feedback.
- Ask the children to TTYP to decide which of the adverts they have looked at is the most successful and why. Remind the children that there isn't a right answer, you are just looking for their own opinions and ideas. Take feedback.

Curriculum link: discussing writing that is similar to that which they are planning to write

Write 1

Purpose: for children to listen to the source material and identify key ideas and language for use in a new advert

- Before the lesson, print a copy of the advert grid from **CD (file 12.5)** for each child.
- Tell the children that they are going to create an advert for a newspaper. Say that they are in charge of collecting information and ideas for an advert that will help Dr Barnardo to raise support for his home in Stepney Causeway.
- Explain that they are going to start by listening to an interview with Dr Barnardo and taking notes so they need to listen carefully.
- Open **CD (file 12.4)** and play the audio of an interview with Dr Barnardo.
- Ask the children to TTYP to talk about the main ideas they can remember from the interview. Take feedback and write their ideas on the board or a flipchart. Now ask them to TTYP to decide what the main message for their advert should be. Ask them to write this in their Daily log. Take feedback.
- Remind the children that a good advert uses language which grabs the reader's attention. Ask them to TTYP to recall any words or phrases from the interview that they could use in their advert. Take feedback and write some of their ideas on the board or flipchart. Ask them to choose some words and phrases to copy into their Daily log.

retrieve and record information from non-fiction; write for a range of real purposes and audiences

- Give a copy of the advert grid from **CD (file 12.5)** to each child. Replay the interview on **CD (file 12.4)** and ask the children to make notes on their grid as they listen to the interview for a second time. Pause the audio at intervals to allow the children to make notes. You may also wish to play the audio a third time.
- Finally, explain that they will need to decide what the purpose of the advert is. Will the advert ask people to give money? If so, how much? Or will it ask them to give support, e.g. furniture, volunteering, food? Ask the children to TTYP to decide what they think they should be asking for. Take feedback and as a class decide on the purpose of the advert.

<table>
<tr><td>

Curriculum link:
discussing and recording ideas and information

</td></tr>
</table>

Daily log

Purpose: for children to keep a personal log of notes, thoughts and ideas, collected from their reading and discussions. Some ideas will be used in their own writing

- Display **CD (file 12.6)** to show some other adverts from the Victorian era over two slides. Ask the children to TTYP to discuss how they are different from adverts they see today. Take feedback.
- Remind the children that the advert they have been making notes for is to raise support for Dr Barnardo's shelter.
- Navigate to the next slide to show an old advert for Dr Barnardo's. Ask them to TTYP to decide how effective they think it is. Take feedback.
- Ask the children to use the notes in their own advert grid and the example adverts that they have seen to plan their advert in their Daily log. Ask them to write a description of a photograph they would like to show alongside the advert. (Children are given the opportunity to design and write up their advert on Day 14.)

DAY 13

<table>
<tr><td>

retrieve and record information from non-fiction; asking questions to improve understanding of a text

</td></tr>
</table>

Deconstruction 2

Purpose: for children to read a newspaper article and identify how it might be improved

- Before the lesson, print a copy of the article from **CD (file 13.2)** for each child.
- Display **CD (file 13.1)** to show the newspaper article and read it aloud to the children. Explain that it is a first draft of an article for their newspaper and needs to be edited.
- Give the children copies of the newspaper article from **CD (file 13.2)** and ask them to TTYP to take turns to read it again.
- Display **CD (file 12.1)** to show the Key features grid that you looked at on Day 12. Read one of the key features, *standfirst*, aloud and model looking for it in the text. TOL as you discuss where it appears in the article and why it is needed. Use the TOL points on printable **CD (file 13.3)** and/or your own ideas to model on the board or a flipchart how the standfirst could be improved.
- Ask the children to TTYP to read the *lead paragraph* again. Ask: 'Does it answer the 5Ws: Who? What? When? Where? and Why?' Ask them to discuss whether the paragraph is easy to understand.
- Turn back to the article displayed on the board and say that you think the *lead paragraph* could be improved. Use the TOL points on printable **CD (file 13.3)** and/or your own ideas to model how the lead paragraph could be improved.
- Ask the children to TTYP to discuss what key features they think are missing from the article. Take feedback. Explain that this is an inside page from a newspaper so they can ignore the key feature *Masthead* at this stage.
- Go through the different key features modelling finding bad examples or lack of examples and orally improving them.
- Explain that as well as adding in and improving the key features, some parts of the article need to be rewritten to make them clearer and to avoid repetition.

- Ask the children to TTYP to make notes on their copy of the text to show where improvements could be made. Take feedback and model how to make further improvements by using their suggestions.
- Let them continue to annotate the text either independently or with a partner. The children shouldn't be rewriting the article at this stage, just suggesting improvements.

Curriculum link: extending the range of sentences with more than one clause

Complex sentences

Purpose: for children to understand how to use a subordinate clause to add information to a sentence

- Before the lesson, print and cut out a copy of the sentences and subordinate clauses from **CD (file 13.5)** for each set of partners.
- Display **CD (file 13.4)** to show a sentence from the article 'A Cloud of Frogs'. Explain that you want to add some additional information to the sentence.
- Click 'Clauses' to show the subordinate clauses. Tell the children that these clauses are not sentences, but when they are added to a sentence they give extra information.
- Choose a clause and TOL as you decide where it fits best, at the middle or end of the sentence. Type up your revised sentence in the box provided. Explain that you need to add punctuation to the clause when you add it into the sentence. Use MT/YT to read the sentence. Ask the children to TTYP to tell each other which part is the main clause and which part is the subordinate clause.
- Repeat the process using another of the subordinate clauses.
- Give the children the cut-out sentence and clauses from **CD (file 13.5)**. Ask them to TTYP and experiment with different ways of changing the sentence until they are happy with their final sentence. Remind them that they might need to change the punctuation or add new punctuation to their sentence.
- Tell them to copy their final sentence into their Daily log.

assessing the effectiveness of others' writing and suggesting improvements

Write 2 PB

Purpose: for children to edit a newspaper article in order to improve it

- Remind the children that they have identified which key features are missing from the newspaper article 'A Cloud of Frogs' and which sections need to be rewritten.
- Explain that they now need to re-read the article and use the notes they have made to try to improve it. Explain that many of the sentences include repetitive information and could be cut down. Tell them that they need to shorten the article to 200 words so that it fits into the space allocated to it in the newspaper.
- Remind the children that one of the key features was *attention grabbing language*. Say that they will need to change some of the language used in the article to ensure that the reader is kept interested.
- Ask the children to turn to p.52 of their Pupils' Book and look at the Write 2 activity. Ask them to TTYP to read through the Top Tips and the Word bank. Explain that you would now like them to re-write the article using the tips and words in their Pupils' Book and the notes they made earlier to help them. (Children are given the opportunity to improve and publish their articles on Day 14.)

DAY 14

Curriculum link:
identifying how language, structure and presentation contribute to meaning

Deconstruction 3

Purpose: for children to learn how to turn notes into a newspaper entry

- Ask the children to turn to p.66 of the Anthology and read the 'Social Diary' and 'This Summer in History' sections of the newspaper. Remind them of the functions of the newspaper: to inform and entertain.
- Display **CD (file 14.1)** to show the notes that the writer made when they were planning the Charles Dickens entry for the 'Social Diary' section of the newspaper. TOL as you explain how they edited all of those notes down to the single sentence in the newspaper. Explain that each entry in the 'Social Diary' gives specific details about the event: Who? What? Where? and When? as well as using language which gently persuades the reader to attend the event.
- Navigate to the next slide to show the notes the writer used to write the entry on the Great Exhibition in the 'This Summer in History' section. Read the notes aloud using MT/YT and then ask the children to TTYP to discuss how the notes were changed to create the entry that appears in the newspaper. Take feedback.
- Ask the children to TTYP to discuss what type of information both these entries included, e.g. proper nouns, dates. Take feedback.
- Navigate to the next slide to show the children the notes you have been given to change into an entry for the 'Social Diary'. Model writing the entry for the children on the board or a flipchart, using TOL to show how you include names, places, dates and times as well as some details to persuade the reader to attend. You can use the entry below as a guide:

  George Sanger is pleased to announce that his celebrated circus will be delighting audiences at the Green Park showground from Tuesday to next Sunday. Matinee performances are from 12–2pm and the evening show will commence at 7pm. "The greatest name in entertainment – prepare to be amazed!" is their proud boast.

- Ask the children to turn to p.53 in their Pupils' Book and look at the Deconstruction 3 activity. Ask them to TTYP to read the notes and to use them to write an entry for the 'This Summer in History' section of the newspaper. Remind them to use proper nouns and specific details as you have done in your example. You may want to support the less able writers during this part of the activity.

write for a range of purposes and audiences; building a varied and rich vocabulary

Write 3

Purpose: for children to use source material to write a section for the class newspaper

- Before the lesson, print copies of the source material from **CD (file 14.2a)**, **(14.2b)**, **(14.2c)** or **(14.2d)**. Each child will need a different sheet depending on which section of the newspaper they chose to write, so print a selection and photocopy more if necessary.
- Tell the children that they are going to be creating their own class newspaper set in the Victorian era. Say that they now have the skills and ideas to write something for their newspaper.
- Tell them that they can write an advert to raise funds for Dr Barnardo, polish the article 'A Cloud of Frogs' that they improved on Day 13, or write entries for the 'Social Diary' or 'This Summer in History'. See printable **CD (files 14.2a** and **14.2b)** for source material for these entries.
- Children who wish to work more independently can use the source material from **CD (files 14.2c** or **14.2d)** to write other adverts or an alternative article.
- Remind the children that they can use the advert grid from **CD (file 12.3)** to help them. Say that they also have the Word bank on p.52 of the Pupils' Book.

- Tell them to remember to include the key features that are relevant for the piece that they are writing. Display the Key features grid from **CD (file 12.1)** as a prompt.
- Remind the children to include interesting and attention-grabbing language to entertain the reader and to use subordinate clauses to give extra information.
- You may need to work with a group of children to support them with their writing.

<table>
<tr><td>**Curriculum link:** discussing and recording ideas</td></tr>
</table>

Daily log

Purpose: for children to keep a personal log of notes, thoughts and ideas, collected from their reading and discussions. Some ideas will be used in their own writing

- Tell the children that they are going to come up with a name for their newspaper. On the board or a flipchart, write some examples of newspaper names from the present day and from Victorian times, e.g. *London News, Illustrated Times, The London Journal.*
- Ask the children to TTYP to talk about which names they like best and why.
- Tell them to note down two ideas of names for their class newspaper in their Daily log.

DAY 15

Write 3 (continued)

Purpose: for children to write their section of the class newspaper as independently as possible

- Continue the process as explained on Day 14 until the children have completed their entries.
- Monitor the children, supporting them if necessary as they write.

<table>
<tr><td>assessing the effectiveness of their own and others' writing</td></tr>
</table>

Evaluate and edit

Purpose: for children to evaluate their own and their partner's work against specific criteria and then discuss how they could improve their work

- Display **CD (file 15.1)** and read through the evaluation points using MT/YT.
- As a model, select an example of work where the writing has met the criteria, and share this with the other children, explaining why it works well.
- Tell the children to take turns to read their partner's writing in pairs and discuss together how well each piece of writing has met the criteria.
- Ask children to discuss at least two changes they could make to improve their work.

<table>
<tr><td>proofread for spelling and punctuation errors</td></tr>
</table>

Proofread

Purpose: for children to proofread their work and make changes to improve the accuracy of their grammar, punctuation and spelling

- Now ask the children to proofread their work. If you have noticed that several children need to improve on a particular aspect of spelling, grammar or punctuation, use this as a focus for the Proofread activity. Write an example which includes common errors from the children's writing and use this as a model.
- The children should always be checking for standard use of punctuation and correct spelling of common exception words.
- The following points would be particularly relevant for this Unit:
  - checking spelling of ambitious vocabulary choices (i.e. those borrowed from the Pupils' Book or Anthology text)
  - making sure paragraphs have been used appropriately to separate information.

Curriculum link:

in non-narrative material, use simple organisational devices such as headings and sub-headings

Publish and present ⓒⅮ

Ideally the children will have access to computers for this activity.

Purpose: for children to prepare and organise their writing for publication

- You can organise the publishing of your newspaper as you feel appropriate for your class. You may choose to organise children into groups according to what they chose to write about, or you may prefer to have more mixed groups so that each group has an article, advert and entry to publish. You may decide that you want each group to produce a separate newspaper or that you want one class newspaper containing all the pieces.

- Appoint an editor in charge of each group to direct the organisation of the separate pieces.

- Remind the children that they need to think carefully about the layout of their newspaper to make sure it is easy to read. Encourage them to think back to the key features that they looked at on Day 12. You may wish to display the key features from **CD (file 12.1)** for the children to refer to.

- Give the children time to write or type up the final version of their piece for the class newspaper.

Timetable

WEEK 1   Reading fiction   *Sugarcane Juice*

Day 1	Day 2	Day 3	Day 4	Day 5
The story store	Visual dictionary	Special phrases 🖨	Re-read a story version 3	Find out about a character
Read a story version 1	Read a story version 3	Word power 🖨	Dialogue and action	Quiz the character
Think and link 1 🖨	Think and link 2	Re-read a story version 3	Daily log	Character fact file 🖨
Read a story version 2	Daily log 🖨	Grammar: nouns and pronouns	Big Question	Daily log
Daily log	Big Question	Read and compare 🖨		Big Question
Big Question		Daily log		
		Big Question		

WEEK 2   Writing fiction   *Sugarcane Juice*

Day 6	Day 7	Day 8	Day 9	Day 10
What if not...?	Build an episode 1	Role-play – build the bus 🖨	Write a story 3	Share a story
Build a sentence 🖨	Build an episode 2	Write a story 1		Evaluate and edit
Tell a story	Build an episode 3 🖨	Write a story 2		Proofread
Daily log	Daily log	Daily log		Very Big Question
Big Question	Big Question	Big Question		

WEEK 3   Reading and writing non-fiction   Persuasive writing

Day 11	Day 12	Day 13	Day 14	Day 15
Introduction	Change it!	Write 1 🖨	Deconstruction 3	Evaluate and edit
Persuasive words 🖨	Watch a trailer	Deconstruction 2	Write 3	Proofread
Read and review 🖨	Deconstruction 1 🖨	Write 2 🖨	Daily log	Perform it
Daily log 🖨	Daily log	Daily log		

🖨: shows that a file should be printed out from the Software.

Overview of the Unit

The children explore a story from another culture: *Sugarcane Juice* by Pratima Mitchell, set in Pakistan. They look closely at the vivid description and action so that they can borrow language, ideas and structure such as dialogue to use in their own writing. They go on to write an additional episode of the story using the ideas and techniques that they have explored.

Linked via a Big Question, the Non-fiction week focuses on developing children's understanding of persuasive techniques used in advertising. For more information about the Non-fiction week and the Non-fiction writing evaluation criteria, see p.181.

Where appropriate, the children will be encouraged to develop an awareness of audience and purpose in relation to the fiction and non-fiction texts they are reading and writing.

Teacher modelling is provided in the teaching notes, Software and the Pupils' Book, supporting the children's writing at every stage in the Fiction and Non-fiction weeks.

The Homework Book provides a homework activity related to the content of this Unit for each of the three weeks.

Fiction

Reading

Children will:

- explore the cultural context of *Sugarcane Juice* to improve their understanding of the plot, setting and characters
- understand how Pratima Mitchell uses the senses to create vivid descriptions
- look closely at how Pratima Mitchell creates tension and pace in a section of the story.

Writing

Key writing purpose to be shared with the children:

To use ideas and characters from Sugarcane Juice *to write a new tension-filled episode of the story.*

Writing evaluation to be shared with the children

My story episode:

- is set on a bus, which is vividly described using simile and metaphor
- uses powerful verbs to describe the action
- has dialogue that creates atmosphere and tension.

Grammar:

- includes correct use of pronouns to avoid repetition, e.g. *he, they*
- uses direct speech, which is set out and punctuated correctly.

See the Planning section of the Software ('Timetables' tab) for a printable version of the Writing purpose and evaluation.

Fiction: Stories from another culture
Sugarcane Juice by Pratima Mitchell

READING FICTION

DAY 1

Curriculum link: listening to and discussing a wide range of fiction, identifying themes

The story store

Purpose: for children to become familiar with another culture

- Ask the children if they know anything about Pakistan. Take feedback.
- Display the Pakistan slideshow on **CD (file 1.1)**.
- Look at the images and facts and discuss them. Ask the children to TTYP (Turn to your partner) and discuss:
  – Is there anything they are surprised about?
  – What else would they like to find out about Pakistan and the people who live there?

predicting

Read a story version 1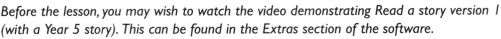

Before the lesson, you may wish to watch the video demonstrating Read a story version 1 (with a Year 5 story). This can be found in the Extras section of the software.

Purpose: for children to become familiar with Story version 1, the bare bones of the story

- Read Story version 1 aloud to the children all the way through. Do not reveal the ending.

  Story version 1
  1. A boy worked in a bus station helping his father.
  2. His father had a stall.
  3. The boy liked watching a conjurer at the bus station.
  4. He followed the conjurer onto a bus to sell his wares.
  5. He became mesmerised by the conjurer's clever tricks.
  6. The bus started up and left the bus station without the boy realising.
  7. The conjurer had already jumped off.
  8. The boy annoyed the passengers and one of them shouted at the bus driver to throw him off the bus.
  9. The boy got off the bus but he was far away from home.

- Use MT/YT (My turn/Your turn) and TTYP for each point. Use exaggerated intonation – e.g. whisper bits – to make the sentences memorable. This will help the children to 'hold' the basic story in their minds.
- Ask the children to TTYP to share what happens in the story.
- Now display Story version 1 on **CD (file 1.2)** so the children can see the text and find out how much of it they have remembered.

building a varied and rich vocabulary

Think and link 1

Purpose: for children to make connections to the story and the setting

- Before the lesson, print a copy of the pictures from **CD (file 1.4)**.
- Tell the children that the story is set in Pakistan, and that the buses there are famous for being amazingly colourful. Explain that bus stations in Pakistan can be exciting places, with people selling food and other goods.
- Display the slideshow of images of Pakistan related to the story on **CD (file 1.3)**.
- Ask the children to TTYP to tell their partner three things that stood out for them in the slideshow. Take feedback.
- Return to the slideshow. Use the Build a sentence technique (see Introduction p.12) to create a descriptive sentence for each picture, for example:

Resources
- **PB** Pupils' Book, pp.54–64
- **A** Anthology, pp.68–80
- **CD** CD on Interactive whiteboard, Unit 6
- **GB** Grammar Bank on CD
- **HB** Homework Book, pp.21–23

    — *This bus is a multi-coloured driving machine.* MT/YT.
    — *This bus is a vibrant multi-coloured driving machine.* MT/YT.
    — *This bus is a wildly patterned, multi-coloured driving machine setting off on a magical journey.* MT/YT.

- Write your completed sentences under the pictures from printable **CD (file 1.4)**, which you can then place on your Story wall for this Unit.

Curriculum link:
predicting;
identifying how
language, structure
and presentation
contribute to
meaning

Read a story version 2   CD

Purpose: for children to examine how Story version 2 provides additional information for the reader and for children to become more familiar with the story before they hear the full version

- Read Story version 2 aloud to the children with appropriate intonation.
Story version 2
  1. Hamid worked in a bus station after school helping his father sell sugarcane juice.
  2. His father had a mobile cart, which was a work of art.
  3. Hamid enjoyed watching Bulbul the conjurer at the bus station.
  4. Hamid followed Bulbul onto a bus to sell sugarcane juice for two rupees a glass.
  5. He became mesmerised as Bulbul made tiny yellow chickens multiply in his hat!
  6. As Hamid applauded, the bus started up and left the bus station to go to Timarpur, without him realising.
  7. However, Bulbul had already jumped off the bus.
  8. By accident, Hamid dropped his tray and the sticky sugarcane juice fell to the floor. An old man was so annoyed that he shouted at the bus driver to throw Hamid off the bus.
  9. Hamid got off the bus at the next stop. He had a little money but he was 10 miles from home.
- Display Story version 2 on **CD (file 1.5)**, over two slides. Point out that we now know that the name of the boy in the story is Hamid. Click 'Highlights' to show the other parts of the story that have changed.
- TOL (Think out loud) and use TTYP to share how this extra information changes the pictures in our minds as we hear the story. Link what the children have read and heard so far with their knowledge of Pakistan, the buses and bus stations.
- Hide the text and ask the children to use TTYP to take turns telling the story to each other, taking one section at a time. You may wish to display the text once or twice during this activity so that they can refresh their memories.

discussing ideas
and predicting

Daily log   PB

Purpose: for children to keep a personal log of notes, thoughts and ideas, collected from their reading and discussions. Some ideas will be used in their own writing

- Ask the children to TTYP and discuss the questions on p.54 of their Pupils' Book.
- Tell them to write down their prediction for the ending in their Daily log.

discussion;
develop, agree
on, and evaluate
rules for effective
discussion

Big Question   CD

Purpose: for children to develop their skills of argument and discussion through a mini enquiry session based on a philosophical question relating to the work of the day

- Display today's Big Question on **CD (file 1.6)**:

  Should we make choices based on the past as well as the present?

- Ask the children to TTYP to talk about this question. Collect feedback and write some responses on the board.
- Click 'Prompts' to show some statements that may help to encourage discussion.

Fiction: Stories from another culture

DAY 2

Visual dictionary (CD)

Purpose: for children to be introduced to vocabulary specific to the culture in the story

- Display the words on **CD (file 2.1)**. Explain that these are words the children may not have heard before and that they are special because they are used in a particular culture. Use MT/YT to read the words aloud.
- Click on a term to take you to its visual dictionary entry. Use MT/YT to read the definition with the children, then to share the sentence containing the word/s.
- Click 'Back to list' to return to the list of words. Repeat for all the terms.
- Next, ask the children to TTYP and discuss how knowing the meanings of these words affects their ideas about the story. Take feedback.

Curriculum link: checking that the text makes sense, asking questions, drawing inferences

Read a story version 3 (teacher only)

Purpose: for children to hear and enjoy the full version of the story for the first time

- Tell the children that they are now going to hear the whole story for the very first time. TOL about which parts you are looking forward to.
- Read the whole of *Sugarcane Juice* from the Anthology pp.68–77 to the children with great enjoyment and appropriate intonation. Make your storytelling a performance, and emphasise the raucous mayhem of the bus station setting.
- Discuss the way the people on the bus speak when they are cross with Hamid. Talk with children about the lady on the bus insulting Hamid, saying '*Hut, badmash*, scoundrel!' *Hut* means *Oi!* or *Oh!* and *badmash* means *naughty* – the lady is telling Hamid off! Explain that a *scoundrel* is someone who is up to no good. Ask the children to TTYP and say these words to their partner, to tell them off!
- Also explain that when Hamid calls the bus driver *Uncle* he is being polite, in the same way that calling an older woman *Bibiji* is polite.
- Link back to the predictions for the story ending the children made in their Daily log. Ask them to TTYP to share their predictions and compare them with the actual ending. Take feedback.

discussing their understanding; asking questions to improve their understanding of a text

Think and link 2 (CD)

Purpose: for children to understand the chronology and main points of the story

- Display the story map on **CD (file 2.2)**.
- Ask the children to TTYP to see if they can remember the main characters and their names: Hamid, Abba, Bulbul, the old man and the kind bus driver.
- Remind the children of the main settings for the story: the bus station and a bus.
- Go through the story map using TOL to discuss what the main events are and where they happen.

retelling stories orally; recording ideas

Daily log

Purpose: for children to keep a personal log of notes, thoughts and ideas, collected from their reading and discussions. Some ideas will be used in their own writing

- Before the lesson, print off a copy of the story map on **CD (file 2.3)** for each child.
- Ask the children to TTYP and use the map to retell the story to their partners.
- Encourage them to annotate their story map by adding any special words that are relevant, to use later on.
- Ask the children to paste their annotated story map into their Daily log.

Curriculum link:
discussion;
develop, agree on,
and evaluate
rules for effective
discussion

Big Question

*Purpose: for children to develop their skills of argument and discussion through a mini
enquiry session based on a philosophical question relating to the work of the day*

- Display today's Big Question on **CD (file 2.4):**

  Is it good to have new experiences?

- Follow the process as explained on Day 1.

DAY 3

discussing words
and phrases
that capture the
reader's interest
and imagination

Special phrases

*Purpose: for children to explore strong descriptive phrases and think about how they help the
reader engage with a story*

> ***thundering towards** Islamabad, Karachi, Faisalabad and other towns*
>
> ***eyes that always looked like they held a secret***
>
> *the bus was ancient and it **groaned and creaked***
>
> ***quick as a flash***

- Display the Special phrases on **CD (file 3.1)**.
- Drag the phrases into the Focus box one by one. TOL for each phrase, describing
  the images and ideas it brings to mind for you as a reader, e.g.

  *'Thundering towards Islamabad, Karachi, Faisalabad and other towns' makes me think of
  the speed the bus is going at and the sound it makes. I can see the bus like a dark cloud,
  coming towards a town with a noise like thunder…boom, boom, boom…getting louder as it
  gets closer. I also think that this bus, like thunder, can't be stopped – it's unstoppable!*

- Make connections with the story as you go, linking the images and ideas created
  by the Special phrases with events and settings in the text. Discuss how the
  phrases help you to picture what happens in the story.
- You can print off the Special phrases from **CD (file 3.2)** and display them on the
  Story wall for this Unit.

discussing words
and phrases
that capture the
reader's interest
and imagination

Word power

*Purpose: for children to learn the meaning of descriptive vocabulary used in the story and to
understand how writers use language for effect*

> *gaudy   lurched   festooned   rattled*

- Tell the children that the writer of *Sugarcane Juice* has used some highly descriptive
  words that are effective because they help us to create clear pictures in our minds.
- Display the **CD (file 3.3)** to show the Power words and their definitions. Use MT/YT
  as you read the sentences aloud, putting special emphasis on the relevant words.
- Take opportunities to use the words during the day in an exaggerated fashion,
  e.g. *'The bad weather is making me feel a bit* rattled *today, children.'*
- Encourage the children to use the words in their everyday conversation so that they
  become embedded in the children's own spoken (and eventually, written) vocabulary.
- Print out these words and their definitions from **CD (file 3.4)** and display them
  on your Story wall for this Unit. Praise the children if they use one of the words.

Curriculum link:
read aloud
showing
understanding
through
intonation, tone
and volume

Re-read a story version 3 🅰

Purpose: for children to gain a deeper understanding of the story and to see the text for the first time

- Ask the children to read the story on Anthology pp.68–77 aloud with their partners. They should read alternate sections each, and ensure they use expression and intonation to convey meaning and impact to their partner. Explain that you will be listening in and looking out for particularly good reading.
- For some groups, you may wish to read aloud to the children first as they follow the text in their own copy so that they can Jump in (see Introduction p.13) to say the Power words and Special phrases.

Year 4 Grammar
choosing nouns
or pronouns
appropriately
for clarity and
cohesion

Grammar: nouns and pronouns ⓒⒹ 🄿🄱 🄷🄱

Purpose: for children to develop their understanding of the appropriate use of nouns and pronouns

- Remind the children that *common nouns* are words that name things (e.g. *palace, country, girl*) and *proper nouns* name particular things (e.g. *Buckingham Palace, Spain, Sophie*).
- Explain that *pronouns* (e.g. *we, she, they, it*) can replace common nouns and proper nouns to make our speaking and writing more natural.
- Display **CD (file 3.5)** to show two sentences and read them aloud using MT/YT.
- Ask the children to TTYP to discuss which sentence sounded the most natural and the closest to how we usually speak. Ask them to answer chorally. Choose two sets of partners to give reasons for their answer.
- Click 'Highlights' to highlight the nouns and pronouns. Clarify that once the nouns have been introduced it sounds more natural to then use pronouns.
- Explain that we have to be careful when we use pronouns because if it is not clear which noun the pronoun is replacing, it can become confusing. Navigate to the next slide and use MT/YT to read the sentence aloud.
- Ask the children to TTYP to say why it is not clear from this sentence exactly what happened, then collect feedback. Click 'Highlights' to show the nouns and pronouns in the sentence. Use the think bubbles to explain the point.
- Navigate to the next slide to show how the sentence could be written more clearly.
- Tell the children that the story *Sugarcane Juice* is packed full of different objects, people and events. Say that the writer has had to be very careful how she uses nouns and pronouns, to make it clear what is happening throughout the story.
- Navigate to the next slide to show a sentence from the story. Read it aloud and explain that it is clear in this sentence that the pronoun *its* is referring to the bus. Navigate to the next slide to show another passage from the story. Tell the children to follow the text on the screen as you read it aloud.
- Say that the writer has had to be very careful here because in this passage we read about different characters and their various belongings. Explain the importance of making it clear what or who each pronoun is referring to.
- Navigate to the next slide to show lists of the characters and their belongings from the passage. Use MT/YT to read through the lists.
- Navigate to the next slide to show the passage with each pronoun highlighted. Point to the first pronoun and ask the children to give a choral answer to the question: *'Which character is this pronoun representing?'* (Bulbul). Repeat the process for each highlighted pronoun, clarifying where necessary.
- Say that you are going to show them the passage written slightly differently. Navigate to the next slide to show the example and ask the children to read it out chorally with you. Now tell them to TTYP to say what is confusing about the passage. Collect feedback.

- Navigate to the final slide to reveal the passage with colour-coded highlights that show how each of the pronouns links to the different nouns. Use the think bubble to explain which word has been changed and how it changes our understanding.
- Now ask the children to look at the Grammar: nouns and pronouns activity on p.55 of their Pupils' Book. Explain that they need to take turns to read through the passage and then TTYP to decide which words are proper nouns and which words are pronouns.
- Choose two or three to share examples of proper nouns they have identified and clarify where necessary. Repeat the process for pronouns. Check that they know which proper noun or common noun their pronoun examples are replacing.

Homework book p.21 provides further practice on pronouns.

Read and compare

Purpose: for children to compare and contrast the two settings in the story

- Before the lesson, print a copy of **CD (file 3.6)** for each child.
- Ask the children to look at the Read and compare activity on pp.56–57 of their Pupils' Book. Say that they are now going to look at two settings from the story.
- Read aloud the paragraph describing the bus station. Display the Settings collector on **CD (file 3.7)** and use it to analyse the bus station setting. TOL as you type in the words and phrases from the paragraph that show smells.
- Ask the children to TTYP to read the description of the bus station on p.56 of their Pupils' Book, then to fill in the first column of their Settings collector from **CD (file 3.6)**.
- Read the other paragraph on p.57, describing the setting inside a bus. Ask the children to TTYP to read and analyse the setting using the same headings as before, filling in the second column of their Settings collector. After a short time, take some feedback and model adding a few words and phrases to your copy of the Settings collector.
- Give the children time to complete their Settings collectors. Remind them that their examples don't need to be the same as yours.
- Ask them to TTYP to compare the information they have collected about the two settings, focusing on the similarities and differences.
- Take feedback and record their responses on the board or a flipchart.
- Now tell the children to TTYP to discuss which description created the most powerful images in their minds and why.
- Collect feedback, making sure they can give reasons and examples from the texts to support their answers.

Daily log

> **Curriculum link:** discussing words and phrases that capture the reader's interest and imagination; building a varied and rich vocabulary

Purpose: for children to keep a personal log of notes, thoughts and ideas, collected from their reading and discussions. Some ideas will be used in their own writing

- Tell the children that the story includes other words and phrases about the two settings: a bus and the bus station. Ask them to look at the story in the Anthology pp.68–77. Model finding an extra detail to describe one of the settings, e.g. *passengers perched perilously on luggage racks* to describe a bus. TOL about what it tells you, e.g. *'This means the bus is so full that some passengers climb on top and sit on the roof!'*
- Ask the children to read the text and add further details about the two settings to their Settings collector.
- Tell the children to paste their work into their Daily log.

Curriculum link:
discussion;
develop, agree on,
and evaluate
rules for effective
discussion

Big Question (CD)

Purpose: for children to develop their skills of argument and discussion through a mini enquiry session based on a philosophical question relating to the work of the day

- Display today's Big Question on **CD (file 3.8)**:

  Is being sad always a bad thing?

- Follow the process as explained on Day 1.

DAY 4

asking questions
to improve their
understanding of
a text

Re-read a story version 3

Purpose: for children to deepen their understanding of a story by increasing familiarity with the text

- Ask the children to read the whole story silently from the Anthology pp.68–77. Tell them that they can stop to record any thoughts, ideas, questions or favourite bits in their Daily log as they read. Explain that it is more important for them to think about what they are reading than to finish first and, as they know the story, it doesn't matter if they don't finish it this time.

showing
understanding
through
intonation, tone,
volume and action

Dialogue and action (CD)

Purpose: for children to explore how the author uses dialogue and description of the action to help the reader visualise how characters behave

- Display the extract on **CD (file 4.1)** which describes Hamid's altercation with the old lady on the bus. Read the extract aloud with appropriate intonation, and use voices for the different characters.
- Ask the children to TTYP and sum up what is happening and who is talking in this extract. Take feedback.
- Say that you want to 'zoom in' on the dialogue. Move to the next slide on **CD (file 4.1)** to show just the dialogue from the extract. Ask the children to TTYP and act out the dialogue, one partner taking the role of Hamid, the other the role of the old lady.
- Move to the next slide on **CD (file 4.1)** to show just the action in this part of the story. Read through the text and TOL to describe how the different characters are moving. Make sure to note that Bulbul gets off the bus without Hamid noticing and that Hamid calls to the driver but the driver does not hear him.
- Tell the partners to join up with another pair and use the text on the slide to help them mime the scene with Hamid, the old lady, Bulbul and the driver. Encourage them to use the details in the text, e.g. the old lady *dabbing the damp patch with a scarf*, to make their mime accurate.
- Now return to the first slide on **CD (file 4.1)**. Read the whole text again. Ask the children to act it out with both dialogue and action.
- As the children act, move around the room observing. Give feedback about how their understanding of the text has improved their interpretation.

discuss and record
ideas; using and
punctuating direct
speech

Daily log

Purpose: for children to keep a personal log of notes, thoughts and ideas, collected from their reading and discussions. Some ideas will be used in their own writing

- Ask the children to recall the ideas and details they used in their acting to write a few sentences describing what happened between Hamid and the old lady.
- Tell the children to TTYP to tell each other an idea before they start to write.
- Remind them that when they write the dialogue between Hamid and the old lady, they should take care to use inverted commas (speech marks) correctly.

Curriculum link:
discussion;
develop, agree on,
and evaluate
rules for effective
discussion

Big Question ⓒ

*Purpose: for children to develop their skills of argument and discussion through a mini
enquiry session based on a philosophical question relating to the work of the day*

- Display today's Big Question on **CD (file 4.2)**:

  If you do something wrong and you say sorry, does that make things better?

- Follow the process as explained on Day 1.

DAY 5

Find out about a character

*Purpose: for children to use evidence from the story to compose questions that will elicit a
deeper understanding of the main character*

- Say that the main character from *Sugarcane Juice*, Hamid, is coming to visit
  the class, and that the children will have a chance to ask him some questions.
  Explain that these questions should be about the story and also about
  Hamid's background.
- Ask the children to TTYP to discuss what they would like more information
  about. Take feedback and note down key ideas on the board or on a flipchart,
  e.g. *what it is like selling sugarcane juice; more information on the bus station; Hamid's
  feelings when he realised he was stuck on the bus.*
- Choose one of the ideas, e.g. *what it is like selling sugarcane juice.* TOL to model
  making it into questions; e.g. '*I want to know:* Is it an easy job? How does Hamid
  make the juice? How much is it? How does he sell it on the buses? *But maybe that's
  too much. I'll narrow it down:* How exactly do you help your father selling sugarcane
  juice? Who buys it and how much is a glass?'
- Now ask the children to TTYP and compose some questions using the ideas on the
  flipchart as a starting point. Ask them to write their questions in their Daily log.
- Take feedback and write some of the children's questions on the board or flipchart.
- Read each question, and ask the children to TTYP to decide whether it is asking
  for a fact, an opinion or a feeling. Mark it 'F', 'O' or 'FE'. Discuss whether there is
  a good range of questions, covering all three areas. If not, involve the children in
  adding some more.
- Leave the questions on display for use during the next activity.

inferring
characters'
feelings, thoughts
and motives from
their actions

Quiz the character 🄰

Purpose: for children to act in role to explore the main character

- Tell the children that they are going to play the role of Hamid, and you are going
  to interview them. Explain that when you ask each question they will have time to
  TTYP to think of their answer, and that they can use the story on pp.68–77 of the
  Anthology to help them.
- Using the list compiled during the previous activity, start by asking easier,
  fact-based questions. Give the children time to TTYP and then take feedback.
  Model writing notes from the answers on the board or a flipchart, so that the
  children have a record they can refer back to later.
- Move on to ask questions about opinions and feelings. Encourage the children
  to find evidence in the text for their answers and to use what they know about
  Hamid to make inferences about how he might feel or behave. Continue to model
  writing interview notes.
- At the end of the interview, use your notes to sum up some of the key
  information you have gathered. Check that 'Hamid' is happy with your findings!
- Leave your notes on display for use during the next activity.

Character fact file

Purpose: for children to use a variety of sources to compile a fact file about the main character in the story

- Before the lesson, print off a fact file for each child from **CD (file 5.1)**.
- Display the Hamid fact file from **CD (file 5.1)**. Read the headings and questions. Point out which answers will be easy to find as they are facts that are given in the story, and which will need the children to use clues from the story and the interview. Model filling in answers for one or two of the questions.
- Ask the children to TTYP and to use the letter from Hamid to his cousin from the Pupils' Book pp.58–59 as an additional source of information to help them complete their fact file.

Curriculum link: discussing and recording ideas

Daily log

Purpose: for children to keep a personal log of notes, thoughts and ideas, collected from their reading and discussions. Some ideas will be used in their own writing

- Ask the children to think back to when they first read the story. Tell them to TTYP and discuss what they enjoyed, what they found exciting, and whether any bits of the story were hard to imagine.
- Ask the children to TTYP and talk about how they feel about the story now – have their feelings changed? If so, how?
- Ask the children to write in their Daily log one thing they enjoyed about the story from the first reading and one thing they were unsure about. Next, tell them to write how they feel about the story now and what parts of it they now enjoy the most.

discussion; develop, agree on, and evaluate rules for effective discussion

Big Question

Purpose: for children to develop their skills of argument and discussion through a mini enquiry session based on a philosophical question relating to the work of the day

- Display today's Big Question on **CD (file 5.2)**:

  Do we have a right to know everything about someone else?

- Follow the process as explained on Day 1.

WRITING FICTION

What if not…?

Purpose: for children to imagine other directions that the story could take

drawing inferences; participate in discussion about books

- Display the What if not…? question on **CD (file 6.1)**: 'What if not *let off the bus*? What if *the driver made Hamid stay on the bus*?' TOL as you explore what the question means, linking it to the story, e.g. '*So if Hamid got stuck on the bus he could end up very far from home. It would be harder for him to get back.*'
- Ask the children to TTYP to discuss the What if not…? question. Take feedback.
- Now ask them to turn to p.59 in their Pupils' Book and to read and discuss the other What if not…? questions. Take feedback, writing their key ideas down on the board or a flipchart to return to later.

Curriculum link:
discussing writing
similar to that
which they are
planning to
write; building a
varied and rich
vocabulary

Build a sentence

Purpose: for children to learn how to compose descriptive sentences about the setting

- Explain that you are going to look at three sentences containing descriptions of the bus going to Timarpur. Display the first sentence on **CD (file 6.2)**. Use MT/YT to read it aloud.
- Comment on how the author uses the simile *it groaned and creaked like an old person in pain* to help the reader to really imagine the noise that the bus made.
- Ask the children to TTYP and make the sound that the bus made.
- Click 'Next' to show a choice of similes that could be used to describe the bus. Drag and drop each simile into the sentence, and read the sentence aloud. Take feedback from the children about the different choices. Discuss their effect on how children imagine the bus.
- Repeat the process for the remaining two sentences.
- Say that you are going to compose a new episode in the story involving Hamid on a runaway bus. Explain that the sentences the children have just been exploring are the inspiration for your description of the bus.
- Now use modelled composition to write a description of the bus for the new episode. As you write each sentence, TOL to explain what you are doing. Orally rehearse and change each phrase before beginning to write. As you compose, use MT/YT for the children to say each sentence, and then write it on the board or a flipchart. A description and TOL prompts are available on printable **CD (file 6.3)**. You may wish to keep these sentences for use on Day 9.
- Once you have finished modelling the writing process, ask the children to read the full text on p.60 of their Pupils' Book, taking turns to read each sentence with appropriate intonation.
- Ask the children, either individually or in pairs, to compose their own sentences aloud, using the prompts in their Pupils' Book. Once they can say each completed sentence aloud, they can write it in their Daily log.
- Ask partners to take turns to develop their sentences. Encourage crossings out, switching words around, etc. Emphasise that this is writing in action.

Tell a story

Purpose: for children to practise oral storytelling

- Tell the children that they are going to help you to think of some ideas for Hamid's new adventure. Show them the map on **CD (file 6.4)** and discuss the route that the bus might take.
- Say that you have decided to use the route through the mountains. Explain that you want this story to be as exciting as possible, so you will need to use accurate verbs to describe the runaway bus and vivid details to make each peril seem terrifying and dangerous.
- Develop the description of the journey orally, using TOL, e.g. *'As the bus sped down the narrow mountain road, Hamid saw the tiny villages like specks in the valley below.'* Then TOL about how to improve the sentence, e.g. *'I want a better word than* sped *like… hurtled or careered.'*
- Ask the children to TTYP to discuss which word to use. Take feedback and incorporate the chosen word in the sentence. Then repeat, e.g. to improve *tiny*.
- Next, ask the children to continue the journey, developing the story orally with their partners using the map on p.61 in their Pupils' Book. Partners should take roles as storyteller and listener, swapping when you say *'Stop and swap'* and carrying on the story. The emphasis should be on building confidence in storytelling and keeping an audience engaged.

Curriculum link:
discussing and
recording ideas

Daily log

Purpose: for children to keep a personal log of notes, thoughts and ideas, collected from their reading and discussions. Some ideas will be used in their own writing

- Remind the children about the What if not…? question they discussed earlier: 'What if not *kind*? What if *the bus driver were cross, or mad, or mean*?'
- Explain that they can use this to generate ideas for their own story. Ask them to TTYP to share some ideas.
- Tell the children to write down two ideas about what might happen in the story in their Daily log.

discussion;
develop, agree on,
and evaluate
rules for effective
discussion

Big Question ⓒⒹ

Purpose: for children to develop their skills of argument and discussion through a mini enquiry session based on a philosophical question relating to the work of the day

- Display today's Big Question on **CD (file 6.5)**:

  Is it weak to change your mind? *

- Follow the process as explained on Day 1.

  * This Big Question will be revisited on Day 11 – the first day of the Non-fiction week.

Build an episode 1 ⓒⒹ

Purpose: for children to be able to see a story grow through three stages of development

- Remind the children that they heard two versions of *Sugarcane Juice* – Story version 1 and Story version 2 – before they heard and read the full story. These helped them prepare to read the full story.
- Explain that you are going to show them some versions of your new episode in Hamid's story, about his adventure on the runaway bus, which you used as preparation for writing the full episode. Explain that this new part of the story should slip effortlessly into the original story and provide a new ending.
- Display the questions on **CD (file 7.1)**. Explain that these questions helped you to decide what to put in the episode. TOL to explore the first question and then click 'Reveal' to show the answer.
- Ask the children to TTYP to discuss the remaining questions. For each, take feedback, then click 'Reveal' to show the answer.
- Move to the next slide to display Build an episode 1. Read it aloud.

plan writing by
discussing writing
that is similar

plan writing by
discussing writing
that is similar;
recording ideas

Build an episode 2 ⓒⒹ

Purpose: for children to be able to see a story grow through three stages of development

- Explain that you are now going to show the next version of your new story episode. This one has additional information and words – it has been developed. Show Build an episode 2 on **CD (file 7.2)**. TOL as you compare this version to Build an episode 1.
- Click 'Highlights' repeatedly to show, in turn, the use of the past tense, additional information, direct speech, and similes (on the first slide) or cultural references relevant to the setting of Pakistan (on the second slide).
- Draw the children's attention to the use of pronouns (e.g. *it, his*) and say that you have used these to avoid repetition of nouns.

Curriculum link: understand the skills and processes that are essential for writing

Build an episode 3

Purpose: for children to be able to see a story grow through three stages of development

- Before the lesson, print a copy of the new episode from **CD (file 7.4)** for each child.
- Put yourself in role as the writer of this story episode. Explain that you have been trying to write the episode so it will fit perfectly into the original story, from the point when Hamid realises he is stuck on a moving bus.
- An example story is provided as a model for writing. Display it on **CD (file 7.3)** and read it aloud to the children.
- Now ask them to TTYP and take turns to read a paragraph of Build an episode 3 from the printout of **CD (file 7.4)**. Using TTYP and oral feedback, ask them to evaluate your writing using the questions on p.62 of their Pupils' Book.

discussing and recording ideas

Daily log

Purpose: for children to keep a personal log of notes, thoughts and ideas, collected from their reading and discussions. Some ideas will be used in their own writing

- Ask the children to TTYP and share ideas for a title for the new episode of the story they've just read. Ask them to record their best idea in their Daily log, explaining why they think it is a good title.

discussion; develop, agree on, and evaluate rules for effective discussion

Big Question

Purpose: for children to develop their skills of argument and discussion through a mini enquiry session based on a philosophical question relating to the work of the day

- Display today's Big Question on **CD (file 7.5)**:

  Should we always make our own decisions?

- Follow the process as explained on Day 1.

DAY 8

Role-play – build the bus

perform, showing understanding through intonation, tone, volume and action

Purpose: for children to develop imagery (similes and metaphors) to describe the bus

- Before the lesson, print off and cut up copies of **CD (file 8.2)**, one piece for each pair of children. These will be used in the role-play.
- Tell the children that they are going to write a new episode in Hamid's story, about the runaway bus.
- Say that in this story the bus is going to be so important it will be like another character. Explain that they are going to develop language and ideas about the bus so that they can use lots of different images to describe it.
- Display the picture of the bus on **CD (file 8.1)**. Click 'TOL' repeatedly and TOL about different ideas which develop imagery for describing the features of the bus. Explain which of the TOL points are metaphors (saying something *is* something else) and which are similes (saying something is *like* something else).
- When you have shared all the imagery, say that the children are going to use these images and work together to 'build' the bus. Explain that there are five different parts, and the children are going to build the bus by 'being' these different parts.
- Give partners a copy of the simile or metaphor for their part of the bus from **CD (file 8.2)**. Ask them to read it and work out if they can make an action and/or a sound to go with it.
- Ask pairs to read out their bit of imagery and to do their action and/or sound. Check that everyone knows what they are doing.

- Tell the children that you are going to play an audio description of the bus's journey as it careers wildly down the mountain. Explain that when the description mentions their part of the bus, they should do the sound and/or movement that they made up. Play the first audio description on **CD (file 8.3)**. The actions and sounds made by the children should match the description, creating the tension and atmosphere of the bus hurtling out of control.
- Next, ask the children to TTYP to come up with a new metaphor or simile describing their part of the bus as it struggles to climb a hill. Take feedback and write ideas on the board or a flipchart.
- Give children time to create actions and/or sounds for their new pieces of imagery.
- Play the second audio description on **CD (file 8.3)** of the bus going up the hill and then down the other side. Repeat the process above with the children performing their new sounds and actions when their part of the bus is mentioned.
- Give feedback and point out good similes and metaphors and appropriate actions or sounds. Ask the children to TTYP to discuss which imagery they thought was the most powerful and how they could use it in their writing.
- Finally, ask the children what other dangers the bus and its passengers could face. Take feedback and write some ideas on the board or a flipchart.

Curriculum link:
composing and rehearsing sentences orally; creating settings, characters, plot

Write a story 1

Purpose: for children to use prompts to develop a plan for a new episode of Hamid's journey

- Tell the children that they are going to write their own version of Hamid's adventure on the runaway bus.
- Explain that you are going to start by using a generic episode plan, which involves Hamid on the bus facing two different dangers, then an ending.
- Display the bare bones episode plan on the first slide of **CD (file 8.4)**.
- Talk through what you might put in your plan. Refer back to the map on **CD (file 6.4)** or p.61 of the Pupils' Book, which the children used for ideas in the Tell a story activity on Day 6.
- Ask the children to use the example plan and the question prompts on p.62 of their Pupils' Book to help them write their own plan in their Daily log.

composing and rehearsing sentences orally; creating settings, characters, plot

Write a story 2

Purpose: for children to develop their plan by adding detail, dialogue and action

- Tell the children that you need to decide where to add detail, dialogue and action to your plan.
- Move to the second slide on **CD (file 8.4)** to display the first stage of the plan, the Build up. TOL as you talk through it, explaining how you can use the description of the bus to create tension as it gets faster and runs out of control. Click 'Reveal' to display ideas for adding description to the plan.
- Navigate to the next slide. TOL as you talk through Problem 1, showing how you would use accurate verbs to show action and dialogue to create tension. Click 'Reveal' to display ideas.
- Repeat for Problem 2 and the Resolution.
- Now ask the children to annotate their own plan, adding ideas and interesting words and phrases.

- Remind the children of the ideas they had when they did the Build the bus activity, which are on the board or flipchart for them to use if they wish.
- Remind them to use dialogue to move the action on and create tension, and not just to say what has already happened.

Curriculum link: write for a range of different purposes

Daily log

Purpose: for children to keep a personal log of notes, thoughts and ideas, collected from their reading and discussions. Some ideas will be used in their own writing

- Ask the children to TTYP to think of something for the driver to say at the beginning of the story to show he is losing control of the bus, and something for him to say later on, to show that he has no control of the bus.
- Ask them to write their ideas in their Daily log.

discussion; develop, agree on, and evaluate rules for effective discussion

Big Question ⓒⒹ

Purpose: for children to develop their skills of argument and discussion through a mini enquiry session based on a philosophical question relating to the work of the day

- Display today's Big Question on the **CD (file 8.5)**:

  Is it good for people to be in control of everything they do?

- Follow the process as explained on Day 1.

DAY 9

Write a story 3 🅿🅱

Purpose: for children to use their developed plan to write their new episode of Hamid's journey

creating settings, characters, plot; monitor whether their writing makes sense

- Tell the children that they are ready to write their own episode of *Sugarcane Juice*. Remind them of the plan setting out the structure of their episode that they wrote and annotated in their Daily log.
- Ask them to use the composition prompts on p.63 of their Pupils' Book to guide them. Remind them that they can use any useful parts of their Daily log to help them.
- Tell the children to use the sentences they wrote as part of the Build a sentence activity on Day 6 to help them write the first paragraph. You may wish to display the sentences you modelled writing during the activity.
- Ask them to look at the Power words on the Story wall and to use a thesaurus for synonyms, especially for verbs describing how the bus moves.
- Remind them of the imagery they created to describe the different parts of the bus in the Role-play activity on Day 8, and how they could use it in their writing for different situations.
- Remind the children to use pronouns where possible to avoid repetition.
- Explain that the dialogue in their story should include some direct speech.
- Encourage children to rehearse their opening sentence in their minds before they begin to write.

DAY 10

Share a story

Purpose: for children to read and share their episode of Hamid's journey

- Ask the children to read through their own episode from Day 9.
- Next, ask them to re-read their episode and underline their favourite or best parts. Ask them to share these with their partners. Collect feedback on best bits from partners.
- Make sure that any powerful words or phrases are written out and added to the Story wall for this Unit.

Evaluate and edit (CD)

Curriculum link: assessing the effectiveness of their own and others' writing

Purpose: for children to evaluate their own and their partner's work against specific criteria and then discuss how they could improve their work

- Display **CD (file 10.1)** and read through the evaluation points using MT/YT.
- As a model, select an example of work where the writing has met the criteria, and share this with the other children, explaining why it works well.
- Tell the children to take turns to read their partner's writing in pairs and discuss together how well each piece of writing has met the criteria.
- Ask the children to discuss at least two changes they could make to improve their work.

Proofread

proofread for spelling and punctuation errors

Purpose: for children to proofread their work and make changes to improve the accuracy of their grammar, punctuation and spelling

- Now ask the children to proofread their work. If you have noticed that several children need to improve on a particular aspect of spelling, grammar or punctuation, use this as a focus for the Proofread activity. Write an example which includes common errors from the children's writing and use this as a model.
- The children should always be checking for standard use of punctuation and correct spelling of common exception words.
- The following points would be particularly relevant for this Unit:
  - checking spelling of ambitious vocabulary choices (i.e. those borrowed from the Pupils' Book or Anthology text)
  - making sure that direct speech is punctuated correctly using inverted commas
  - checking that capital letters have been used for proper nouns.

Very Big Question (CD)

discussion; develop, agree on, and evaluate rules for effective discussion

Purpose: for children to develop their willingness to broaden or revise their opinions through exploring one of the Big Questions in more depth

- See Unit 1 Day 10 for teaching notes on the Very Big Question (p.41).

READING AND WRITING NON-FICTION

Linked via a Big Question, the Non-fiction week focuses on developing children's understanding of persuasive techniques used in advertising so that they can create their own marketing campaign with a clear message. The children will analyse a film trailer and poster and design their own versions for a new film. See p.164 for the daily timetable for the Non-fiction week.

Non-fiction

Reading

Children will:

- explore the way that advertising is used to change people's minds or persuade them to do something
- understand that adverts have a purpose, message and intended audience
- discover how persuasive techniques are used in adverts, e.g. *emotive language, questions*
- explore different forms of advertising including a film review, poster and film trailer.

Writing

Key writing purpose to be shared with the children:

To write a trailer script to advertise a film to a specific audience.

Writing evaluation to be shared with the children

My trailer script:

- is attention-grabbing
- uses persuasive techniques to encourage the audience to see the film
- is appropriate for a primary school-aged audience
- is based on my storyboard and combines text with ideas for images and audio to give a clear message
- is laid out correctly using film script conventions.

Grammar:

- includes at least one question to engage the reader, which is punctuated correctly.

See the Planning section of the Software ('Timetables' tab) for a printable version of the Writing purpose and evaluation.

DAY 11

Curriculum link:
discussing a
wide range of
non-fiction

Introduction

Purpose: for children's interest in persuasive texts to be stimulated via one of the Big Questions they have explored

- Display the Big Question from Day 6 on **CD (file 6.5)**:

  Is it weak to change your mind?

- Tell the children that adverts are created especially to change people's minds or to persuade them to choose one product rather than another.
- Display the slideshow of adverts on **CD (file 11.1)**. Explain that each advert has a purpose, a message and an intended audience. TOL as you analyse the first advert by explaining the purpose, message and intended audience.
- Show the rest of the slideshow, stopping on each advert and asking the children to TTYP to discuss the purpose, the message and the intended audience.
- Take feedback after each advert.

learn the
conventions of
different types of
writing; building
a varied and rich
vocabulary

Persuasive words

Purpose: for children to become familiar with some of the key features of persuasive writing

- Show the children the words on **CD (file 11.2)** and read them using MT/YT.
- Click on a word to see its definition. Share the definition with the children using MT/YT and then read the sentence below.
- Click 'Back to list' to return to the word list. Repeat for all the words.
- Next, display **CD (file 11.3)**. Share the first sentence with the children, then ask them to TTYP to decide which word fits the sentence best. Take feedback.
- Drag and drop the word into the sentence. Click the marking icon to show a tick or cross, indicating whether the right word has been used. Click again to turn off the marking and continue until you have completed the activity.
- Print out the words and their definitions from **CD (file 11.4)** to display on the Persuasive writing wall for this Unit.
- Use the words with the children throughout the day, especially the trickier ones such as *emotive* and *imply*.

Read and review

Purpose: for children to read and identify the key features of persuasive writing in a variety of texts

- Before the lesson, print a copy of **CD (file 11.6)** for each child, plus an enlarged version to use to collect and display feedback.
- Display the poster on **CD (file 11.5)**. Ask the children to TTYP and discuss what they think the purpose of the poster is. Take feedback and write their ideas on the board or a flipchart.
- Now ask the children to TTYP and discuss who the poster's audience is. Take feedback as before.
- TOL as you explain how the poster appeals to the audience. Draw their attention to the word *ruthless* and explain that it is an emotive word used to make us feel that VIPER are bad. Ask the children to TTYP to find any other emotive words or phrases in the poster. Take feedback.
- TOL as you explain what the words are trying to make the reader feel, e.g. 'At the mercy of *makes the country seem helpless – it makes us feel fear and worry.* In their power *makes us feel that VIPER will do terrible things if they get their way.*'

- Draw children's attention to the question '…but does Danny Brown have the nerve and enough time to outwit them?' TOL as you explain that a question is a persuasive technique used to make the reader start to wonder how the film might end, e.g. *'This technique gets the reader emotionally involved in the film before they even see it. They are persuaded that they need to find out what happens.'*
- Display an enlarged Read and review chart from **CD (file 11.6)**. Model filling in the first two answers and examples for the *VIPER!* poster, but don't give marks out of ten yet. Ask the children to TTYP to complete their own copy of the first chart. Make sure children link the heading 'Persuasive techniques' with your earlier explanation about the use of a question in the poster.
- Next, tell the children to read the film review of *VIPER!* on p.78 of their Anthology.
- Ask the children to TTYP and discuss what the viewpoint of the reviewer could be. Take feedback. Make sure that the children understand that the review is trying to persuade the reader to go to see the film.
- Now ask the children to fill in their second Read and review chart from **CD (file 11.6)** for the review. Tell them not to give marks out of ten yet.
- Take feedback and write their ideas on the second enlarged chart. Next, compare the texts (the poster and the review). Use TTYP and feedback to decide as a class what marks out of ten to give each aspect of the two persuasive texts.
- Display the completed charts and ask the children to copy the marks out of ten onto their own charts. Ensure children keep their charts for later use.

Curriculum link: assessing the effectiveness of others' writing

Daily log

You will need to have collected film reviews and poster-style film adverts from the Internet, newspapers and magazines in preparation for this activity.

Purpose: for children to keep a personal log of notes, thoughts and ideas, collected from their reading and discussions. Some ideas will be used in their own writing

- Print off one copy of **CD (file 11.6)** for each child.
- Give each set of partners a film review and an advert. Ask the children to use their charts to analyse each one. Encourage the children to make judgements about the effectiveness of these persuasive texts and to give a mark out of ten for each row of the chart.
- Share the children's findings, drawing out their reasons for their judgements.
- Ask the children to paste their adverts and charts into their Daily log.

DAY 12

Change it!

Purpose: for children to gain an awareness of the effect of persuasive language

- Display **CD (file 12.1)** to show the text from the film review of *VIPER!* that the children read previously. Remind them that it is a positive review, persuading people to see the film.
- Tell the children that you are going to change the review so that it is negative: so it persuades people *not* to see the film.
- Navigate to the next screen and model changing the first sentence of the review by dragging and dropping in the alternatives. Use MT/YT to share each choice. Decide which one to use by asking the children to TTYP, then taking feedback.
- Repeat the process on the next two screens. TOL to describe how the word choices change the tone of the review from positive to negative.

- Now ask the children to complete the Change it! activity on p.64 of their Pupils' Book, writing their new sentences in their Daily log. As they write, note good examples of negative sentences and write them on the board or a flipchart to use in your feedback.
- Share the good ideas you have seen and encourage the children to share any sentences they are particularly proud of.

Watch a trailer (CD)

Purpose: for children to watch a trailer critically, thinking about the persuasive techniques used to appeal to the audience

- Tell the children that the film *VIPER!* has a trailer as well, and that you want them to watch it with a *critical eye* (explain this term if necessary). Ask them to look out for any persuasive techniques they can spot.
- Before they watch the trailer for the first time, remind them of the persuasive techniques they know about by referring to the Persuasive writing wall.
- Show the children the trailer for *VIPER!* on **CD (file 12.2)**.
- Ask them to TTYP and discuss any persuasive techniques they noticed. Take feedback and write key ideas on the board or a flipchart.
- Ask the children to TTYP and discuss who they think the trailer is aimed at (the audience) and what its main message is. Take feedback and write responses on the board or flipchart.
- Tell the children that they are going to watch the trailer again, this time looking out for the images used to make the film seem exciting.
- Show the trailer again, then take feedback. TOL as you make a link between the image of the snake (a viper) and how the audience is meant to feel about the criminal gang VIPER. Ask the children to TTYP and discuss why they think the last image in the trailer is of the viper. Take feedback.
- Tell them that they are going to watch the trailer once more, and this time they need to look out for how the music and narration (the *voice-over*) link together.
- Show the trailer again and take feedback. Ask the children to TTYP and discuss which of the words used in the narration are the most important. Take feedback and write the key words on the board or flipchart.

Deconstruction 1 (CD)

Purpose: for children to read and identify the key features in a variety of persuasive texts and analyse their success

- Before the lesson, print a copy of **CD (file 12.3)** for each child.
- Ask the children to TTYP and take turns to read the script for the *VIPER!* trailer on pp.79–80 of their Anthology.
- Next ask the children to fill in one of their Read and review charts from **CD (file 12.3)** to help them find the key features of persuasion used in the film trailer. Tell them not to give marks out of ten yet.
- Ask them to fill in the row about the use of sound and visuals in the trailer.
- Show the children the *VIPER!* trailer on **CD (file 12.2)** again.
- Ask the children to TTYP to add their final ideas to their chart. Ask them to complete it by giving each feature a mark out of ten. Take feedback.
- Tell the children to get out the Read and review charts they completed the previous day for the *VIPER!* poster and review. Ask them to compare their marks for the poster and review with the marks they gave the trailer. Tell them to TTYP and discuss which of the three – the poster, review or trailer – was the best at persuading someone to see the film, and why. Take feedback.

> **Curriculum link:** discussing writing that is similar to that which they are planning to write

Curriculum link:
exploring,
discussing and
recording ideas

Daily log (CD) (A)

Purpose: for children to keep a personal log of notes, thoughts and ideas, collected from their reading and discussions. Some ideas will be used in their own writing

- Tell the children that they are going to watch the *VIPER!* trailer on **CD (file 12.2)** again, this time noting how the images and music combine.
- Show the trailer, then ask the children to TTYP and discuss how the music and images made them feel.
- Ask them to turn to the script for the trailer on pp.79–80 of their Anthology. Tell the children to watch once more, and to note down in their Daily log their feelings and what the music was like at different points in the trailer.
- Take feedback and discuss the children's responses to the trailer.

DAY 13

write for a range
of real purposes
and audiences

Write 1 (CD) 🖨

Purpose: for children to plan the message and purpose of their advertising campaign and design a poster for it

- Before the lesson, print one copy of **CD (file 13.2)**.
- Tell the children that they have been asked to promote a film version of the story they wrote in the second week, to be called *Hamid's Adventure*. They will need to make a poster and a trailer, both for an audience of primary school-aged children.
- Ask the children to TTYP to discuss what the purpose and message of the campaign are. Take feedback and write some ideas on the board or a flipchart.
- Ask the children to TTYP to write a checklist of what their adverts need to contain. Remind them to use the knowledge they have built up from analysing the different adverts and persuasive texts on Days 11 and 12. Take feedback and make a list on the board or flipchart.
- Tell the children that they will start by making the poster. Ask them to TTYP to discuss what the poster should have on it. Take feedback.
- Show the children some images they could use in their poster for *Hamid's Adventure* on **CD (file 13.1)**. Explain that different boys are playing Hamid in each of the images. Ask them to TTYP to talk about what message each image is giving. Take feedback and write a message below each image on the printout from **CD (file 13.2)**.
- Remind the children that a poster does not have much text but it does have a very clear message. Explain that it often has a *tag line* which plays with words and is very memorable. TOL as you suggest some ideas for tag lines for *Hamid's Adventure*, using repetition: 'One boy, one bus…one amazing adventure!' alliteration: 'Hang on Hamid!' or suspense: 'Just an ordinary day…until it ran out of control…'
- Ask the children to TTYP to come up with more tag lines. Take feedback and write some ideas on the board or flipchart.
- Display the image on **CD (file 13.3)**. Click 'TOL' repeatedly and TOL about the choices you made to create a poster for the film *Hamid's Adventure*.
- Ask the children to choose one image from **CD (file 13.1)** and to design a rough poster in their Daily log, including a clear message and a tag line.

discussing
writing in order
to understand
and learn from
its structure,
grammar and
vocabulary

Deconstruction 2 (CD) (A)

Purpose: for children to see a model of a storyboard for a film trailer

- Return to the *VIPER!* trailer on **CD (file 12.2)**. Tell the children that they are going to plan their own trailer for the film *Hamid's Adventure*. First they will choose which key moments to show. They will then build up a script for the trailer, including voice-over and dialogue for the characters, and finally they will choose music that will build up the excitement and drama.

- Show the children the storyboard for the *VIPER!* trailer on **CD (file 13.4)**. Draw their attention to the technical terms such as *shot, close-up, zoom* and *voice-over*. TOL as you explain each term and how it is used in the trailer.
- Explain that the images used in the trailer are carefully chosen to give the main ideas in the film and create excitement. Explain that the shots of the village set the scene, while the shot of the *road closed* sign shows that there is a problem.
- Navigate through the slides. Ask the children to TTYP and decide what the shots of the science lab and London tell the audience. Take feedback.
- Ask the children to re-read with their partners the *VIPER!* trailer script from their Anthology pp.79–80, using lots of expression to convey drama and impact.
- Tell them to TTYP to discuss which key things they would put in a trailer for *Hamid's Adventure*. Take feedback and write their ideas on the board or a flipchart.
- Ask the children to TTYP and discuss how they would show the setting for *Hamid's Adventure*, and how they would begin to show the danger and excitement in the film. Take feedback and write their ideas on the board or flipchart.
- Display **CD (file 13.5)**. Say that you have chosen some images and key words and phrases for your trailer, and now you are going to build up a voice-over script. Navigate through the slides and use the TOLs and the Voice-over prompts to build up your storyboard (you can change and edit these on the CD file if you wish).

Write 2

Purpose: for children to plan a trailer using a storyboard

- Before the lesson, print a copy of **CD (file 13.6)** for each child.
- Ask the children to TTYP to remind their partner about the main action in the story they wrote in the second week, about Hamid and the runaway bus. Take feedback for two or three stories.
- Tell the children that they will need to show between three and six exciting *clips* from their story in their trailer for *Hamid's Adventure*. Ask them to TTYP and tell their partner what they will include. Take feedback and write some ideas on the board or a flipchart.
- Give the children a copy of **CD (file 13.6)** and ask them to make notes about which image clips they would like to include in their trailers, and to note some key words and phrases about their story. Remind them that they will need to set the scene by introducing the main ideas of the story and possibly their main character. They will also want to focus on some dramatic moments and some *hooks* such as questions that will leave the audience in suspense.
- Ask them to TTYP to share their plans so far. If they need to do so, encourage them to change the moments they include or the order of the scenes to make the story clearer or the trailer more persuasive.

Curriculum link: think aloud to explore and collect ideas; drafting and re-reading to check their meaning is clear

exploring, discussing and recording ideas

Daily log

Purpose: for children to keep a personal log of notes, thoughts and ideas, collected from their reading and discussions. Some ideas will be used in their own writing

- Remind the children that, so far, the film has had the title *Hamid's Adventure*. Suggest that it may not be the best or most exciting title that they could use.
- Ask the children to TTYP and talk about other titles that they could use instead. Take feedback, asking the children to give reasons for their suggested titles.
- Tell the children to choose their favourite title and write it in their Daily log.
- Explain that their poster and trailer will need to use this title from now on.

DAY 14

Deconstruction 3

Purpose: for children to see a model of using music, images and words to create a trailer

Curriculum link:
identifying how
language, structure
and presentation
contribute to
meaning

- Show the children your storyboard with key words on **CD (file 14.1)**. Explain that you are going to choose some music and sound effects to go with your trailer.
- Click on the first audio icon and ask the children to listen carefully to the music. Tell them to TTYP and think of two words to describe the music. Popcorn feedback (see Introduction p.17).
- Ask the children to TTYP and discuss which story square they think the music should go with. Take feedback and discuss.
- Repeat this with the other audio icons, deciding which story squares the audio should go with. Focus on how you might build drama and suspense through the trailer to persuade the audience that it will be an exciting film. You may want to contrast dramatic music with sudden moments of silence to create impact.
- Ask the children to TTYP and discuss what sound effects you could include in your trailer. Take suggestions, and decide that you will use a squeal of brakes after '…but at what expense?' to create a moment of drama.
- Tell the children that you are now ready to make your storyboard into a trailer script. Navigate to the next slide on **CD (file 14.1)** and use the guided script and TOL prompts to talk through your trailer script over three slides, including voice-over text, dialogue and descriptions of music and sound effects.

Write 3

Purpose: for children to improve their storyboard by deciding how to combine images, words and music

write for a range
of purposes and
audiences; building
a varied and rich
vocabulary

- Tell the children that they are almost ready to write their trailer script, but first they will choose their music and sound effects. Using their trailer storyboard from **CD (file 13.6)** as a guide, ask them to TTYP and discuss what type of music or sound effects they could include for the different shots. Take feedback, encouraging them to justify their answer, e.g. *I'm going to use loud, fast-paced music here because it's a dramatic chase scene so I want the audience to be feeling tense.*
- When children have chosen their music and sound effects and noted them on their plans, tell them that they are ready to write their final trailers.
- Tell the children to look at pp.79–80 of the Anthology to see how the script for the *VIPER!* trailer has been set out. Explain that the children should set their script out in the same way and use some technical language such as *shot, close-up, zoom in, zoom out* and *voice-over*.
- Remind them that they are trying to get their message across to a particular audience, in this case primary school-aged children.

Daily log

assessing the
effectiveness of
their own writing
and suggesting
improvements

Purpose: for children to keep a personal log of notes, thoughts and ideas, collected from their reading and discussions. Some ideas will be used in their own writing

- Now that they have completed their work for the trailer, ask the children to look back at their initial plans for a poster for the film in their Daily log. Does it reflect the main message of their trailer? Can it be improved?
- Give the children time to add some ideas about how they could improve their poster designs.
- If there is time or at a later date, the children could make a final copy of their poster, using their Daily log notes on how to improve it.

DAY 15

Evaluate and edit (CD)

Purpose: for children to evaluate their own and their partner's work against specific criteria and then discuss how they could improve their work

- Display **CD (file 15.1)** and read through the evaluation points using MT/YT.
- As a model, select an example of work where the writing has met the criteria, and share this with the other children, explaining why it works well.
- Tell the children to take turns to read their partner's writing in pairs and discuss together how well each piece of writing has met the criteria.
- Ask the children to discuss at least two changes they could make to improve their work.

Proofread

Purpose: for children to proofread their work and make changes to improve the accuracy of their grammar, punctuation and spelling

- Now ask the children to proofread their work. If you have noticed that several children need to improve on a particular aspect of spelling, grammar or punctuation, use this as a focus for the Proofread activity. Write an example which includes common errors from the children's writing and use this as a model.
- The children should always be checking for standard use of punctuation and correct spelling of common exception words.
- The following points would be particularly relevant for this Unit:
  - making sure the trailer script is laid out with the correct conventions
  - checking spelling of ambitious vocabulary choices (i.e. those borrowed from the Pupils' Book or Anthology text).

Perform it (CD)

Purpose: for children to work effectively with a partner to perform a film trailer and to develop critical awareness

- Tell the children that when trailers are made, it is really important that the voices for the voice-over and dialogue sections are very expressive and dramatic, because these Storyteller voices draw the audience into the film and persuade them that they want to watch it.
- Ask partners to choose one of their scripts and work together to practise reading out the voice-over and dialogue. They should use their most effective Storyteller voices to convey meaning and impact. Walk around as they work, monitoring their progress and giving feedback.
- Then ask one set of partners who feel confident to read out their trailer script to the class.
- Ask the children to TTYP and discuss what features of the trailer would be successful in persuading the audience to want to see the film, and what could be improved? Take feedback. Draw out answers relating to the use of emotive language, persuasive techniques and use of sound and visuals.
- If you wish to extend this activity, partners could act out their trailer as well as reading it. If you have access to suitable equipment and audio editing software, they could even film their trailers.

Curriculum coverage chart

England	*Literacy and Language* Year 4 is closely matched to the Programmes of study for the new *National Curriculum in England* from 2014 and the Year 4 grammar requirements listed in its Grammar appendix. See the overview chart on p.18 and the curriculum link boxes in the teaching notes for details. *Literacy and Language* is suitable for children working at National Curriculum level 2a and above and aims to take children to level 5 and beyond. See **www.oxfordprimary.co.uk** for curriculum updates.
Scotland	Primary 5 *Curriculum for Excellence* Second level
Wales	*Literacy and Language* enables children to become accomplished in oracy across the curriculum reading across the curriculum writing across the curriculum. See **www.oxfordprimary.co.uk** for further details and a free downloadable correlation chart when the new *National Literacy and Numeracy Framework* is introduced.
Northern Ireland	Primary 5/Year 5 The following points from the *Language and Literacy* curriculum are covered in each unit of *Literacy and Language*: *Unit 1* Talking and listening: 1, 2, 3, 5, 7, 8, 9, 10, 12, 13, Reading: 1, 3, 4, 5, 6, 7, 8, 9, 10, 11, 13 Writing: 1, 2, 4, 5, 6, 7, 8, 9, 10, 12 *Unit 2* Talking and listening: 1, 2, 3, 5, 7, 8, 9, 10, 12, 13 Reading: 1, 3, 4, 5, 6, 7, 8, 9, 10, 11, 13 Writing: 1, 2, 3, 4, 5, 6, 7, 8, 9, 10, 12 *Unit 3* Talking and listening: 1, 2, 3, 5, 7, 8, 9, 10, 12, 13 Reading: 1, 3, 4, 5, 6, 7, 8, 9, 10, 11, 13 Writing: 1, 2, 4, 5, 6, 7, 8, 9, 10, 12 *Unit 4* Talking and listening: 1, 2, 3, 5, 7, 8, 9, 10, 13 Reading: 1, 3, 4, 5, 6, 7, 8, 9, 10, 11, 13 Writing: 1, 2, 4, 5, 6, 7, 8, 9, 10, 12 *Unit 5* Talking and listening: 1, 2, 3, 5, 7, 8, 9, 10, 12, 13, 14 Reading: 1, 3, 4, 5, 6, 7, 8, 9, 10, 11, 13 Writing: 1, 2, 4, 5, 6, 7, 8, 9, 10, 12 *Unit 6* Talking and listening: 1, 2, 3, 5, 7, 8, 9, 10, 12, 13 Reading: 1, 3, 4, 5, 6, 7, 8, 9, 10, 11, 13 Writing: 1, 2, 4, 5, 6, 7, 8, 9, 10, 12